Functional Behavior Analysis

CASE STUDIES AND PRACTICE

Kylan Turner

Bassim Hamadeh, CEO and Publisher

Laura Pasquale, Acquisitions Editor

Gem Rabanera, Project Editor

Berenice Quirino, Associate Production Editor

Jess Estrella, Senior Graphic Designer

Trey Soto, Licensing Associate

Don Kesner, Interior Designer

Natalie Piccotti, Director of Marketing

Kassie Graves, Vice President of Editorial

Jamie Giganti, Director of Academic Publishing

ISBN: 978-1-5165-7157-4

Functional Behavior Analysis

CASE STUDIES AND PRACTICE

CONTENTS

DISCLAIMER

The recommendations regarding ethical practice throughout this textbook are based on the experience and training of the author(s) and do not represent an official statement from a behavior analysis organization, specifically not the Behavior Analyst Certification Board® or the Association for Behavior Analysis International. The recommendations provided to conduct ethical practice are not provided with the assertion that these are the only solutions, but instead are provided as suggestions based on the authors' interpretation of the ethical code. Instructors using this text are encouraged to provide additional examples and training in ethical problem-solving and effective clinical practice. Finally, the subject matter in all case studies were written as aggregates of various clinical experiences, and any identifiable information has been disguised to protect the privacy of individuals and organizations.

CHAPTER 1

The Ethical Assessment of Behavior

**Christina King, Ph.D., BCBA, LABA
and Kylan Turner, Ph.D., BCBA-D, LABA**

As you have likely observed after reading the title, this book will cover the underlying concepts and principles as well as the practical implementation of a functional behavior assessment (FBA). Prior to discussing the ethical considerations of FBA in this chapter, it is necessary to briefly define FBA and its objectives. The premise of most of this discussion will involve acknowledging the assertion in behavior analysis that all behaviors serve a purpose (or multiple purposes) for the individual performing the behavior. In other words, behaviors do not occur at random or for no reason. Behavior analysts call this purpose a **function of behavior**, and fortunately, there is a finite number of functions that a behavior may serve. Most simply, behaviors generally occur because, as a result of performing the behavior, the individual gains attention, gains access to a preferred item or activity, is able to escape an activity or a demand that is nonpreferred, and/or is able to provide themselves reinforcement (i.e., without requiring the involvement of other people)—a function known as automatic reinforcement (Iwata, Dorsey, Slifer, Bauman, & Richman, 1994).

The FBA is an assessment process with multiple stages and tools, which is why the FBA is often referred to as a **multimodal** assessment. This continuum of procedures ranges from least to most intrusive and assists in identifying the function of the behavior in order to then tailor behavior-change procedures to influence whether the behavior continues to occur or not. The least intrusive approaches involve simply collecting data from multiple informants who have observed the behavior occurring (including from the individual themselves) as well as directly observing occurrences of the behavior as they naturally occur. More intrusive methods involve **experimental manipulation**, wherein relevant environmental variables that occur before or after the behavior are manipulated systematically to observe the behavior's occurrence in relation to the presence of those variables. When the experimental manipulation involves attempting to isolate the variables that may be responsible for evoking the behavior, the manipulation is called a **structural analysis**, and when the experimental manipulation involves attempting to isolate the variables that occur after the behavior—and therefore may increase the likelihood of the behavior occurring in the future—the manipulation is referred to as a **functional analysis**.

Because experimental manipulations are designed to increase the probability of an undesired behavior occurring in the context of the assessment, important ethical considerations arise. When conducting experimental manipulations, it is necessary to plan for and implement **procedural safeguards** to protect the individual being assessed, as well as those present during the assessment, from harm. In addition to minimizing physical or emotional harm to the individual or bystanders, it is necessary to also minimize other adverse effects that could arise from temporarily increasing the behavior's occurrence. For this reason, there are guidelines regarding the level of formal training and experience, as well as supervision, a practitioner should possess prior to conducting experimental manipulation within an FBA. In the appendix of this chapter, recommended readings on this topic (specifically those authored by Bailey and Burch) are provided that outline more specific information regarding the levels of experience and training needed to conduct various stages of the FBA process and, specifically, experimental manipulation. For example, when evaluating who may be qualified to conduct a procedure in a manner that presents minimal risk to all involved, an early-career Board Certified Behavior Analyst® (BCBA) may be considered to have the required training to conduct a functional analysis on behaviors that do not present physical harm, whereas a doctoral-level behavior analyst with at least 10 years of experience would be the type of professional considered sufficiently well-trained to complete a functional analysis on extremely self-injurious behavior with minimal risk to all involved (Bailey & Burch, 2016). It is therefore the responsibility of the individual designing the FBA to carefully and honestly evaluate one's level of experience prior to attempting to conduct any stage of the process and to seek the services of those with more extensive experience if needed. These considerations will be addressed initially in this chapter and its appendices but will also be explored in greater detail in Chapter 10 of this book.

Now that we have briefly defined FBA and its objectives, it is important to take a step back and explore the foundation of the field from which FBA originated: behavior analysis (BA). BA is the empirical study of behavior and learning as well as the application of those findings, and it is guided by the conceptual analysis of behavior (also referred to as the "philosophy of the science of behavior"). The conceptual analysis of behavior is based on the following assertions: that all operant behavior may be explained through learned stimulus-response associations, resulting in reward and/or punishment; that verbal behavior is operant (or operates on the environment); and finally, that private events such as thinking and feeling are behavioral. Within that philosophical and historical context, other branches of BA have been developed, including a focus on empirical research, application, and service delivery.

Stated more directly, the four major foci of behavior analysis are the **conceptual analysis of behavior (CAB)**, the **experimental analysis of behavior (EAB)**, **applied behavior analysis (ABA)**, and **service delivery (SD)**. As was previously mentioned, CAB provides the guiding philosophy of the science of BA and focuses on the analysis of philosophical, historical, methodological, and theoretical issues. The EAB branch of BA consists of the research activity that empirically explores basic behavioral processes. ABA is the branch of BA that applies the principles and processes identified through the repeated empirical findings of EAB, and its objective is to influence socially significant behavior through systematic assessment of environmental events and application of behavior-change procedures indicated by that assessment. Finally, service delivery focuses on the work of practitioners who most often conduct behavior assessment, use experimental design, analyze and interpret data, write and revise behavior-analytic treatment plans, train others to carry out behavior-intervention plans, and oversee the implementation of these plans. Service delivery also includes a focus on the models through which ABA is disseminated.

Given that the discipline of behavior analysis is deeply rooted in empiricism, the roles and relationships connecting EAB and ABA are areas of consideration for further focus when discussing what makes behavior analysis unique. Baer, Wolf, and Risley (1968) carefully discuss the roles of the branches of EAB and ABA and how they relate to and inform one another. Instead of simply classifying basic and applied research in terms of EAB focusing on basic research and ABA focusing on application, Baer et al. (1968) suggested that both EAB and ABA are areas of scientific study, but the distinction between the two should be based on what controls the behavior being studied. In other words, EAB is not necessarily discriminatory in selecting behaviors and variables on which to focus: the very nature of basic research is to ask and attempt to answer (using scientific methods) questions that could reveal more information about behavioral processes and new variables for consideration. This is in contrast to the more narrow selection of behaviors to be studied in ABA, as these must focus only on variables that will result in behavioral improvement. In other words, EAB researchers are limited simply to that which scientific principles and technology (and ethical parameters) will allow them to study, while ABA researchers are more restricted to the focus on behaviors that are socially important. Both branches of behavior analysis are critical, but their roles and scope within the discipline present different areas of utility. This textbook has been developed based on these foci of behavior analysis, with the conceptual analysis of behavior as the guiding philosophical approach.

In this first chapter, you will be asked to review case studies and complete end-of-chapter activities. This chapter, like all others in this textbook, includes a focus on the "See one, do one, teach one" model of mastering important skills and concepts. Therefore, it is important that you take all opportunities to complete these varied stages of activities to deepen your understanding and broaden your skill set.

LEARNING OBJECTIVES

After completing the chapter's activities, learners should be able to do the following:

- Briefly define behavior analysis, conceptual analysis of behavior, systematic manipulation of behavior, applied behavior analysis, and service delivery

- Discuss the role of the BACB® in providing standards and accountability to the field of behavior analysis

- Discuss the purpose of the *Professional and Ethical Compliance Code for Behavior Analysts* and its relevance to functional behavior-assessment practices

- Identify the codes contained in the *Professional and Ethical Compliance Code for Behavior Analysts* that relate to functional behavior-assessment practices

- Identify the conduct codes that align with the case study vignettes provided

Behavior Analysis

The following diagram (Figure 1.1) illustrates behavior analysis and its four subcomponents: CAB, EAB, ABA, and SD.

Figure 1.1 Behavior Analysis

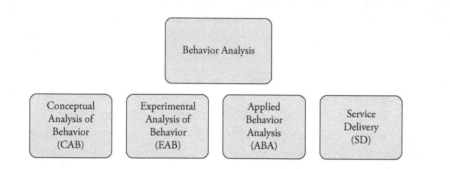

In an effort to establish training standards for ABA practitioners and ethical guidelines for the practice of ABA, as well as to provide accountability for consumers, the Behavior Analysis Certification Board®, Inc. (BACB®) was formed in 1998. The BACB® provides tiered certification to behavior analysts across education levels (from postsecondary to doctoral-level education), accreditation to institutions providing coursework in ABA, and resources and standards for supervised fieldwork for practitioners seeking certification. One of the most critical projects the BACB® has undertaken has been the establishment of the *Professional and Ethical Compliance Code for Behavior Analysts* (2014). This document—referred to by most practitioners as "The Code"—provides expectations for professional behavior and outlines, in detail, standards for ethical conduct in order to protect consumers and practitioners alike (Bailey & Burch, 2016). The goal of creating this Code and requiring adherence to its standards is to ensure that consumers seeking behavior analytic services, research subjects, behavior analysts themselves, and the profession itself are protected from harm. All individuals certified through the BACB® are obligated to comply with The Code or face disciplinary action as outlined by the BACB®. The Code is referenced throughout this book, as it is helpful in guiding the ethical practice of all practitioners conducting FBA, whether they are behavior analysts or not.

Since it is possible for a variety of professionals or paraprofessionals to be involved in a particular learner's assessment process, it is necessary to also consider who could or should be responsible for conducting the FBA process and interpreting the data that will drive important decisions. Despite the fact that FBA is mandated both by special education law in the United States and by the BACB® as a part of a comprehensive and evidence-based assessment process, there are not clear guidelines in education law about who can or should conduct an FBA (i.e., the qualifications or training they must possess) or what exactly defines the FBA. It is therefore important for practitioners to seek continued education, training, and supervision to ensure that competence standards, as well as legal and ethical requirements, are being met.

Because the practice of FBA involves repeated and extended observation of individuals' behavior in a variety of contexts and settings, this particular assessment process presents ethical considerations that must be clearly understood and addressed. For instance, a behavior analyst may be asked to conduct an FBA on a variety of socially important behaviors, such as self-injury, self-stimulation in the form of masturbation, food hoarding, aggression, incontinence, property destruction, pica, or other behaviors that require additional consideration and protection of the individual's privacy and dignity. Given the vulnerable nature of many of the potential behaviors that an ABA practitioner may encounter, it is critical that ethical guidelines are followed to protect all individuals involved. Additionally, properly conducted FBA involves interacting with individuals in the learner's life who can provide insight on the behavior. Although these interviews and indirect assessment practices are critical for identification of the variables controlling the behavior of concern, the practice of interacting with others about a learner's behavior presents ethical challenges when it comes to the protection of privacy and confidentiality.

Informed Consent

Prior to conducting any assessment (including FBA), it is necessary for the assessor to obtain informed consent from the individual being assessed (or from the party responsible for their care, such as a parent or legal guardian). Informed consent is considered to have been obtained when the individual being assessed (or responsible party, if the individual is a minor or unable to provide consent themselves) is informed of the nature of the assessment (and the risks and benefits that may occur as a result of the assessment) and provides permission for the assessment to take place. It is best practice for the assessor to provide information about the assessment (verbally, as well as in writing) and to respond to questions about the process prior to conducting any part of the assessment. During the informed consent process, the assessor should evaluate whether the individual providing consent is fully aware of the risks and benefits of each aspect of the process (including more intrusive procedures, such as structural or functional analysis) and has the opportunity to ask questions. Assessors must also make it clear to those providing consent that participation in the assessment is voluntary and that they have the opportunity to end the assessment at any time without adverse consequences or retribution from the assessor. Behavior analysts collecting informed consent for an FBA do so using a form such as the one included in the appendix of this chapter (though this should be customized to include specific assessments and procedures used, particularly if systematic manipulations are to be conducted), which addresses the ethical requirement outlined in The Code for obtaining written informed consent prior to carrying out an assessment.

In the comprehensive Code, 10 separate code items refer to the standards required for behavior analysts when conducting FBA: 3.01 Behavior-Analytic Assessment; 3.02 Medical Consultation; 3.03 Behavior-Analytic Assessment Consent; 3.04 Explaining Assessment Results; 3.05 Consent-Client Records; 4.02 Involving Clients in Planning and Consent; 4.03 Individualized Behavior-Change Programs; 4.04 Approving Behavior-Change Programs; 4.07 Environmental Conditions that Interfere with Implementation; and 10.05 Compliance with BACB® Supervision and Coursework Standards. In this chapter, these compliance codes will be reviewed and explored with real-world case examples and ethical dilemmas. Finally, a sample consent form for the ethical practice of conducting FBA will be provided. Further reading and training is recommended regarding ethical assessment when conducting FBA. For that reason, at the end of this chapter, a recommended-reading list is provided.

The following excerpts were taken directly from the 2014 BACB® Code. Note that the BACB® Code uses the term "client," while this text uses the word "learner" to indicate a student or a target consumer of behavior-analytic services; "BCaBA" is an acronym used to denote the role of a Board Certified Assistant Behavior Analyst; and "RBT" is an acronym designated for individuals who have completed required training hours to become a Registered Behavior Technician. The RBT is held to comply with a select number of the codes below (indicated in superscript where applicable), whereas the BACB® and BCaBA are required to comply with all codes.

3.01 Behavior-Analytic Assessment[RBT]

(a) Behavior analysts conduct current assessments prior to making recommendations or developing behavior-change programs. The type of assessment used is determined by client's needs and consent, environmental parameters, and other contextual variables. When behavior analysts are developing a behavior-reduction program, they must first conduct a functional assessment.

(b) Behavior analysts have an obligation to collect and graphically display data, using behavior-analytic conventions, in a manner that allows for decisions and recommendations for behavior-change program development.

3.02 Medical Consultation

Behavior analysts recommend seeking a medical consultation if there is any reasonable possibility that a referred behavior is influenced by medical or biological variables.

3.03 Behavior-Analytic Assessment Consent

(a) Prior to conducting an assessment, behavior analysts must explain to the client the procedure(s) to be used, who will participate, and how the resulting information will be used.

(b) Behavior analysts must obtain the client's written approval of the assessment procedures before implementing them.

3.04 Explaining Assessment Results

Behavior analysts explain assessment results using language and graphic displays of data that are reasonably understandable to the client.

3.05 Consent-Client Records

Behavior analysts obtain the written consent of the client before obtaining or disclosing client records from or to other sources, for assessment purposes.

4.02 Involving Clients in Planning and Consent

Behavior analysts involve the client in the planning of and consent for behavior-change programs.

4.03 Individualized Behavior-Change Programs

(a) Behavior analysts must tailor behavior-change programs to the unique behaviors, environmental variables, assessment results, and goals of each client.

(b) Behavior analysts do not plagiarize other professionals' behavior-change programs.

4.04 Approving Behavior-Change Programs

Behavior analysts must obtain the client's written approval of the behavior-change program before implementation or making significant modifications (e.g., change in goals, use of new procedures).

4.07 Environmental Conditions that Interfere with Implementation

(a) If environmental conditions prevent implementation of a behavior-change program, behavior analysts recommend that other professional assistance (e.g., assessment, consultation or therapeutic intervention by other professionals) be sought.

(b) If environmental conditions hinder implementation of the behavior-change program, behavior analysts seek to eliminate the environmental constraints, or identify in writing the obstacles to doing so.

10.05 Compliance with BACB® Supervision and Coursework Standards[RBT]

Behavior analysts ensure that coursework (including continuing education events), supervised experience, RBT training and assessment, and BCaBA supervision are conducted in accordance with the BACB®'s standards if these activities are intended to comply with BACB® standards.

When reading the following vignettes, keep the above excerpts of The Code in mind. Ask yourself which section(s) of The Code might have been implemented for a better outcome.

Case Study 1: Clara's FBA at School

Clara is a 7-year-old girl attending a full-time kindergarten general education class. She's been diagnosed with autism spectrum disorder and disruptive behavior disorder. For 3 weeks, Clara has been pulling other children's hair approximately five times per day. Other children have begun to avoid Clara and have asked their teacher to avoid seating them next to her. Clara's school team held an emergency meeting to discuss this behavior. The individuals in attendance were Clara's general education teacher, her special education teacher, the school principal, and the school psychologist. Together, they discussed the need to conduct an FBA to determine the relevant environmental events and stimuli and the function of the behavior to decrease its occurrence in the future.

The FBA (which included an intrusive structural analysis and a functional analysis, both of which temporarily increased the occurrence of this aggressive behavior) was conducted over the next eight school days, and the data were used to inform a behavior-intervention plan. The function of the behavior was determined to be gaining attention, and the intervention proposed was for the teacher and all other class members to ignore all occurrences of hair pulling while specifically reinforcing intervals of time where Clara does not pull others hair and instead taps her peers on the shoulder to initiate conversation.

The general education teacher, Ms. Flaggs, was very pleased with the results of the behavior-change plan. Clara's frequency of engaging in hair pulling decreased from five times per day to once per month in just 5 weeks following initial implementation of the intervention. Because this was such a dramatic improvement, Ms. Flaggs thought it would be appropriate to call Clara's parents and let them know about her incredible progress. When she did so, she was faced with an unexpected response: Clara's parents reported they felt shocked that an FBA had been conducted on a behavior they did not even know was occurring at school. Further, they stated that they were frustrated that they were not consulted about the intervention plan implemented.

Ms. Flaggs was equally surprised by Clara's parents' response. She stated that she knew Clara's family had been indicating they were stressed due to Clara's behaviors at home and that she did not want to cause them undue stress until the hair-pulling-at-school behavior had been fully addressed. She expressed that she thought that Clara's parents would be happy to know the behavior had improved so significantly and that sharing this good news, and how the behavior was successfully addressed, was intended to help them.

Case Study 2: Jordan's Nutritional-Fact Sharing

Jordan is a 34-year-old man who works 4 days per week as a shelf stocker at his family's neighborhood grocery store. He has a diagnosis of mild autism spectrum disorder, obsessive-compulsive disorder, and generalized anxiety and depression. He lives with both of his parents, who monitor his medication compliance, help him pay his bills, and assist him in the completion of other daily tasks.

Following several instances of aggressive behaviors toward customers, Jordan's family sought the services of Dr. Sullivan, a behavior analyst, to monitor his job performance and provide intervention to address his behavior. During one of her initial observations, Dr. Sullivan observed Jordan talking to customers about their selection of foods to purchase. He pulled packages of food out of their carts and asked them why they would plan to purchase foods with high fat, salt, and sugar content. After reading aloud the nutrition facts on the labels of various packages of food, Jordan stood very close to the customers' faces, proceeded to berate them for their selection of items, and vocally shared his hypotheses about their body mass indexes.

Knowing that she needed to take action promptly to address Jordan's behavior, Dr. Sullivan held a meeting that evening with Jordan, his employer, and Jordan's parents. The team discussed the behaviors recently observed. To prepare for the meeting, Dr. Sullivan printed out copies of a colleague's behavior-change plan (originally written to teach a 4-year-old girl not to talk to strangers) after changing the learner's name in the plan to Jordan's name. Dr. Sullivan assumed that this plan would work well for Jordan's situation as well because, essentially, Jordan needed to learn to not talk to people he did not know at the store. If that behavior could be decreased, Jordan would be able to focus on his work-related tasks and would not have challenging conversations with customers.

Case Study 3: Mason's Great Escapes

Mason is a 9-year-old boy who lives with his parents and two older sisters in a rural area of Idaho. Mason was recently diagnosed with attention-deficit-hyperactivity disorder and experiences severe sleep disturbances. On most nights, he sleeps less than 2 hours total. During the remaining night hours, he engages in property destruction in the form of carving holes out of his bedroom walls, pulling stuffing out of his plush toys, and overturning his mattress in order to flip off of his bed. In addition to these behaviors, Mason has managed to open and crawl out of the windows of his second-floor home. He also stealthily makes his way to the kitchen and exits the house through the front door to play in the backyard.

These behaviors were incredibly alarming to his parents, and they swiftly implemented several safety measures. Currently, there are alarms on all the windows in the house and on Mason's bedroom door. Additionally, Mason's parents take turns sleeping in his bed with him to attempt to prevent him from leaving the room or engaging in dangerous behaviors. Despite these measures, Mason is still managing to escape his bedroom and the family home an average of twice per week by disabling the alarms on his bedroom door and exiting the home through the dog door located in the home's kitchen entry door.

Mason's family contacted a behavior analyst, Ms. Jenna Miller, for assistance with addressing this dangerous behavior. Ms. Miller immediately determined that, as a part of the FBA she would conduct to address this behavior, she would directly contact Mason's school. Given the rural area in which Mason resides and goes to school, Ms. Miller is familiar with nearly every teacher and behavior clinician in the area. To expedite the process of conducting the FBA, she contacted Mason's teacher, who gathered all behavior and academic records and shared them with Ms. Miller.

Ms. Miller then conducted the FBA and designed a behavior-intervention plan that included the family setting a timer and waking every 10 minutes to reinforce Mason remaining in his room. This intervention plan was agreed upon by the family, but once implementation began, it was incredibly challenging for them to remain consistent. Inevitably, Mason would pretend to fall asleep, and when his parents fell asleep, Mason would leave the room using the same methods previously indicated. It was clear, after only a few nights of implementation, that Mason's parents were facing challenges implementing the intervention, but Ms. Miller insisted they continue with the plan as written.

After a period of continued challenges regarding this behavior and the intervention plan's failure to successfully address this behavior, Mason left the home one evening and was not located for the next 20 hours. When he was located, he was found in the woods 1 mile from the family home, excitedly playing in a tree with only minor scratches from spending so much time outside. Following the extreme panic that this episode caused (which involved recruiting law enforcement and search teams to locate

Mason), his parents were justifiably concerned about the nature of the behavior consultation provided by Ms. Miller. Further investigation determined that Ms. Miller had not maintained her certification as a behavior analyst and had not attended any continuing education events or activities pertaining to behavior-analytic practices or ethical conduct in the previous 5 years.

Case Study 4: Parker's Bathroom Visits

Parker is a 6-year-old boy with nonverbal learning disability. He attends a general education classroom at his local public school and does not require special education services. He has a peer in his class, Jason, who also has autism, and they share many of the same interests. Parker and Jason have often described themselves as "best friends" and played together in and out of school. Parker's parents and teachers have had few concerns about his academic progress or social development. However, there is one behavior that has been causing concern: Parker's bladder incontinence, which has been a chronic issue since Parker was a toddler. Although he successfully uses the toilet for bowel movements, Parker continues to urinate in his pants at least once daily. His parents often attempt to send him to school in a diaper designed for older children to prevent him needing to change his clothing, but Parker has frequently removed it while on the bus on the way to school.

Other students have begun to engage in name calling, including "peeing Parker" or "baby Parker," which frequently results in Parker running away or crying. Given the social stigma that has developed around Parker's diaper wearing and frequent accidents, Parker's best friend has begun to avoid interacting with him during the school day. His teachers and parents have therefore begun to seek the consultation of a behavior analyst to conduct an FBA. The behavior analyst concluded that this behavior serves the function of escape, as each time that Parker engages in incontinence, he consequently escapes the academic or social situation he is in because he needs to change his clothing. A medical consultation to explore biological reasons for his incontinence was not completed, as it was immediately assumed to be a behavioral concern.

Summary

This chapter provided an introduction to the scope and parameters of ethical functional behavior assessment. The goal of this chapter is to ensure that all future practitioners and students of ABA recognize that all practices in our discipline must align with the *Professional and Ethical Compliance Code for Behavior Analysts.* As is necessary when any ethical practice is taught and discussed, this chapter focused on real-world case examples and dilemmas. It is through consideration of real scenarios that could take place that the guidance and protection provided by The Code—for both consumers and practitioners—becomes clear.

The elements of The Code that directly relate to functional behavior assessment were reviewed, and it is highly recommended that you discuss them using the team-discussion exercises outlined at the end of this chapter. It will also be important for you to review the sample consent form for use when preparing to conduct an FBA with a consumer. Reviewing the provided case vignettes demonstrating the consent process will also highlight the importance of adhering to a specific process for obtaining informed consent.

Definition of Key Terms

- **function of behavior:** the purpose a behavior serves for the individual; the answer to the question "Why is this behavior occurring?"
- **multimodal:** involving multiple modes of assessment within the FBA process (e.g., interviews, direct observation, systematic manipulation).
- **experimental manipulation:** to determine the function of the behavior, relevant environmental variables are systematically manipulated within an experimental design, and the effect on behavior is closely observed.
- **structural analysis:** a type of experimental manipulation that involves systematically manipulating the variables that are present prior to the typical occurrence of a behavior.
- **functional analysis:** a type of experimental manipulation that involves systematically manipulating the variables that are present following the typical occurrence of a behavior.
- **procedural safeguards:** measures taken to minimize the risk of physical or emotional harm to an individual being assessed, the assessor, or any bystanders present during the assessment process (procedural safeguards are particularly necessary to plan for and implement when an experimental manipulation is being conducted).
- **conceptual analysis of behavior:** the philosophy of the science of behaviorism.
- **applied behavior analysis (ABA):** applies the basic principles of behavior analysis with the objective of influencing socially significant behavior through systematic assessment of environmental events and application of behavior-change practices.
- **experimental analysis of behavior (EAB):** provides the scientific foundation for applied behavior analysis and is the basic science of behavior analysis.
- **service delivery (SD):** focuses on the practitioners who deliver ABA services and models through which ABA is disseminated.

Test Your Understanding

Level 1: Knowledge

1. True or False: Behavior-change programs can be developed at the same time as conducting a functional behavior assessment.
2. True or False: Consent must be obtained prior to conducting a functional behavior assessment, and, in cases of extremely dangerous behaviors, verbal consent is sufficient.
3. True or False: Assessment results need to be explained to the learner in easily understandable language, and learners need to be involved in the development of the behavior-change plan.
4. True or False: Consent needs to be obtained from the learner prior to accessing school, hospital, or other providers' protected records for the learner.
5. True or False: Learners whose behaviors have been identified through functional behavior assessments as having the same function can be given the exact same behavior-change plan, as long as only the names are changed on the plan itself.

6. True or False: Learners need to provide written approval if a significant change will be made to the behavior-change plan.

7. True or False: If environmental constraints exist that hinder implementation of the behavior-change plan, the constraints should be removed if possible, or they should be documented in writing.

8. True or False: Behavior analysts should ensure that their course work and supervision experiences comply with the BACB®'s standards.

Level 2: Comprehension

1. The *Professional and Ethical Compliance Code for Behavior Analysts* outlines
   a. specific requirements and guidelines for behavior analysts to follow with respect to their work conducting functional behavior assessments as well as other activities typically performed by behavior analysts.
   b. specific suggestions and tips for behavior analysts to follow with respect to their work conducting functional behavior assessments as well as other activities typically performed by behavior analysts.
   c. general guidelines for behavior analysts to follow when in need of direction regarding the decisions they make as they conduct functional behavior assessments.
   d. none of the above.

2. Written consent is needed when performing which of the following activities relating to functional behavior assessment?
   a. Written consent is only necessary in the event that the learner is capable of reading at a fourth-grade level.
   b. Prior to conducting the functional behavior assessment but not prior to accessing learner records from other sources.
   c. Prior to accessing learner records from other sources but not always prior to conducting the functional behavior assessment.
   d. Prior to conducting the functional behavior assessment and prior to accessing learner records from other sources.

3. Written approval must be obtained from the learner prior to which of the following activities relating to functional behavior assessment?
   a. Prior to planning the functional behavior assessment procedures and prior to planning the behavior-change procedure or modifications to the behavior-change procedure.
   b. Prior to implementing functional behavior assessment procedures and prior to implementing the behavior-change procedure or modifications to the behavior-change procedure.
   c. Prior to conducting indirect assessments or interviews with individuals other than the learner and prior to implementing the behavior-change procedure or modifications to the behavior-change procedure.
   d. Written approval is only needed if the individual's assessment results will be used in a research publication or presentation.

4. The learner should be involved in which of the following activities relating to functional behavior assessment? (Select the response that is most comprehensive.)
   a. The behavior analyst should include the learner in determining the assessment procedures to be used and obtain written approval before implementing assessment procedures; behavior analysts should explain assessment results in a reasonably understandable way; learners should provide consent for the behavior analyst to access protected records from other sources.

b. Behavior analysts should explain assessment results in a reasonably understandable way; learners should provide consent for the behavior analyst to access protected records from other sources; learners should be involved in the planning of behavior-change programs and should provide consent for the program as well as any significant modifications to the program.

c. The behavior analyst should include the learner in determining the assessment procedures to be used and obtain written approval before implementing assessment procedures; behavior analysts should explain assessment results in a reasonably understandable way; learners should provide consent for the behavior analyst to access protected records from other sources; learners should be involved in the planning of behavior-change programs and should provide consent for the program as well as any significant modifications to the program.

d. It is in learners' best interest not to be involved in the assessment or behavior-change planning process because their involvement will hinder the potential effects of the behavior-change program.

Level 3: Application

1. Consider the case study illustrating Clara's hair-pulling behavior at school. Are there any codes outlined in the *Professional and Ethical Compliance Code for Behavior Analysts* that were clearly addressed in the case study? Were there any codes that were violated? Why have you identified these codes? Are there any actions that the behavior analysts (or others) in the case study could take to resolve any violations you identified?

2. Consider the case study illustrating Jordan's nutritional-fact sharing while working at the grocery store. Are there any codes outlined in the *Professional and Ethical Compliance Code for Behavior Analysts* that were clearly addressed in the case study? Were there any codes that were violated? Why have you identified these codes? Are there any actions that the behavior analysts (or others) in the case study could take to resolve any violations you identified?

3. Consider the case study illustrating Mason's nighttime escape behavior. Are there any codes outlined in the *Professional and Ethical Compliance Code for Behavior Analysts* that were clearly addressed in the case study? Were there any codes that were violated? Why have you identified these codes? Are there any actions that the behavior analysts (or others) in the case study could take to resolve any violations you identified?

4. Consider the case study illustrating Parker's incontinence at school. Are there any codes outlined in the *Professional and Ethical Compliance Code for Behavior Analysts* that were clearly addressed in the case study? Were there any codes that were violated? Why have you identified these codes? Are there any actions that the behavior analysts (or others) in the case study could take to resolve any violations you identified?

5. Select a previously covered case study in this chapter. Make a video recording with an oral explanation of the reasons why certain professional and ethical codes are necessary for consideration. Submit this recording for review. General tips: Students should take care to address the camera as though they are speaking with either a consumer of ABA services or a supervisee (imagine that the camera is the individual with whom you would be speaking). Students may elect to use props to demonstrate the way in which data should be collected or other materials relating to how the behavior-change procedure should be implemented. In the event that these props or data-collection sheets are referenced in the video, these items should be made visible on camera.

In-Class Small-Group Discussion Questions/Exercises

Create small groups (perhaps four or five students) and discuss the following topics, allowing 10 to 15 minutes to complete the response.

1. What are your thoughts on the case studies presented in this chapter?
    a. Do you believe that the case studies presented highlight the need for the *Professional and Ethical Compliance Code for Behavior Analysts*? Why or why not?
    b. What factors about the individual's scenario make you agree or disagree with the approach taken by the behavior analyst in each case study?
    c. What additional questions would you want to ask about the situations presented in the case studies?
2. Consider the role that the BACB® plays in the work of behavior analysts as well as the purpose for the *Professional and Ethical Compliance Code for Behavior Analysts*. Consider the 10 compliance codes highlighted in this chapter and discuss the real-world implications and consequences that would occur if each of those compliance codes were not provided or followed. What effect could the absence of each code have on individual learners, behavior analysts, and the profession of behavior analysis as a whole? (Be sure to frame your discussion in terms of each compliance code with relation to each party identified in this question.)

Reference

Baer, D.M., Wolf, M.M., & Risley, T.R. (1968). Some current dimensions of applied behavior analysis. *Journal of Applied Behavior Analysis, 1*, 91–97.

Bailey, J., & Burch, M. (2016). *Ethics for behavior analysts* (3rd ed.). New York, NY: Routledge.

Behavior Analyst Certification Board®. (2014). *Professional and ethical compliance code for behavior analysts*. Retrieved from http://www.bacb.com/Downloadfiles//BACB_Compliance_Code.pdf.

Iwata, B.A., Dorsey, M.F., Slifer, K.J., Bauman, K.F., & Richman, G.S. (1994). Toward a functional analysis of self-injury. Journal of Applied Behavior Analysis, 27(2), 197–209.

Recommended Readings

Baer, D.M., Wolf, M.M., & Risley, T.R. (1968). Some current dimensions of applied behavior analysis. *Journal of Applied Behavior Analysis, 1*, 91–97.

Bailey, J., & Burch, M. (2016). *Ethics for behavior analysts* (3rd ed.). New York, NY: Routledge.

Bailey, J., & Burch, M. (2010). *Twenty-five essential skills and strategies for the professional behavior analyst.* New York, NY: Routledge.

Skinner, B.F. (1953). *Science and human behavior.* New York, NY: Macmillan.

Appendix

Sample Functional Behavior Assessment Consent Form

I, _____, give consent for the completion of a functional behavior assessment (FBA) on [LEARNER'S NAME].

A functional behavior assessment is the process of

- identifying problematic behavior(s);
- identifying environmental events that impact problematic behavior(s);
- determining the cause/function of the problematic behavior(s); and
- outlining the necessary changes needed to be made by the school, teacher, student, parent/guardian, and any other member of the therapeutic-treatment team in order to allow the learner to successfully access the general curriculum and/or function more independently.

An FBA may include, but is not limited to, the following components:

- Interviews regarding the student's behavior, in which the learner (if applicable), teacher(s), parent(s)/guardian(s), and other relevant team members server as informants
- Information-gathering tools (e.g., cumulative file review, teacher-rating scale, and learner self-assessment)
- Observations of learner behavior in school, home, and community settings
- Data collection on learner behavior
- Structural analysis, wherein the learner will be systematically exposed to or placed in the presence of different stimuli to evoke the occurrence of the problem behavior to assess which stimulus is likely to be present before the behavior occurs. (If a structural analysis is deemed necessary, an addendum to this consent form will be provided, and benefits and risks of that specific procedure will be discussed and consented to prior to the structural analysis being conducted.)
- Functional analysis, wherein the learner will be systematically exposed to or placed in the presence of different consequences (e.g., receiving attention, the opportunity to leave a task, or being left alone to engage in the behavior) following occurrence of the problem behavior to assess which consequence is likely to keep the behavior occurring. (If a functional analysis is deemed necessary, an addendum to this consent form will be provided, and benefits and risks of that specific procedure will be discussed and consented to prior to the functional analysis being conducted.)
- Ongoing data collection to evaluate intervention effectiveness
- Safety or crisis plan, if necessary

The benefits of completing the above-described assessment include the ability to select function-based behavioral interventions for treating the problem behavior. There are minor risks associated with the completion of this FBA. An unintended side effect may be that [LEARNER'S NAME] may engage in challenging behavior as a result of being observed. The evaluator will develop protocols to make this event unlikely and to insure the safety of all, especially [LEARNER'S NAME], is maintained. Physical records with identifiable information regarding [LEARNER'S NAME]'s behavior will be protected in a locked filing cabinet, and electronic data will be stored in a password-protected file; nevertheless, there is always the potential for confidentiality to be compromised. The evaluator will make every effort to minimize these risks.

I have read the above information and understand that I can ask questions at any time regarding the assessment procedures by contacting [NAME OF EVALUATOR] at [PHONE NUMBER/ EMAIL ADDRESS]. I also understand that assessment is voluntary and that I can request that it be discontinued at any time without any adverse effects on [LEARNER]'s programming. I understand that the results of the assessment may be used to develop a behavior-intervention plan for [LEARNER'S NAME].

☐ I give consent for my child, _____, to participate in a functional behavior assessment.

☐ I do not give consent for my child, _____, to participate in a functional behavior assessment.

_____   _____
            Parent/Guardian Signature   Date

CHAPTER 2

Determining Social Significance

A functional behavior assessment (FBA) is recommended when an individual learner's behavior becomes concerning. The first step in behavioral assessment is to identify what behavior analysts call a **target behavior**, which is an observable and measurable action the learner emits that is identified as needing to be changed. A comprehensive discussion of the process to define target behaviors will be provided in Chapter 4 of this text; however, determining what constitutes an appropriate target for behavior change is necessary to outline prior to that point.

Cooper, Heron, and Heward (2007) presented many critical considerations in selecting a target behavior, including an evaluation of the impact the behavior has with respect to the learner's (or others') health and safety, reinforcement for significant others, an evaluation of who will benefit from the behavior being changed, and a cost-benefit analysis of the time and effort required to complete the behavior change. Additionally, there are aspects of the behavior itself that should also be evaluated, such as the frequency of the behavior's occurrence, the longevity of the behavior, and the likelihood of success in changing the behavior. Finally, one should consider the direct impact on the learner as a result of the target behavior change, including the potential for the learner to gain higher rates of reinforcement, the importance of the behavior for the learner, and if a reduction of negative attention will occur.

Once the target behavior has been identified, the first question to ask is whether it is socially significant or if it is important for the individual to experience change in the behavior. Behavior analysts are required to seek to change only behaviors that will result in a significant improvement in the learner's safety, adaptive, social, academic, or physical functioning. **Social significance** is measured by the degree to which changing the identified behavior will improve the individual's life. Behavior analysts are discouraged from seeking to change behaviors that will not result in meaningful improvement in the individual's life, even if it is within the behavior analyst's ability to change the behavior.

As we delve into the discussion of social significance when selecting target behaviors, social validity should also be discussed, as it has farther-reaching implications. **Social validity** is a measure of the acceptability and appropriateness of the target behavior, behavioral goal, intervention procedure(s), and ultimate effect of behavior change. In other words, not only should the target behavior be socially significant, but the social validity of each element of the behavior-change process and its effects are critical to examine to justify the need for behavior change. Hanley (2010) has argued that social validity can be evaluated using direct measurement with the recipients of intervention (learners) themselves. An objective way to evaluate the social validity of an intervention would be to measure how long a particular behavior-analytic intervention is used over time, which follows the assumption that individuals only continue to use an intervention if they find it to be acceptable. Another option would be to provide the learner a choice of interventions and measure the frequency of their selections, which suggests that interventions selected frequently are more acceptable than those selected less frequently. Although individual target behaviors or interventions are often assessed for social significance, the evaluation of social validity includes consideration of each of the decisions involved in assessment and intervention.

When considering the behaviors on which to focus behavior-change, imagine that a seven-year-old displaying deficits in adaptive functioning (e.g. emits minimal functional language, he has not been toilet-trained, and only follows 1-step instructions 50% of the time) has been assessed for his language and earned a low score in the area of grade-level vocabulary. In particular, he is unable to expressively identify most colors, letters, or shapes and is therefore failing to meet his academic goals. During a program-planning meeting with his Individualized Education Plan (IEP) team, his speech therapist suggests that, in light of these assessment data, it would be worthwhile for this learner to engage in an intensive training program to increase his vocabulary in these areas, taking additional instructional time from other areas of the learner's programming. Although there are numerous areas of deficit for the learner in the area of adaptive skill development and additional language instruction would likely improve an area of need, one must determine whether creating a goal to focus on colors, letters, and shapes should take priority over a more intensive plan of improving independent adaptive functioning. The answer to that question will depend on the perceived social significance and social validity of each target behavior and the process by which such behaviors will be addressed.

In this chapter, case studies and exercises will be presented that will ask the reader to evaluate whether the scenarios would call for behavior intervention to be implemented. Be sure to complete the activities outlined at the end of the chapter to complete another iteration of the "See one, do one, teach one" process to fully master the skills involved in identifying and evaluating the social significance of target behaviors.

LEARNING OBJECTIVES

After completing the chapter's activities, learners should be able to do the following:

- Determine the degree of social significance of a variety of behaviors
- Identify whether changing a target behavior would lead to significantly greater independence and improved functioning than a different target behavior

- Specifically state whether changing a particular behavior would lead to improved safety for the individual, and/or increased adaptive, social, academic, or physical functioning

- Justify this position with information relating to the individual's environmental context and with indicators of current functioning

Case Study 1: Marla's Finger-Tapping Behavior

Marla is a 10-year-old girl with autism spectrum disorder. She attends a general education classroom full time and is functioning at grade level. She engages in repetitive finger tapping when she is completing her math worksheets in class. The finger-tapping behavior consists of extending her index finger of her left hand, lowering it to the edge of the seat of her chair, and repetitively tapping once per second until she has completed her math worksheet. There is one classmate who sits next to her, and this classmate reports that the finger tapping is not noticeable or distracting to him or other classmates.

In the scenario above, Marla's finger-tapping behavior would not be considered socially significant nor would it warrant a functional behavior assessment or behavior intervention plan. This is because Marla's finger-tapping behavior does not apparently interfere with Marla's completion of her academic work (she is successfully completing her math sheet). Additionally, Marla's behavior is not hindering her peers' learning (the classmate who sits next to her is apparently not bothered by this behavior and successfully completes his work without difficulty). Therefore, even though a behavior analyst could conduct a functional behavior assessment and develop an effective behavior change plan to decrease the occurrence of finger tapping in this situation, it would not be worthwhile to do so, as it will not result in a meaningful improvement in either student's life. Marla's academic and social functioning is not impacted adversely by this behavior; therefore, the behavior can be left unaddressed.

Case Study 2: Carlos's Face-Slapping Behavior

*Carlos is a five-year-old boy with a diagnosis of Oppositional Defiant Disorder who attends a full-day pre-kindergarten program operated in his community's church. Carlos engages in open-hand face slapping when he is provided with a **task demand** from one of his teachers. This behavior occurs an average of thirteen times per class day (a period of seven hours) and is usually accompanied by screaming the word "No!" or the statement "Don't want to!" Approximately fifty percent of the time, the face-slapping behavior results in a red mark or bruise on the other individual's face. The face slap can occur immediately following the provision of the task demand or up to five minutes following the provision of the task demand (depending on the physical proximity of the teacher to Carlos's reach). About ten percent of the time, Carlos will slap the face of one of his peers instead of the teacher who presented the task demand. His teachers remark, anecdotally, that it appears he will face slap peers only when he is unable to reach the teacher's face.*

It is clear that Carlos's behavior is significantly different than Marla's behavior in Case Study 1, in that Carlos's behavior is socially significant in several ways. First, Carlos is engaging in a potentially dangerous behavior that is causing harm to those around him. This adversely impacts the safety of those around him (both that of his teachers and, on occasion, his peers). Aggressive behaviors, especially those that are severe enough to cause harm (as indicated by the red marks being left behind following the face slapping), need to be addressed immediately and a **zero-tolerance policy** should be adopted with respect to any aggressive acts (including self-injury and behaviors that are injurious to others, such as in Carlos's case).

Second, it is critical to consider the social impact this behavior causes. As Carlos engages in this aggressive behavior, his teachers and peers will be less likely to seek interaction with Carlos. Even though his teachers are required to present task demands to him (as a matter of carrying out academic programming in the classroom), they may be reluctant to ask Carlos to do more than is absolutely necessary to keep him on task. This is because even the teachers are responding to environmental events, and, whether purposefully or not, they may likely seek to avoid the possibility of being injured by Carlos. Ultimately, this may have an impact on his academic performance (due to fewer academic challenges being presented to him in the school day), but also on his social relationship with his teachers. Additionally, his peers may begin to distance themselves from social interactions with Carlos to avoid the possibility of injury.

Finally, Carlos's face-slapping behavior limits the development of his adaptive functioning and independence. It is critical for young children to develop the ability to either communicate their displeasure or lack of preference with a certain task appropriately (and eventually comply) or request help if the task is too difficult. As Carlos's aggressive behavior occurs frequently over time, he might miss out on opportunities to be taught alternate means to communicate his needs. For all these reasons (but, most importantly, for the safety of the entire classroom community), Carlos's face-slapping behavior must be addressed immediately with a functional behavior assessment and behavior intervention plan.

Case Study 3: Benjamin's Repetitive Questioning

Benjamin is a fourteen-year-old boy with a diagnosis of Autism Spectrum Disorder and Obsessive Compulsive Disorder. Benjamin demonstrates particularly intense **perseveration** *on the topic of the weather. He displays extreme anxiety when thunderstorms occur (he begins to scream and cry, and he seeks a closet or enclosed space to sit in and will not leave the space until the storm has passed). Benjamin's anxiety that a thunderstorm will occur is near constant, and given that he and his family reside in a coastal town in Florida, the probability for inclement weather of this kind is relatively high.*

Benjamin engages in repetitive questioning (mostly directed to his mother) about the weather forecast. From the moment Benjamin wakes up in the morning until he falls asleep, Benjamin asks questions about the weather forecast for the day and week ahead as well as questions about what will happen if he is caught in the storm (e.g., "Is it supposed to storm today?", "There is a forty percent chance of showers; do you think it will rain and then thunder?", "Will the thunder be so loud I will need to cover my ears?", "If it rains, will we be swept into the ocean?", "What if it storms when I'm on the bus?", "What if I cannot get inside and lightning hits me?"). Benjamin asks these questions once nearly every two to five minutes and will increase the frequency of his question-asking, breathe heavily, and begin rocking and eventually crying if he does not receive a response within ten seconds of his questions. If his mother (or the individual he is asking) is able to answer his questions within ten seconds of him asking the question, he will not increase his rate of question-asking from once every two to five minutes. The only time Benjamin will typically refrain from asking these questions is if he is eating a snack or a meal or if he is drawing pictures of storms in his notepad. This behavior became so significant that his mother chose to home school Benjamin due to his frequent tantrums regarding riding the school bus and walking into the school building on days when inclement weather was expected.

Benjamin's repetitive questioning about storms is a socially significant behavior of concern. Though this is not a behavior that concerns his immediate safety, it is a behavior that negatively impacts his social interactions with his mother (and anyone around him, as he engages in the repetitive questioning with most communicative partners) and limits his ability to engage in academic tasks. Additionally, Benjamin has been removed from the least restrictive environment for him (his school) and is currently in an environment where he has extremely limited opportunities to interact with peers his own age. Therefore, this questioning should be addressed in a behavior intervention plan such that these opportunities for increased independent social functioning can be presented to Benjamin once again.

Case Study 4: Jean's Non-Preference for Dish Washing

Jean is a thirty-four-year-old woman with Mild Intellectual Disability. She resides in a group home with four other adults with various disabilities. As a part of her membership in the group home, Jean is expected to engage in household chores that contribute to the cleanliness, organization, and general operations of the group home. Among these chores include making one's bed, washing one's clothes and putting them away in one's closet, cooking simple meals for oneself, and washing one's dishes in the communal kitchen. Jean avoids touching soapy water (she has successfully overcome this when bathing herself by using a loofah and showering instead of taking baths), but she engages in extreme avoidance when required to wash dishes by hand (e.g., she will scream, cry, and hit those around her when asked to wash dishes). Though the staff at her group home has attempted to teach her to use rubber gloves to complete this task, Jean remains resistant and engages in challenging behaviors when required to do so. One of the other residents in Jean's group home, Gloria, has a great affinity for running her hands under water and prefers to wash dishes instead of preparing meals for herself. The staff at the group home decided to schedule Jean and Gloria's meal times to coincide, and they have taught Jean to prepare two meals or snacks at a time (to share one with Gloria), and have taught Gloria to clean both her own and Jean's dishes. The group home staff perceived this to be a mutually beneficial, symbiotic solution to Jean's challenging behaviors when asked to wash her own dishes, as both group home members ultimately receive a prepared meal and their dishes end up being cleaned.

The question of whether Jean's avoidant behavior when asked to wash her own dishes is socially significant is relatively more complex than the previous case scenarios presented in this chapter. Although finding a way for Jean to independently wash her own dishes would result in greater independence and adaptive functioning, the fact that Gloria resides with Jean and is not only willing, but prefers, to wash dishes, ensures that the task is still accomplished and that Jean's quality of life is not adversely impacted by being forced to engage in a task she does not prefer. Additionally, encouraging Jean to prepare meals for Gloria ensures that Jean is still contributing equally to the household chores. Ultimately, though this solution does not directly address teaching Jean to comply with the task demand of dish washing, the behavior analyst should ask him or herself if it is worthwhile for this behavior to be addressed at this time. In this case, there is sufficient evidence that this is currently not a socially significant behavior of concern. However, if Gloria were to leave the group home in the future or eventually refuse to wash additional dishes in the future, it will be necessary for Jean's reluctance to wash dishes to be addressed (by overcoming the resistance directly through behavior change procedures, or by using rubber gloves, using disposable plates and utensils, or with some other workaround). In this way, Jean's scenario illustrates that some behaviors may vary in their degree of social significance depending on the context in which the behavior occurs and on other relevant factors in the individual's life at different times.

Questions for Determining Significance

Often, behavior analysts are faced with the challenging truth that despite being able to modify nearly any given behavior (within the capacity of their control), they must determine if it is socially important for them to do so. Wolf (1978) explored the issue of social importance in the selection of target behaviors in a commentary meant to further develop the scientific discipline and community of applied behavior analysis. Ultimately, he indicated, if, after examining the significance of a certain behavior, it is determined that the behavior is not as significant as initially perceived, it is important that the behavior analyst shift her or his attention onto a different, higher priority behavior. This discussion is relevant to the topic of determining social significance in the sense that it is *possible* for behavior analysts to change a wide variety of behaviors across various dimensions, but they still must ask themselves whether it is necessary for them to do so.

As was demonstrated in the case studies in this chapter, there are several different types of questions that need to be asked when determining a behavior's social significance and selecting a target behavior for change. For instance, "If the behavior is changed, how will the individual's life improve (in terms of their safety, adaptive functioning, social interactions, academic performance, or physical mobility)?" If the answer is that the individual will be able to be safer in their natural environment, independent when engaging in daily living activities, that peers will want to spend more time with the individual, and/or that the individual will improve their performance in an academic task or have increased mobility, it would be important to make this behavior a focus of behavior change.

Another question that behavior analysts should ask is, "What would happen if the behavior were *not* targeted for change?" If the answer to this question was that the individual would experience an adverse effect in his or her level of independence, frequency or quality of social interactions, academic standing, or physical mobility, it would be critical to address this behavior. Often, the role of educators is not only to teach students the skills they need to succeed and gain independence, but also to work to remove barriers that prohibit students from mastering those critical skills.

Behavior analysts also should ask themselves, "Would it be better to focus their efforts on a different behavior that, if changed, will result in more significant improvement in the individual's life?" If the answer is that another behavior takes immediate priority over the selected target behavior, it is critical that the behavior analyst shift their focus to the higher priority behavior. The time constraints and limitations on resources that educators and behavior analysts face are two pragmatic concerns that impact their ability to carry out lengthy assessment and intervention processes.

Summary

This chapter covered the question of social significance when selecting a target behavior to change. The more that a behavior analyst focuses on targeting behaviors that will result in meaningful change in the individual's life, the greater positive impact they will have in their practice.

Definition of Key Terms

- **target behavior:** a behavior selected for change
- **social significance:** the degree of relative importance the behavior change will have on the learner
- **social validity:** a measure of the acceptability and appropriateness of the target behavior, behavioral goal, intervention procedure(s), and ultimate effect of behavior change
- **task demand:** a directive presented to a learner (in verbal, visual, or textual form) signaling that the availability of reinforcement will follow the completion of an activity or that reinforcement is no longer available for a certain period of time
- **zero-tolerance policy:** a policy indicating that no instances of the behavior are acceptable and the behavior must reach a rate of zero
- **perseveration:** repetitive utterances or actions that occur following an initial stimulus that has since passed

Test Your Understanding

Level 1: Knowledge

1. True or False: The social significance of a behavior is best identified by examining the individual's social abilities exclusively.
2. True or False: A target behavior can be any behavior selected for change.
3. True or False: Prior to selecting a target behavior, a behavior analyst should evaluate the social significance of the behavior.
4. True or False: Determining social significance should include an evaluation of whether the behavior change will improve the lives of those around the individual learner, as well as the learner themselves.
5. True or False: Determining social significance does not require consideration of the context in which the behavior occurs; if the behavior could be problematic in any hypothetical context, it is socially significant and needs to be changed.
6. True or False: Behaviors that have the potential to cause harm to those around the individual learner are highly socially significant and need to be changed.
7. True or False: Changing a person's behavior to maximize their academic ability is automatically more socially significant than changing their behavior to maximize their adaptive ability.
8. True or False: Members of the individual's environment (school, home, or community) can contribute to the evaluation of the social significance of a particular behavior of concern.

9. True or False: Behavior analysts must focus on socially significant behaviors because those are the only behaviors that are possible for them to change.
10. True or False: Behavior analysts have a duty to focus on socially significant behaviors because those are behaviors determined to have the greatest positive impact on the individual's life.

Level 2: Comprehension

1. Social significance is determined by evaluating the potential for the behavior change to improve the individual's
   a. safety
   b. adaptive functioning
   c. social functioning
   d. all of the above
2. When attempting to determine the social significance of a behavior, it is important to discuss the following factors:
   a. The intensity of the behavior
   b. The frequency and duration of the behavior
   c. Who is affected by the behavior
   d. All of the above
3. Out of the situations provided, select which of the following would be an example of a socially significant behavior that should warrant immediate focus for behavior change:
   a. An individual's jumping behavior that occurs in front of the television during leisure time at home
   b. An individual's jumping behavior that occurs in the middle of a sixth grade science class, despite ridicule from peers
   c. An individual's jumping behavior while out on the playground at recess with one other peer who also enjoys jumping
   d. None of the above
4. Out of the situations provided, select which of the following would be an example of a socially significant behavior that should warrant immediate focus for behavior change:
   a. An individual's behavior of eating with his or her mouth open and not using a napkin to wipe his or her mouth while at the lunch table at school with peers. This behavior has caused peers to sit at a different table
   b. An individual's behavior of eating with his or her mouth open and not using a napkin to wipe his or her mouth while at dinner with his or her older siblings who do not seem to notice the behavior
   c. An individual's behavior of eating with his or her mouth open and not using a napkin to wipe his or her mouth while eating alone at breakfast at home
   d. None of the above
5. Out of the situations provided, select which of the following would be an example of a socially significant behavior that should warrant immediate focus for behavior change:
   a. An individual's insistence on discussing sports statistics while attending a professional baseball game with friends
   b. An individual's insistence on discussing sports statistics while watching a football game on television with a neighbor
   c. An individual's insistence on discussing sports statistics with strangers in the bathroom at the community pool
   d. None of the above

Level 3: Application

1. Consider the case study illustrating Marla's finger tapping. Are there any modifications to either the severity of the behavior or its impact on the classroom environment that would increase the social significance of this behavior (rendering it in need of behavior change)? What would those modifications be and why would they make the behavior more socially significant?
2. Consider the case study depicting Carlos's aggressive face-slapping behavior occurring in his classroom environment. Are there any factors associated with this behavior that, if changed, would decrease the social significance of this behavior (such that it would not be a prioritized focus of behavior change)? Why or why not? Support your perspective with evidence from the case study.
3. Consider the case study discussing Benjamin's repetitive questioning about the weather. This behavior seems to be isolated to the context of interactions between Benjamin and his mother and only sometimes other individuals. Does the lower frequency of individuals seemingly affected by this behavior factor into your determination of its social significance? Why or why not?
4. Consider the case study outlining Jean's avoidance of dish washing in her group home environment. This behavior was indicated not to be in immediate need of behavior change due to the presence of a group home member who would assist Jean in meeting her own needs. However, can you imagine other factors that would suggest that this behavior could remain unaddressed? What would those be and why would they indicate that the behavior need not be the focus of behavior change?
5. Consider the variety of scenarios explored across the case studies in this chapter. Are there certain behaviors that seem more socially significant than others? Why or why not? When responding to this question, specifically state the relevant factors in your determination of each behavior's social significance.
6. Select one of the case studies covered in this chapter or create one yourself. Imagine you need to explain the social significance of the behavior outlined in the case study to a team member also working with the learner. Create a video recording of the oral explanation of the behavior's social significance and submit this recording for review. General tips: Students should take care to address the camera as though they are speaking with either a consumer of ABA services or a supervisee (imagine that the camera is the individual with whom you would be speaking). Students may elect to use props or other materials to demonstrate the way in which data should be collected or relating to how the behavior change procedure should be implemented. In the event that these props or data collection sheets are referenced in the video, these items should be made visible on camera.

In-Class Small Group Discussion Questions/Exercises

Create small groups (perhaps four or five students) and discuss the following topics, allowing 10 to 15 minutes to complete the response.

1. What are your thoughts on the case studies presented in this chapter?
    a. Do you agree or disagree with the analysis of the social significance for each behavior? Why or why not?
    b. What factors about the individual's scenario make you agree or disagree with the analysis provided?
    c. Are there additional questions would you want to ask about the behaviors presented in the case studies?

2. List behaviors that you engage in daily. Pick a few and justify why you believe that they would or would not be socially significant behaviors worth changing and identify other behaviors that are not worth changing.

3. Consider the behaviors of either a learner or another individual in your life. (It is suggested that you keep the identity of the person confidential, rather than sharing it with the group.) Then,
   - identify three socially significant behaviors that you would attempt to change, if you were working professionally with that individual;
   - identify three socially significant behaviors that though somewhat concerning, would not warrant behavior change, if you were working professionally with that individual; and
   - image any other factors that might cause you to change your position and explain.

References

Cooper, J.O., Heron, T.E., & Heward, W.L. (*2007*). *Applied behavior analysis* (2nd ed.). Upper Saddle River, N.J.: Pearson Prentice Hall.

Hanley, G.P. (2010). Toward Effective and Preferred Programming: A Case for the Objective Measurement of Social Validity with Recipients of Behavior-Change Programs. *Behavior Analysis in Practice, 3*(1), 13–21.

Wolf, M.M. (1978). Social validity: The case for subjective measurement or how applied behavior analysis is finding its heart. *Journal of Applied Behavior Analysis, 11*(2), 203–214.

Recommended Reading

Bannerman, D.J., Sheldon, J.B., Sherman, J.A., & Harchik, A.F. (1990). Balancing the right to habilitation with the right to personal liberties: The right of persons with developmental disabilities to eat too many doughnuts and take a nap. *Journal of Applied Behavior Analysis, 23,* 79—89.

CHAPTER 3

Functional Behavior Assessment: An Overview

Functional behavior assessment (FBA) is a comprehensive, multi-modal process used to gather various types of data from different sources to arrive at hypotheses about the relation between the person and environment in order to guide behavior-change methods (Ramsay, Reynolds & Kamphaus, 2002). This chapter will discuss each element of the FBA process and its relation to other elements in the development of a functional hypothesis. But, before doing so, it is important to discuss some of the historical background of the FBA.

Behavior analysts have long known that the environment influences the behavior of organisms. Early assessments to identify the function, or the reason, a behavior occurs relied on analysis of those environmental variables and their relation to the behavior. These initial assessments involved primarily indirect and direct assessment methods to amass data to generally determine the function. The degree to which a method is considered to be direct or indirect depends on how closely it captures data on the behavior as it occurs in the natural environment. An **in-vivo observation** is a real-time observation of the behavior's occurrence and is a direct assessment whereas indirect assessment gathers data in a manner more removed from the behavior's actual occurrence. When taken together, indirect and direct assessments comprise what is called "**descriptive assessment**", as the data provide a description of what is occurring in the environment surrounding the occurrence of the behavior.

Limitations of the descriptive assessment arise when the resulting analysis of those data are unclear or ambiguous, the behavior presents risk of harm that require additional clarity about the function prior to intervening, or indicate multiple functions are underlying the behavior. In 1982, Iwata and colleagues published the results of a seminal study (that was re-printed in the same journal in 1994), which provided a methodology to experimentally evaluate the potential function(s) of behavior by systematically manipulating consequences following the occurrence of a target behavior. The resulting methodology was referred to as **functional analysis** (FA) and was proposed as a stage of the FBA process to prove the hypothesized function following an initial descriptive assessment. An FA is a brief single subject research study, the results of which aim to indicate that the target behavior (dependent variable) is systematically changing in the presence of a particular consequence (independent variable). This repeated and systematic change in the target behavior occurring only in the presence of one (or multiple) consequence(s) is a **functional relation**. Identifying the functional relation between a target behavior and its reinforcing consequence is the goal of the FA.

The development, further replication, and validation of the FA as a reliable method prompted the FA to be a mainstay among behavioral assessment technologies. Following the development of the FA process, behavior analysts also aimed to experimentally analyze the variables that precede a behavior and therefore could play a role in evoking a target behavior. This type of experimental analysis is called a **structural analysis (SA)** and it follows the same principles as a FA in terms of designing an experiment to systematically evaluate variables influencing the behavior. The results of an SA allow one to identify interventions that will likely prevent the behavior from occurring, whereas the results of an FA indicate what is likely increasing the likelihood of the behavior occurring in the future. Both the FA and SA will be discussed in great detail in Chapter 10 of this text.

The value of the FBA, including the use of FAs and SAs, is that it can be used with any population and targeted behavior. In fact, a core philosophical principle underlying the FBA process–and argument for conducting FBA in general–is that every behavior serves a function (or multiple functions) and the identification of such functions is critical for a behavior analyst to be able to design and implement an effective behavior-change intervention. This **function-based intervention** approach additionally implies that any information we have about the prevalence of certain behaviors in a specific population or even diagnostic information regarding specific disorders may be useful in terms of determining eligibility for services (for example), but is not particularly relevant toward our development of a behavioral intervention (e.g., knowing that individuals with a formal diagnosis Oppositional Defiance Disorder typically ignore verbal directions provided to them is not an explanation that is directly helpful toward identifying an intervention to change the behavior). This does not mean that biological explanations for the occurrence of a behavior (e.g., ear infections, a rotting tooth, gastrointestinal symptoms, migraines, or any other biological indicators) should be ignored. Instead, biological or medical explanations for the occurrence of the behavior should be fully explored first and either ruled out or addressed by relevant medical professionals before determining if conducting FBA is warranted. More on the function-based behavior intervention process is discussed in Chapter 11 of this text.

Now that we have reviewed some of the historical and philosophical background of the FBA process, it is necessary to examine each component of the process more closely. A graphical overview of the various steps in the FBA process is provided in this chapter. First, a team is assembled, the social significance of the behavior is discussed, and a definition of the behavior is formed. Once data are collected on the target behavior through descriptive assessment methods, they are analyzed and a hypothesis about the function or purpose of the behavior is formulated. At this point, the team can determine if experimental manipulation (FA or SA) is needed to further test or prove the functional relation to confirm its accuracy. If the target behavior presents a low risk of harm and/or the team determines that the descriptive assessment results indicate the likely function of the behavior, it is possible for the team to not proceed with an experimental manipulation. However, if the descriptive assessment results are ambiguous or if there is any risk of harm in proceeding with descriptive assessment results alone, experimental manipulation should be conducted with (as always) procedural safeguards in place and careful attention to and compliance with the Code (BACB®, 2016). (Determining whether to conduct experimental analysis will be discussed further in Chapter 10.) Following verification of the function of the behavior, a **behavior intervention plan (BIP)** is developed to change the behavior. As is the case with all attempts at behavior change, it is critical to then monitor and evaluate progress to ensure the behavior change is maintained.

After reading this chapter, please complete the end-of-chapter activities to fully complete the "See one, do one, teach one" process to enhance your progress toward mastery of these concepts.

LEARNING OBJECTIVES

After completing the chapter's activities, learners should be able to do the following:

- List and discuss the steps of the FBA process and their relation to one another in the development of a functional hypothesis

- Identify parties responsible for completing each step of the FBA process Define key terms.

- Consider the need to teach skills to decrease problem behavior

- Consider the example hypothesis statements and their implications for guiding the development of behavior intervention

- Consider the example behavior intervention plan and the implications of its implementation and progress monitoring

Functional Behavior Assessment Process

Figure 3.1 Functional Behavior Assessment Process

Step 1: Establish a Team

Since challenging behaviors do not often occur in isolation, it is critical to gather information from individuals who observe the behavior across environments in which they occur. For this reason, it is very useful to establish a team specifically designated to

- collect data on the occurrence of the challenging behavior in the context in which they observe it, and
- interact with the learner over time.

This type of team has the potential to take a variety of forms; it may be comprised of professionals (e.g., school educators and staff, psychologists, related services therapists, etc.), family members (e.g., parents, legal guardians, extended family, and adult siblings), and even community members who observe the target behavior within their interactions with the learner (e.g., school bus driver, swim teacher, camp counselor, vocational coach, etc.). Behavior analysts are usually included in the team when there is a behavior of concern and the team may or may not have already defined the behavior.

Step 2: Identify the Target Behavior

Once a team has been assembled, it is critical to come to a common understanding of the target behavior. This step usually happens after having talked with several team members and after directly observing the behavior. To ensure all members of the team hold the same perspective of the target behavior, a formal, written definition of the target behavior should be crafted. This definition should outline the behavior's form, specifically outlining what the behavior looks and sounds like and outlining whether the behavior results in a change in the environment (e.g., property destruction, etc.). An objective and measurable definition of the target behavior is essential for the team to collect reliable and meaningful data to effectively change the target behavior. The required elements of an objective, measurable, and observable behavior definition will be discussed in detail in Chapter 4. For now, please note that because behavior is lawful, and therefore subject to the laws of science (namely predictability and cause- and effect-relations), it is possible for the analysis of behavior to take place when specific information is gathered about the behavior.

Step 3: Collect Baseline Data

There are two types of data required to conduct an FBA: indirect and direct assessment methods. **Indirect assessment** includes reviewing the learner's current and previous records (from education, medical, and related therapists' reports). Additionally, indirect assessment methods include formal and informal interviews with the team of individuals observing the target behavior in the natural environment. There are several formal interview tools that have already been established and empirically validated and that vary in format (i.e., ranging in form from structured interviews, questionnaires, rating scales, self-report instruments, to checklists). These tools will be explored extensively in Chapter 6 of this book.

   Direct assessment includes **in-vivo observation** of the learner as they engage in the target behavior. Most commonly, direct observation data consists of recording the occurrence of the target behavior over the course of several days and across locations in which the behavior occurs. Specifically, for each occurrence of the target behavior that is observed, data on the environmental stimuli and events that occur *immediately before* the occurrence of the behavior, **antecedents**, and *immediately after* the occurrence of the behavior, **consequences**, are recorded. This **temporal sequence** of potentially dependent events is referred to as the **antecedent-behavior-consequence (ABC) contingency** or the **three-term contingency** in behavior analysis. The three-term contingency is the basic unit of analysis of operant behavior.

Essentially, because behaviors are influenced by the environmental stimuli and the events that occur before and after the behavior's occurrence, recording those events repeatedly can result in identification of a pattern wherein certain stimuli or events are found to be more or less likely to occur around the behavior. In other words, determining the most commonly occurring antecedents and consequences preceding and following a behavior will provide critical objective information about why the individual might engage in the behavior. It is the objective of the direct assessment to capture as many instances of the three-term contingency pertaining to the target behavior as is possible in order to later analyze the data to determine those patterns.

This type of data is usually recorded in an **antecedent-behavior-consequence (ABC) chart** for ease in analysis. Additionally, **scatterplots** are used to present a matrix of the occurrence of the behavior across locations and times to more accurately identify temporal patterns of behavior (Touchette, MacDonald, & Langer, 1985). Other tools such as time sampling, duration, and latency recordings can be employed during the direct assessment phase of the FBA to obtain precise data on the behavior's occurrence. Finally, standardized behavior rating scales, learner motivation assessments, and reinforcer preference assessments can be used at this stage in the FBA process to identify additional dimensions and factors relating to the occurrence of the behavior. Direct assessment methods will be discussed in detail in Chapter 7.

Step 4: Develop a Hypothesis Statement

Following the collection of indirect and direct assessment data, it is important to analyze the data to determine the potential function of the behavior. All behaviors serve a particular purpose in an individual's life—whether the individual is aware of the purpose or not, learners only *repeatedly engage* in a behavior if the consequence to the behavior is valuable in some manner. In fact, the repeated engagement, or future frequency of engagement, in a behavior is the crux of a critical behavioral principle, **reinforcement**. In many ways, identifying the function of the behavior is the same as identifying the source and type of reinforcement for a specific behavior. Therefore, it is important to briefly discuss the various types of reinforcement that learners could be seeking as a result of their behavior.

Reinforcement occurs when a learner engages in a behavior, experiences a particular consequence, and then engages in the behavior again in the future under similar conditions (Cooper, Heron, & Heward, 2007). The very definition of reinforcement is focused on the frequency of future occurrences of behavior. Therefore, if a behavior is repeated and the same consequence is observed to have occurred, then we would say that the behavior was *reinforced*. Reinforcing consequences can be classified in essentially two ways: either: 1) something is *added* to the environment after the behavior occurs (i.e., the learner *gets something* like attention from another person or people or an item or access to an activity, or any other stimulus); or 2) something is *removed* from the environment after the behavior occurs (i.e., a non-preferred task demand is not required or any other aversive stimulus is removed). When the consequence following a behavior is that something is added to the environment and the behavior continues to occur in the future and results in the same consequence, it is called **positive reinforcement**. Alternatively, when the consequence following a behavior results in the removal of a stimulus and the behavior continues to occur in the future and results in the same consequence, **negative reinforcement** is said to have occurred.

Additionally, there is a final type of reinforcement, called **automatic reinforcement**, wherein, reinforcement occurs as the result of a behavior the learner performs him or herself, without other people being involved. An example of this would be humming to oneself over an extended period of time. In this case, since the humming behavior is being repeated, it is therefore *reinforcing*; and, it is *automatic* in the sense that the individual is providing him or herself the stimulus of the humming sound (there is not a reliance on someone else to provide that sound). Automatic reinforcement can also be positive, in the sense that a stimulus was added to the environment (in the case of humming) or negative, in the event that an aversive stimulus is removed from the environment (for example, covering one's ears when loud music is being played).

A **hypothesis statement** is a statement, comprised of four components, indicating the team's "best guess" as to the function, or purpose, that a target behavior serves for the learner. This statement includes information on the setting, immediate antecedent and consequence variables, a restatement of the definition of the target behavior, and the proposed function of the behavior. Usually, a particular target behavior might have one of four possible functions:

- Attention (positive reinforcement)
- Escape (negative reinforcement)
- Access to tangible Items or activities (positive reinforcement)
- Automatic reinforcement/sensory (reinforcement not mediated by another person)

Accurately determining the function of a target behavior allows for the team to select an appropriate—and effective—intervention to change the learner's behavior. These four possible behavioral functions will be discussed in much greater detail later in this book.

Step 5: Test the Hypothesis

At this stage in the FBA, the team is only capable of providing a *hypothesis* of the function of the behavior. To be more certain about the function that the behavior serves, as was discussed earlier in this chapter, it may be necessary to *test* the hypothesis and prove a functional relation. This process involves systematically modifying the environment/setting to increase the probability that the behavior will occur in that setting. If the behavior reliably occurs more frequently in the purposefully manipulated setting than in other settings, the team is justified in proceeding in the assumption that the functional relation has been proven. This specific process is called a **functional analysis**, which can vary somewhat in terms of specific procedural elements and will be discussed at length in Chapter 10.

Step 6: Develop Interventions

Many evidence-based interventions are **function-based**, meaning that the intervention has been empirically demonstrated to specifically address a particular function of behavior. Once the function of the behavior is identified, the team can select an evidence-based intervention to address the target behavior. The intervention(s) selected should include strategies specifically identified to decrease occurrences of the target behavior as well as to teach a behavior that serves the same function as the challenging behavior (replacement behavior). A behavior intervention plan (BIP) should be written that provides clear guidelines on where, when, and by whom the behavior interventions should be implemented. The BIP should also include guidelines regarding what should take place in the event adverse event(s) occur to ensure the safety of the learner as well as those in the same environment.

Step 7: Monitor Intervention Effectiveness

At any point when a behavior intervention is implemented, it is critical to have a system for data collection and monitoring in place to ensure that the intervention is effective in changing the behavior. This data collection and monitoring system should have clear guidelines indicating where, when, by whom, and how exactly, data will be collected on the target behavior. Additionally, it is crtitical to continue to assess and monitor the maintenance (the continuation of the behavior change over time) and generalization (promoting the behavior change to occur across different settings, with different people and stimuli) of the behavior.

Summary

This chapter provided an overview of the various steps in the functional behavior assessment process, the parties responsible for carrying out each step, and the relationship between each step. Additionally, an overview of the four functions of behavior and the role of teaching new skills to decrease problem behavior were provided.

Definition of Key Terms

- **Functional Behavior Assessment (FBA):** a set of procedures implemented in a specific manner to determine the reason a particular behavior occurs. There are three categories of methods used within the FBA including indirect assessment, direct assessment, and experimental methods
- **in vivo observation:** real-time direct observation of the target behavior
- **descriptive assessment:** direct observation of behavior and environmental events
- **functional analysis:** a procedure wherein the assumed function of the behavior is tested by systematically manipulating the learner's conditions to determine which environmental condition is most likely to evoke and maintain the behavior (i.e., which condition is reinforcing the target behavior)
- **functional relation:** when a well-controlled experiment systematically demonstrates that when a change in the independent variable occurs, a change in the dependent variable reliably occurs
- **structural analysis:** a procedure wherein the learner will be systematically exposed to or placed in the presence of different stimuli to evoke the occurrence of the problem behavior
- **function-based intervention:** an intervention specifically designed to enable the individual learner to engage in a behavior to serve the same function of the target behavior
- **Behavior Intervention Plan (BIP):** a plan that is comprised of specific behavior change procedures based on the findings of the FBA. The plan is developed by the treatment team and implemented by various members of the team
- **indirect assessment:** a process whereby information is gathered about the target behavior through indirect means (interviews, questionnaires, and anecdotal reports) by those who have observed the behavior or the individual themselves
- **direct assessment:** observation of the target behavior's occurrence wherein frequency, duration, and magnitude data are collected. Additionally, notes regarding the environmental variables surrounding the behavior and temporal patterns are collected

- **antecedents:** environmental conditions, events, or stimuli that occur immediately prior to a target behavior's occurrence
- **consequences:** environmental conditions, events, or stimuli that occur immediately following a target behavior's occurrence
- **temporal sequence:** a sequence of events in time
- **Antecedent-Behavior-Consequence (ABC) contingency/three-term contingency:** a temporal sequence of the antecedent, behavior, and consequence that is potentially dependent (i.e., the behavior may be dependent on certain antecedents or consequences being present). It is the basic unit of analysis of operant behavior
- **Antecedent-Behavior-Consequence (ABC) chart:** a chart for recording the antecedent, behavior, and consequence of each occurrence of the target behavior. It usually contains three columns (one for the antecedent, behavior, and consequence, respectively) and an additional column for notes or comments. This chart is analyzed carefully for the purposes of determining the function of the behavior
- **scatterplot:** a matrix used to plot direct assessment data to assist in determining the function of the behavior. Scatterplot specifically indicates the timing of the behavior and allows for it to be analyzed for patterns over time
- **reinforcement:** occurs when the future frequency of a behavior increases following a particular consequence
- **positive reinforcement:** occurs when the future frequency of a behavior increases following the presentation of a stimulus
- **negative reinforcement:** occurs when the future frequency of a behavior increases following the removal or termination of an aversive of a stimulus
- **automatic reinforcement:** occurs when the future frequency of a behavior increases following the presentation, removal, or termination of stimulus independent of the mediation of others
- **hypothesis statement:** an educated guess regarding the function of a behavior
- **topography:** the form of a behavior (what it looks or sounds like)

Test Your Understanding

Level 1: Knowledge

1. True or False: Professionally trained behavior analysts and educators are the only individuals to be included in the FBA process.
2. True or False: Clinically competent behavior analysts should develop an intervention plan without determining the function of the behavior.
3. True or False: A teacher's report of the occurrence of a behavior in the school setting counts as direct observation, since all teachers are trained in behavioral observation.
4. True or False: To be most effective, a behavior intervention must be based on addressing the function of the behavior.
5. True or False: The maintaining consequence for a behavior is the consequence that occurs most frequently immediately following the behavior.

Level 2: Comprehension

1. Identify which are functions of behavior:
   a. social reprimands
   b. frustration
   c. escape/avoidance
   d. all of the above
2. If a target behavior is occurring in the school setting only, it would be most appropriate to interview which of the following group of individuals:
   a. classroom teacher, paraprofessionals in the classroom, art teacher, and recess aide
   b. principal, classroom teacher, grandmother, and younger sister
   c. bus driver, art teacher, recess aide, and principal
   d. parents, aunt, neighbor, and gymnastics coach
3. The four components of a hypothesis statement include
   a. information on the location where the behavior takes place, the variables surrounding the behavior, various beliefs about the behavior's occurrence, and the proposed function of the behavior.
   b. information on the setting, immediate antecedent and consequence variables, a restatement of the definition of the target behavior, and the proposed function of the behavior.
   c. information on the setting, immediate antecedent and consequence variables, a restatement of the definition of the target behavior, and various beliefs about the behavior's occurrence.
   d. none of the above.
4. Which is an accurate characterization of a function-based intervention:
   a. A function-based intervention consists of developing an intervention to focus on the form or topography of a behavior.
   b. A function-based intervention consists of developing an intervention to change the behavior using strategies demonstrated by the evidence base to effectively address behaviors of the same function.
   c. A function-based intervention consists of basing the intervention on the function.
   d. A function-based intervention is a series of strategies focusing on improving the individual's independent functioning.
5. A thorough functional behavior assessment should consist of which of the following:
   a. Thorough interviews with all individuals who observe the behavior, multiple direct observations of the target behavior across settings and times when the behavior is likely to occur, an accurate analysis of the maintaining antecedent and consequence data, and a function-based intervention
   b. Thorough interviews with a sample of those who observe the behavior, multiple direct observations of the target behavior across settings and times when the behavior is likely to occur, an educated guess of the maintaining antecedent and consequence data, and a function-based intervention
   c. Thorough interviews with all individuals who observe the behavior, multiple direct observations of the target behavior across settings and times when the behavior is likely to occur, an accurate analysis of the maintaining antecedent and consequence data, and a topography-based intervention
   d. Thorough interviews with all individuals who observe the behavior, multiple direct observations of the target behavior across settings and times when the behavior is likely to occur, and a function-based intervention.

Level 3: Application

1. Consider the FBA process as a whole and the role that each step plays in the process. Describe each step in the process and provide a statement of its purpose and importance. Why is this process completed in this particular sequence? Select two to three steps in the process and describe what would happen if you failed to complete any of them.

2. Imagine you are being asked to complete an FBA on a learner's behavior that occurs across all settings (home, school, and community). Compile a list of individuals you would interview for the indirect assessment step and provide a rationale for their inclusion in your data collection.

3. Consider the requirement for monitoring intervention effectiveness following implementation of the behavior plan. Of what does this process consist? How long do you believe monitoring should continue following initial implementation? Why?

4. Function-based interventions are critical to ensure effective behavior change. Consider the need for a behavior intervention to be based on the function of a behavior. What would happen if a behavior intervention were focused on the behavior's topography or form? Why are function-based interventions more effective?

5. Consider the need to conduct multiple direct observations when completing an FBA. Why is this a critical aspect to the process? What risks might occur if fewer direct observations were conducted?

6. Make a video recording of the oral explanation of each stage of the FBA process and submit this recording for review. General tips: Students should take care to address the camera as though they are speaking with either a consumer of ABA services or a supervisee (imagine that the camera is the individual with whom you would be speaking). Students may elect to use props to demonstrate the way in which data should be collected or use other materials relating to how the behavior change procedure should be implemented. In the event that these props or data collection sheets are referenced in the video, these items should be made visible on camera.

In-Class Small Group Discussion Questions/Exercises

Create small groups (perhaps four or five students) and discuss the following topics, allowing 10 to 15 minutes to complete the response.

1. Consider a learner (either one with whom you work or have worked with, or a hypothetical learner you may encounter in your professional practice) who may be in need of behavior change. Who would be the members on the team that would be established to conduct the functional behavior assessment? Why?

2. Identify a socially significant challenging behavior and provide a behavior definition for that behavior for that individual. Be sure to write this definition in a manner that allows anyone reading the definition to reliably measure the behavior and to objectively observe each occurrence.

3. Briefly explain the differences between indirect and direct assessment data. What would be an example of each type of data collected?

References

Alberto, P.A. & Troutman, A.C. (2013). *Applied behavior analysis for teachers* (9th ed.). New York, NY: Pearson.

Behavior Analyst Certification Board®. (2014). *Professional and ethical compliance code for behavior analysts*. Retrieved from http://www.bacb.com/Downloadfiles//BACB_Compliance_Code.pdf.

Cooper J.O, Heron T.E, Heward W.L. *Applied behavior analysis* (2nd ed.) Upper Saddle River, NJ: Pearson; 2007.

Iwata, B.A., Dorsey, M.F., Slifer, K.J., Bauman, K.F., & Richman, G.S. (1994). Toward a functional analysis of self-injury. *Journal of Applied Behavior Analysis, 27*(2), 197–209.

Ramsay, M.C., Reynolds, C.R., & Kamphaus, R.W. (2002). *Essentials of behavioral assessment* (Vol. 37). John Wiley & Sons.

Touchette, P.E., MacDonald, R.F., & Langer, S.N. (1985). A scatter plot for identifying stimulus control of problem behavior. *Journal of applied behavior analysis, 18*(4), 343–351.

CHAPTER 4

Defining Behavior

In any academic or professional discipline, the precise and accurate use of terminology is important. Using language effectively helps to reduce miscommunication and also has the potential to increase the effectiveness of one's interactions with others. In Applied Behavior Analysis (ABA), the need for language to be precise and accurate when describing behavior can have a direct impact on the reliability and validity of assessment results and the effectiveness of a behavior-change intervention. Writing an objective and measurable definition of **behavior**, complete with examples and non-examples of what the behavior looks like, is also called an **operational definition**, is a required skill for all behavior analysts and is the first step in a functional behavior assessment (FBA). To advance closer to mastery of this critical conceptual stage in the FBA process, carefully review all of the examples provided and complete all of the end-of-chapter activities to round out this chapter's use of the "See one, do one, and teach one" model.

LEARNING OBJECTIVES

After completing the chapter's activities, learners should be able to do the following:

- Describe the requirements for an operational definition of a behavior to be objective and measurable

- Explain the difference between overt and covert behavior

- Discuss the requirement that a behavior definition pass the Dead Man Test (DMT) to qualify as a behavior

- Provide examples of how behaviors pass or fail the Dead Man Test (DMT)

- Define and identify Criterion for Acceptable Performance (CAP) for behaviors

- Define types of behavioral measures and provide examples

- Define the required components of a behavioral objective and provide examples

- Discuss the role a behavior definition plays in the functional behavior assessment process

- Review and identify the required elements of operational behavior definitions by reviewing the exemplars and non-exemplars provided

- Create measurable and objective operational behavior definition exemplars and non-exemplars

- Teach someone to identify and create measurable and objective operational behavior definition exemplars and non-exemplars

Operational Definitions

Chapter 1 stated that behaviorism is the philosophy of the science of behavior, which includes a focus on the observable relations between stimuli and responses. To this end, in the research and practice of ABA, operational behavior definitions must be **objective** and **measurable** to maintain behaviorism's focus on that which is observable. Objective and measurable definitions are especially useful as we conduct direct assessment observations. For a behavior to be objectively defined, it must be described in such a way that anyone observing an individual is able to indicate unequivocally whether the specific target behavior occurred (without needing to rely on inference, past experience, feelings, or opinion). Objectivity in behavior definitions also implies that the behavior is observable and that there is an absence of **mentalistic** descriptions of the behavior. By focusing on objective behavior definitions, behavior analysts are able to accurately record the actions that an individual performs and avoid the inaccuracies that often arise from attempting to infer others' emotional states or thought processes.

For a behavior to be measurable, any person can use the objective behavior definition and specific metric to record the behavior's occurrence, duration, or magnitude with accuracy. An important aspect of a behavior definition is that it clearly describes the **_topography_**—or form—of a behavior. One convenient way to determine if a behavior meets the requirements of measurability is to ask whether the behavior can be _counted_ or _timed_ and whether others can be given the same definition and record the same information about a behavior's occurrence. For instance, let's imagine that the behavior we're measuring is clapping. Let's suppose that a clap is defined as each instance when an individual raises both hands (with fingers extended and palms facing one another) to their midline and makes contact with both palms with sufficient force to make a sound audible from five feet away. In this case, it is fairly simple for most individuals to read the behavior definition provided, observe an individual, and count discrete occurrences of clapping. The same could be said about the ability to measure the duration of singing behavior—when given an objective definition of singing—it is possible for one to use a timer and record the duration of episodes of singing. Both clapping and singing in this case are behaviors that could be measured by counting or timing their occurrence. However, let's suppose we're attempting to measure a more complex phenomenon of human experience, for instance, a person's sadness. How would you measure the occurrence of another person's sadness? Perhaps you would attempt to measure it by counting the number of times the person cries, or perhaps the duration of time they cry? By focusing on crying, it would allow for some degree of measurability, since we can count or time the actual behavior. However, this raises additional questions: Are we certain that a person's crying behavior is a valid way of measuring a person's sadness? In other words, might there be other reasons why a person would be crying?

A person may cry for several possible reasons—not all of which would indicate they are feeling sad. First, lots of people cry when they report feeling happy or even when they report feeling surprised. Another reason a person could be crying may be because they report feeling embarrassed or ashamed, but not necessarily sad. One could also argue that it is possible to make oneself cry, allowing for the possibility that a person engaging in that behavior is seeking attention or appealing to the emotions of others who witness the crying behavior. Aside from the array of emotional states that could be represented by the behavior of crying, there are also physical reasons, such as allergic reactions or even because they are eating spicy food. Finally, there are times when people report feeling sad, but do not necessarily cry. Taken together, it appears that measuring crying behavior is not necessarily the most reliable way for us to infer any information about an individual's emotional state after all. These examples suggest that sadness—or any emotional state, for that matter—is not a phenomenon that can be measured objectively or measurably by another person. Instead, crying is an example of a behavior that can be considered a **behavioral correlate** to sadness.

Overt vs. Covert Behaviors

You may be wondering, why is it that while other disciplines such as cognitive psychology or psycho-analysis focus on an individual's self-report of sadness, behavior analysts restrict their work only to behaviors that can be observed directly? First of all, behavior analysts reject mentalism (the perspective that thoughts and feelings as an internal dimension are capable of being measured reliably on their own) and instead adhere to the principles that there are **overt** and **covert** behaviors (Skinner, 1969).

To explain further, overt behaviors are objective and measurable, and covert behaviors cannot be observed or measured directly—but are still behaviors. Examples of overt behaviors would be eating, talking, or stomping one's feet—because these are events that can be directly observed. However, internal states like one's thoughts or feelings, or behaviors that do not happen in the environment where and/or when observation is taking place are considered to be covert. As was stated previously, behavior analysts would consider behaviors such as laughing or crying as behavioral correlates to a covert event internal to the person. Behavior analysts are careful to consider only the laughing or crying behavior as observable actions that *might indicate* an internal emotional or mental state and might be information used in addition to the direct observation data.

Covert behaviors can also be those that occur without us observing them. A behavior such as nighttime bed-wetting, for example, may be considered covert because it is not observed directly, but the evidence that the behavior occurred will be present in the environment the next morning. Another example of covert behavior might be evasive alcohol consumption, as the behavior may be occurring in private but evidence of empty containers or intoxication will be apparent. Exploring this example further, we can say that if one were in the room when drinking took place (in a position of observability), the behavior would be considered overt. However, the fact that this behavior takes place without the ability to observe it, requires that the behavior be considered covert.

Historically, behavioral assessment has focused exclusively on the analysis of overt behaviors; however, that perspective has changed over time and indirect assessment measures have been used to help identify the occurrence of covert behavior as well. Although direct observation of overt behaviors is considered the more reliable method in functional assessment, covert behaviors should not be discounted as they can be equally socially significant and indirect measurement procedures assist toward capturing data on their occurrence.

Dead Man Test (DMT)

Another critical consideration in the selection and definition of target behaviors includes the need to focus on what an individual actually does when attempting to define and eventually change a behavior. In addition to being objective and measurable (and therefore, overt), we need to ask ourselves whether a behavior passes the "Dead Man Test" (DMT). The DMT is essentially a rule of thumb used to determine if a behavior is one that we can focus on in our work as behavior analysts. Malott and Suarez (2003) stated this heuristic well: "If a dead man can do it, it ain't a behavior, and if a dead man can't do it, then it is a behavior" (pg. 9). Or, put another way, from Malott and Shane (2014), "[B]ehavior is anything an animal (including the human animal) does" (pg. 6). Essentially, the DMT poses a very simple question to behavior analysts as we craft our behavior definitions; once a target behavior is identified and preliminarily defined, we need to ask ourselves "Can a dead man do it?" If the answer is yes, then we need to choose a different behavior or, more likely, re-define the target behavior.

Table 4.1 Examples of the Dead Man Test

Behavior	Does it pass the DMT?	How could this behavior definition be corrected to pass the DMT?
Jason will sit still at circle time.	No. A dead man can sit still at circle time.	Jason will sit upright on mat, keep his arms and legs within the designated space, vocally respond when called on by the teacher, and participate in singing the opening and closing songs.
Cara will be quiet at nap-time.	No. A dead man can be quiet at nap-time.	Cara will either sleep on her mat or will lie on her mat, without talking to peers or to the teacher, and look at a book.
Jack will not hit others at recess.	No. A dead man cannot hit others.	Jack will wait his turn in line to play on the playground equipment and will keep his hands in his pockets while standing in line.

Criterion for Acceptable Performance (CAP)

Finally, a critical component relating to the use of behavior definitions in the field includes providing a **criterion for acceptable performance** (CAP). Even when behavior analysts have an objective and measurable definition of an overt, observable behavior, it is necessary to establish criteria to determine if the occurrence of the behavior (or the performance) was acceptable. CAP provides a benchmark or goal for a minimum performance standard and allows behavior analysts to include in a definition the frequency, duration, or magnitude at which we expect to see the behavior occur in order for it to be counted in our data collection. When formulating CAPs, we should take into account the nature of the behavior itself, the learner's abilities, and the learning opportunities provided.

Table 4.2 Examples of CAP Statements

Types of CAPs	Behavior Definition	Example of CAP (to be included in the definition)
Percentage of correct responses	When asked what he would like for lunch, Marco will vocally state his choice and abstain from crying or yelling.	Marco will appropriately respond, indicating his choice of food 100 percent of the time when asked.
Duration: Length of time individual performs the behavior	After using the restroom, Jamal will thoroughly wash his hands.	Jamal will wash his hands for a minimum of 1 minute after using the restroom.
Latency: Duration of time between the instruction being provided and individual engaging in the behavior	When told to get ready to get into the car, Sarah will put on her shoes and jacket.	Sarah will begin to get ready to get into the car within one minute of being asked.

Let's consider an example of an individual learning to write his or her name. Initially, the legibility of their writing will not be completely clear. It is a natural aspect of the learning process that an individual would start writing their name with a **baseline level** of legibility and then progress to greater legibility with additional instruction and reinforcement. For this reason, it's necessary to consider determining CAPs for the behavior's occurrence when the behavior is initially observed and then to modify the criterion at later stages in the learning process to ensure that the occurrence of the behavior—in whatever iteration in the learning process is currently being shown—is captured through baseline data collection. Perhaps, with the case of writing one's name, the CAP would state that half of the letters are legible, and later in the learning process the CAP would be raised to all letters being legible.

With respect to challenging or disruptive behaviors, it is necessary to consider the CAP that would be most appropriate for the individual in the context in which they are performing the behavior. For instance, let's consider screaming as a behavior that is occurring in a classroom. A CAP indicating zero tolerance for screaming would be appropriate in a high-school classroom, but not necessarily in a preschool classroom (where it is relatively common and, to some extent, developmentally appropriate, for screaming to occur from time to time). Often, in attempting to decrease a challenging behavior, it is necessary to teach a new social or adaptive skill to replace the problematic behavior. Let's imagine that an individual is learning to greet others as a social skill to replace unwelcomed hugging of strangers in a work setting. Setting a criterion of greeting one hundred percent of the people they encounter may be excessive in a corporate office but may be appropriate in a department store when one is an employee creating a welcoming environment for customers.

Behavioral Measurement

There are many ways to measure behavior, and the method used must be stated in a behavior definition. There are three **dimensional qualities** of measuring behavior: repeatability, temporal locus, and temporal extent. Each of these dimensional qualities can be measured using a variety of procedures. The chart that follows provides an overview of the methods used to capture each dimensional quality. For example, if one is attempting to capture the *repeatability* of a specific behavior, such as hand-raising (instead of calling out in class), one could record the frequency of the behavior within a class period at school. Or, to identify the *temporal locus*, one could measure the latency, or elapsed time, for the learner to complete a task after being asked to do so. An additional behavior that is a measure of *temporal locus* is inter-response time, or the amount of time elapsed between one behavior and a successive behavior. Finally, to capture the *temporal extent* of one's sitting behavior, a behavior specialist could time the duration of the behavior's occurrence. Including a behavioral measure within an operational definition allows others to read the definition and determine the metric used to collect data on the behavior.

Table 4.3 Three Dimensional Qualities of Behavior

Dimensional Quality	Measure
Repeatability	• Count • Rate or frequency • Celeration
Temporal locus	• Latency • Inter-response Time
Temporal extent	• Duration

Behavioral Objective

A major element of the operational definition of behavior includes the **behavioral objective.** A behavioral objective includes the four components: the target behavior, the condition, the name of the learner or individual, and the CAP. The target behavior is the name of the behavior that will be the focus of the objective (e.g., clapping, singing, biting, etc.). The condition is essentially the environment or setting where the behavior should be observed and provides important context for the behavior. The learner is the individual expected to engage in the behavior. And the CAP, which was discussed earlier in this chapter, is included in the behavioral objective to ensure a minimum standard for the occurrence of the behavior is included. Tables 4.4 through 4.7 provide various examples and non-examples of how the components of a complete behavior definition may be formulated.

Table 4.4 Behavior Definition: Sharing a Toy with a Peer

Example	Non-Example
Target Behavior: Sharing a toy with a peer	Target Behavior: Wanting to share a toy with a peer
Operational Definition: Sharing a toy with a peer includes picking up the toy and moving one's body close to the peer and placing the toy into the other peer's hands or placing it on the floor or table within twelve inches of the peer.	Operational Definition: Wanting to share a toy with a peer includes seeing that a peer would like to play with the toy, wanting to share, and giving the toy to the peer.
Behavioral Measure: Frequency count will be used to record how many times Jack shares a toy with a peer.	Behavioral Measure: The number of times that the toy is shared will be recorded.
Behavioral Objective: During free play at day care in the block area (condition), Jack (learner) will share three toys (target behavior) with at least one peer, four out of five days (CAP).	Behavioral Objective: Whenever the opportunity arises (condition), Jack (learner) will share all his toys (target behavior) on most days (CAP).

PROBLEMS WITH THE NON-EXAMPLE

- The target behavior is not observable, objective, or measurable.
- The operational definition includes mentalistic language and not objective/observable/measurable statements. One cannot assess what a person "sees" or "thinks"; we can only observe behavior and record it objectively.
- Additionally, this operational definition should not mention that the peer "wants the toy"—we are only concerned with how many times the learner demonstrates sharing behavior (whether the peer "wants the toy" is not a qualifier for sharing to have occurred).
- Finally, "giving the toy" is not very clear, as there are multiple ways that this could be interpreted. It's best to list what physically occurs (what it looks like) when one gives an object to another person.
- The behavioral measure does not indicate what type of measurement will be used (i.e., frequency count). Though the type of measurement is implied, it's not specifically stated.
- The condition in the behavioral objective is very vague (when do the most common opportunities arise?). Also, the objective would not likely be for him to share all of his toys necessarily (it's not realistic nor is it necessarily socially appropriate). Finally, "most days" is not very specific, which makes it challenging to know when Jack will have met the goal.

Table 4.5 Behavior Definition: Having a Conversational Exchange with a Sibling

Example	Non-Example
Target Behavior: Having a conversational exchange with a sibling	Target Behavior: Having a conversation with a sibling
Operational Definition: Having a conversational exchange with a sibling includes answering a question that is presented by a sibling and then asking a question of the sibling on the same topic (e.g., when Sally's sister asks Sally about her favorite "My Little Pony," Sally will respond with an answer to the original question and then pose a question based on the topic of "My Little Pony"). One conversational exchange will consist of Sally's sibling presenting a question, Sally responding to the question, and then Sally presenting a question to her sibling.	Operational Definition: Having a conversation includes going back and forth while talking to someone else. Questions, comments, and changes of topic would be required.
Behavioral Measure: Frequency count will be used to measure how many times Sally engages in a conversational exchange with her sibling. This frequency count will be divided by the number of opportunities provided to Sally to interact with her sibling, and will be multiplied by one hundred to calculate the percentage of opportunity.	Behavioral Measure: Duration would be used to measure how long the conversation lasts.
Behavioral Objective: In the car ride home from school with her sister Jenny (condition), Sally (learner) will engage in 90 percent of the opportunities for conversational exchanges (target behavior) with her sister, four out of five days (CAP).	Behavioral Objective: Whenever in the presence of another individual (condition), Sally (learner) will engage in at least a two-minute conversation with another person (target behavior); days would vary (CAP).

PROBLEMS WITH THE NON-EXAMPLE

- The target behavior is not sufficiently precise to account for the beginning and ending points of the behavior; it would not allow for a discrete measurement.
- The operational definition is not very clear—what does it mean to "go back and forth while talking to someone else"? How could this be measured by anyone who reads this definition? It also includes too many possible responses to be precise; it could be more useful to either count the number of questions, comments, or changes of topics separately or carefully define how the questions and responses tie together in the ideal representation of the behavior (in the "example").

- The behavioral measure of duration would not capture the behavior that is being sought from Sally. The objective for Sally is to improve her conversational exchanges in terms of the development of that skill—it may be too early to work on increasing the duration in which she engages in these conversations (duration measures the degree to which she has *long* conversations, but the goal is to measure the *quality* of her conversation at this point, which is best measured by frequency of specific questions/responses and percentage of opportunity).

- Additionally, it would be best, when it comes to conversational exchanges, that there be a response provided to the sibling in a certain amount of time (such as ten seconds). Successful conversations usually have a short time period between one individual's response and the other individual's response (a delay in response of more than ten seconds would seem odd to most partners in conversation). That time period between exchanges should be properly labeled using **latency** as the measurement.

Table 4.6 Behavior Definition: Remaining Clothed

Example	Non-Example
Target Behavior: Remaining clothed	Target Behavior: Not taking clothing off
Operational Definition: Remaining clothed includes not removing shoes, socks, pants, underwear, or shirt during the school day.	Operational Definition: Not taking clothing off includes avoidance of stripping behavior.
Behavioral Measure: Duration will be used to measure how long Stephen keeps his clothing on while at school.	Behavioral Measure: Duration will be used to measure how long Stephen avoids stripping.
Behavioral Objective: During the entire eight-hour school day at Ben Franklin Middle School (condition), Stephen (learner) will keep his clothing on (target behavior), three out of five days (CAP).	Behavioral Objective: At school (condition), Stephen (learner) will avoid stripping (target behavior) everyday (CAP).

PROBLEMS WITH THE NON-EXAMPLE

- The target behavior focuses on what the learner should not be doing (i.e., not removing clothing). Instead, the target behavior should be written in the affirmative (i.e., keeping clothing on) to maintain a focus on the behavior that should be expected.

- The operational definition should never include a statement that essentially rephrases the name of the behavior (we would never state that the definition of "yelling" is "screaming"; it's not very descriptive). Therefore, stating that "keeping clothing on" includes the "avoidance of stripping" is not very useful toward our definition of keeping clothing on. It would be necessary to define what "clothing" includes—do we just want Stephen to keep on his jacket or **all** of his clothing? The need to be specific and precise with a behavior such as this is critical.

- Though it's great that duration was selected as the behavioral measure, the behavior of "avoiding stripping" has been re-stated, but is still not very clear.

- The behavioral objective is quite vague: Which periods of the school day? Are we concerned about this behavior during the whole school day or just particular segments? Also, "everyday" is not likely to be what is being sought since school is in session only five days/per week—what about the weekend?

- Also, the behavioral objective could be improved by specifying "in the classroom" or "outside of the bathroom" so that if Stephen pulls his pants/underwear down to use the restroom he can still meet the objective.

Table 4.7 Behavior Definition: Using an "Indoor" Voice

Example	Non-Example
Target Behavior: Using an indoor voice	Target Behavior: Using an indoor voice
Operational Definition: Using an indoor voice includes using a soft but audible voice, while indoors ("soft but audible" is defined as loud enough for a person standing within five feet of the individual to hear what is being said, but not so loud that others need to cover their ears or physically move away from the individual; and not so soft that individuals need to come within six inches of the individual speaking in order to hear).	Operational Definition: Using an indoor voice includes using a level of volume that is appropriate for being indoors and doesn't make people uncomfortable.
Behavioral Measure: Frequency count will be used to measure how often Kelly uses an "indoor" voice while inside. This frequency count will be divided by the total number of utterances Kelly made while she was indoors and will be multiplied by one hundred to calculate the percentage of opportunities	Behavioral Measure: Frequency count will be used to measure how often Kelly uses an "indoor" voice while inside. This frequency measure will be divided by the total frequency of times when Kelly is indoors and will be multiplied by one hundred to calculate the percentage of opportunities.
Behavioral Objective: During visits to the library, the grocery store, and church (condition), Kelly (learner) will use an indoor voice during eighty percent of her utterances (target behavior), four out of five visits (CAP).	Behavioral Objective: When inside and it's necessary to use an indoor voice (condition), Kelly (learner) will use an indoor voice (target behavior) most of the time (CAP).

PROBLEMS WITH THE NON-EXAMPLE

- The operational definition is almost adequate, but it needs more qualification and subjective statements need to be removed. What does "a level of volume that is appropriate for being indoors" mean? How can we objectively determine that people are "uncomfortable"? An extra sentence or two clearly qualifying this statement would be very useful.
- Also, when defining an element of behavior that is a little more subjective (some people may interpret varying volumes as loud or soft), it is **always** useful to provide an example of "too loud" and "too soft"—the example indicates these extremes in the context of this behavior for this individual, which allows for readers of the behavior definition to properly determine the range of acceptable volume (i.e., "loud enough so that someone standing within five feet can hear, but not so loud that they need to cover their ears/move away" and "not so soft that individuals need to come within six inches of the individual speaking to hear").

Summary

If there is one message to be gleaned from reading this chapter, it is that *precise and accurate use of language is vital in the process of behavioral assessment and intervention.* The first step in the FBA process is crafting a behavior definition that is objective and measurable, focused on an overt behavior, and passes the Dead Man Test. Throughout the course of this chapter, each of these required components has been defined and reviewed. Additionally, multiple examples and non-examples have been provided to highlight the specificity and precision required when defining behavior. Accurate and precise language will directly influence the reliability of assessment results and the effectiveness of a behavior-change intervention. To further master this practice, it will be important for you to engage in the review activities at the end of this chapter to create original behavior definitions and teach others to do the same.

Through the process of reviewing examples of behavior definitions, practicing creating your own, and helping to shape others' definitions, you will become a master in defining behaviors—putting you well on your way to conducting reliable and valid functional behavior assessment.

Definition of Key Terms

- **behavior:** anything a person does (an action)
- **operational definition:** a written definition that describes the topography of a behavior in clear terms
- **objective:** defining behaviors in a manner that is free from influence of personal feelings or opinions
- **measurable:** the ability to measure a behavior in quantitative terms (i.e., counting or timing the behavior)
- **mentalistic:** focus on mental perception or thought processes to describe behavior
- **topography:** the form a behavior takes
- **behavioral correlate:** an overt behavior that reliably occurs under the conditions in which the covert behavior is perceived to be occurring (per client report, other physical measures, or other biological measures)
- **overt behavior:** behavior that can be directly observed (e.g., singing or coughing)
- **covert behavior:** behavior that cannot be directly observed and take place inside the person's skin (e.g., thinking or feeling)
- **Dead Man Test (DMT):** a litmus test to determine whether the phrasing of a behavior definition fits the requirements for a behavior to be measured. *If a Dead Man can do it, it should not be considered a behavior*
- **Criterion for Acceptable Performance (CAP):** a statement included in a behavior definition that indicates parameters regarding a target duration or the frequency of a behavior to acceptably meet a behavioral objective
- **behavioral measure:** the measurement dimension that will best capture the occurrence of the behavior (count, rate or frequency, celeration, duration, latency, etc.)
- **behavioral objective:** a statement in a behavioral definition that includes three components: name of the learner, behavioral measure, and CAP

Test Your Understanding

Level 1: Knowledge

1. True or False: Behaviors can be defined in terms of a person's perceived cognitive processes and emotions.
2. True or False: Behaviors can be measured by observing what a person does.
3. True or False: Covert behaviors can be measured by listening to a person's report of their thoughts or feelings.
4. True or False: The Dead Man Test is a rule of thumb to determine if a behavior definition is phrased in a manner to allow for the behavior to be measured.
5. True or False: A criterion for acceptable behavior is a statement indicating the minimum standard for a behavior's occurrence to be acceptable.

Level 2: Comprehension

1. Identify which are overt behaviors:
   a. wondering
   b. hoping
   c. chewing
   d. frustration
2. Identify which are covert behaviors:
   a. scratching
   b. smelling
   c. feeling cold
   d. jumping
3. A behavior objective should include
   a. the learner's name and age, the behavior measure, and CAP.
   b. the learner's name, the behavior measure, and CAP.
   c. the behavior measure, the objective statement, and CAP.
   d. the behavior measure, the objective statement, and covert behavior measure.
4. The topography of jumping is outlined by which of the following descriptions:
   a. José enjoys jumping because it helps him release some of his energy.
   b. José bends both of his knees and at the waist to sit in a crouching position and rapidly extends his body straight up in the air until both of his feet leave the ground.
   c. José feels happiest when he is jumping.
   d. José jumps to avoid academic tasks that are challenging for him to complete.
5. Writing an objective and measurable behavior definition is important in the functional behavior assessment process because
   a. doing so allows for the reliable and valid measurement of the behavior.
   b. doing so ensures that behavior interventions that are developed based on the data collected are likely to be effective.
   c. both A and B.
   d. neither A nor B.

Level 3: Application

1. Consider the need for behavior definitions to be objective and measurable and to focus on overt behaviors. Explain what could happen if data were collected using a behavior definition that was not objective, measurable, or specifically focused on an overt behavior. How would the data collected vary from an objective, measurable, and specific focus on overt behavior? How would this impact the subsequent steps in the functional behavior assessment process? (Please review Chapter 1 for the complete overview of the functional behavior assessment process and consider how each step would be impacted.)
2. Imagine you are being asked to complete an FBA on a learner's aggressive behavior. Create a complete behavior definition that is objective, measurable, passes the Dead Man Test, and includes a complete behavioral objective.
3. Behavior analysts at times have their own hypotheses (or best guesses) as to why a behavior is occurring. Sometimes those who are new to the field are tempted to incorporate the hypothesized

function of a behavior into the behavior definition. For instance, if you have been observing a learner for several weeks and note that 100% of the time when they engage in crying behavior they have experienced an absence of attention and receive attention immediately upon crying, you may assume the function of the behavior is to gain attention. Although this could be a correct assumption, what are some reasons you would not allude to that assumption in your behavior definition and instead focus a behavior definition strictly on the topography of the behavior?

4. Consider a socially significant behavior you would like to target for change. Create a complete behavior definition so that anyone with the definition would be able to observe your behavior and unequivocally determine if the behavior occurred.

5. Make a video recording of the oral explanation of the process of creating a behavior definition and submit this recording for review. General tips: Students should take care to address the camera as though they are speaking with either a consumer of ABA services or a supervisee (imagine that the camera is the individual with whom you would be speaking). Students may elect to use props to demonstrate the way in which data should be collected or use other materials relating to how the behavior change procedure should be implemented. In the event that these props or data collection sheets are referenced in the video, these items should be made visible on camera.

In-Class Small Group Discussion Questions/Exercises

Create small groups (perhaps four or five students) and discuss the following topics, allowing 10 to 15 minutes to complete the response.

1. Consider the theory of mentalism and its approach to describing and explaining phenomena. Within your small group, generate five examples of mentalistic explanations of behaviors. Then, discuss and provide an explanation for why each definition may not result in reliable or valid behavior measurement.

2. Within your small group, generate five examples of behavior defintions that are objective, measurable, pass the Dead Man Test, and include a complete behavioral objective. Discuss the challenges associated with meeting each of these requirements for a behavior definition.

3. Imagine you have been asked to teach a new classroom teacher to write behavior definitions. Each member of your small group should identify a hypothetical behavior for a learner and role play teaching another member of your small group how to write a complete behavior definition.

References

Malott, R.W., Malott, M.E., & Suarez, E.A.T. (2003). *Principles of behavior* (5th ed.). Upper Saddle River, NJ: Pearson Education.

Malott, R.W., & Shane, J.T. (2014). *Principles of behavior* (7th ed.). Upper Saddle, NJ: Pearson.

Skinner, B.F. (1969). *Contingencies of reinforcement*. New York: Appleton-Century-Crofts.

CHAPTER 5

Data Collection Tools

D ata collection is a critical aspect of nearly every activity in ABA, and this is especially the case in the process of FBA. Collecting valid and reliable data requires carefully defining the behavior (which was covered in Chapter 4) and selecting the appropriate measurement method to capture meaningful information about the behavior's occurrence. Proper data collection is paramount to the FBA process, as all subsequent decisions regarding identification of the behavior's function and subsequent behavior-change interventions are based on the data obtained.

This chapter will review considerations of behavioral measurement and will provide opportunities for you to determine the appropriate method of measurement for a specific behavior. Specifically, the principles of appropriate scientific measurement, **reliability** and **validity**, and the purpose of indirect and direct assessment processes will be discussed. Finally, various computer-assisted measurement procedures and applications will be explored to ensure reliability and convenience when collecting behavioral data. After completing this chapter and the activities at the end of the chapter, you will have had the opportunity to see examples, work with data collection tools, and teach others to do the same, completing another iteration of the "See one, do one, teach one" process.

LEARNING OBJECTIVES

After completing the chapter's activities, learners should be able to do the following:

- Briefly define measurement and its purpose in FBA

- Briefly define reliability and validity in the assessment process

- Define inter-observer agreement

- Define behavioral measures and procedures for indirect assessment data collection

- Define behavioral measures and procedures for direct assessment data collection
- Identify various computer-assisted behavior measurement procedures and their purpose

Selecting Appropriate Behavior Measurement

Johnston and Pennypacker (1993) defined **measurement** as the "the process of assigning numbers and units to particular features of objects or events …. [It] involves attaching a number representing the observed extent of a dimensional quantity to an appropriate unit. The number and the unit together constitute the measure of the object or event" (pp. 91, 95). Practitioners of ABA use measurement for a variety of purposes to ultimately address their overarching goal of improving the lives of their learners and consumers. Measurement of specific behavioral levels and thresholds allow practitioners (i.e., teachers and behavior analysts) to make decisions about whether intervention is necessary; and, if intervention is implemented, it is critical for determining the degree to which the intervention changed the behavior. Measurement also allows practitioners to capture several aspects of the behavior change—from the extent of change in the behavior's frequency, duration, or magnitude, to the variability or stability of the behavior prior to and following intervention implementation.

Ongoing measurement of a behavior, through the process of careful data collection, allows practitioners to accomplish several objectives. First, through close contact with the data regarding the behavior's occurrence, practitioners are able to make decisions regarding the selection of intervention. These data are also used when modifying aspects of the intervention to improve effectiveness.

Another purpose of careful and consistent data collection is that practitioners who have data to support their decision making are able to be accountable to all parties who are affected by those decisions. The client, learner, consumer, employer, and society with and for whom the practitioner works are best served when the practitioner is able to clearly explain and justify treatment decisions based upon objective behavioral data. In this way, the practitioner is accountable for the decisions they make and is therefore in compliance with the ethical guidelines required of his or her credential and professional practice.

Finally, when considering FBA specifically, data collection is paramount to ensuring that the FBA is conducted properly and that its results are used effectively. Many times, practitioners have assumptions regarding the function of a behavior but must still complete the process of the FBA to empirically verify the function to then craft an intervention. Failure to properly identify the function of a behavior will likely result in failure to develop a function-based intervention, which, consequently, may lead to a suboptimal—if not completely ineffective or harmful—approach to addressing the behavior. It is therefore the practitioner's ethical and scientific responsibility to appropriately measure behavior and collect it carefully.

Because FBA is usually a step that precedes the development of a behavior-change intervention, the focus of the measurement process in an FBA is to *contextualize the occurrence of the behavior*. Essentially, this involves identifying the environmental variables that make the behavior likely to occur. This process involves collecting data before and after the behavior's occurrence. Prior to discussing this process and various procedures of data collection involved in FBA, a few basic principles of scientific measurement will be discussed in general terms.

Reliability

Reliability in scientific measurement is an indication of the consistency of a measurement procedure to capture the same result over time (Cooper, Heron, & Heward 2007). For instance, let's imagine you have a bathroom scale that you use to measure your weight on a daily basis. Suppose you were unsure if your scale was reliable and you wanted to test it. You could step on your scale at 8:00 a.m. and record your weight. Then, a few minutes later, at 8:04 a.m., you could measure your weight again; during this second trial, you should assume that the scale will report the same weight as was indicated just four minutes prior. If it does, you can state that the consistent measurement is an indication that the scale is reliable in its measurement.

However, let's suppose that your 8:04 a.m. measurement was significantly different than the 8:00 a.m. measurement. Whether that difference was just one pound or ten pounds across the two trials, there is clearly concern that the scale lacks consistency, or reliability, in its measurement, since body weight does not vary significantly in just a four-minute period of time. In an empirical investigation of the scale's reliability, one would want to conduct more trials by stepping on the scale multiple times in a short period of time to determine the scale's consistency, or by placing other physical objects on the scale whose mass do not vary (e.g., your FBA textbook).

Because science relies on all sorts of measurement tools to capture a great variety of data, it is necessary to ensure that the measurement tools are reliable in all cases. Behavior analysis, as a scientific discipline, therefore needs to undergo the same scrutiny in terms of evaluating and ensuring reliability in our behavior measurement processes.

The challenge practitioners face, however, is that most behavior cannot be measured using a physical measurement tool, such as a bathroom scale, a ruler, or a thermometer, for instance. Direct observation conducted by other humans is required in order for a behavior to be measured. In this way, their own observation capability and efficient recording instruments become a practitioner's best tools.

However, this data collection and measurement approach clearly introduces potential variability, as we all know that different people have the potential to view the exact same event and draw different conclusions. It is for this reason that practitioners focus intently on creating objective and measureable behavior definitions (as covered in Chapter 4) and work to practice the skills of direct observation and objective data recording to ensure data collected are consistent. In fact, there is a specific term used in ABA that pertains to the amount of agreement between two different observers of the same behavior, **inter-observer agreement (IOA)**. IOA is calculated using several different formulae, each of which will be discussed.

Interobserver Agreement (IOA)

The following formulae outline the various methods by which to calculate IOA data. For a more comprehensive review of this information, please refer to the examples outlined by Cooper, Heron, and Heward (2007).

TOTAL COUNT IOA.

The most common and straightforward approach to assessing inter-observer agreement is by calculating the Total Count IOA, which is calculated using this formula:

$$\frac{\text{Number of times the observers agree}}{\text{Total number of observations}} \times 100$$

Let's imagine there are two observers recording the occurrence of a kindergartener's face-slapping behavior. They stand in a corner of the classroom where the learner cannot see them, but they have a direct line of sight of the child, five feet away from where he is seated during a craft activity (when the behavior is most likely to occur). Using clipboards, pencils, and a vibrating timer set to alert them of every thirty-second period, they each record either a "yes" to indicate the occurrence of a face slap or a "no" if there was not a face slap in the thirty-second period. Their observations are shown in the following table:

Table 5.1 Inter-observer Agreement Data Summary

Thirty-second period	Observer 1	Observer 2	Agree/Disagree
1	Yes	No	Disagree
2	No	No	Agree
3	No	No	Agree
4	No	No	Agree
5	No	No	Agree
6	Yes	Yes	Agree
7	Yes	Yes	Agree
8	No	Yes	Disagree
9	No	No	Agree
10	Yes	Yes	Agree

Upon reviewing the data above, there are eight times when the observers agreed and two times when they disagreed (in the first and the eighth thirty-second period). The percent agreement formula previously provided indicates that this would be the following:

$$(8/10) \times 100 = 80 \text{ percent agreement}$$

In this case, IOA could be improved by the two observers discussing the occasions of disagreement and potentially resolving them by reviewing and clarifying the behavior definition and then coming to an agreement on the behavior's occurrence. Additionally, a weakness of total count IOA calculations is that even with high numbers of agreement, one cannot be fully assured that the observers rated the same occurrences the same way. Therefore, there is another formula that we can consider, using the same data obtained via event recording: the mean count-per-interval IOA, which addresses this weakness by breaking the observation period into smaller increments to gain more specific information about which occurrences of the behavior were counted.

MEAN-COUNT-PER-INTERVAL IOA

This calculation allows practitioners a more specific understanding of the reliability of the observations, as it allows for the agreements to be evaluated in smaller increments of time. This is done by first dividing the total observation period into smaller intervals (i.e., instead of evaluating all agreements and disagreements across a twenty-minute period, one could divide the observation into twenty individual one-minute intervals). Then, the observers would record instances of behavior that occur within each shorter interval. Once those data are collected, the agreement between the two observers' counts is calculated. Finally, the agreements per interval are used to calculate IOA across the entire period of observation. Mean-count-per-interval IOA can be calculated using the following formula (Note: "Int" represents "interval" and "n" stands for the total number of intervals in the complete observation period):

$$\frac{\text{Int 1 IOA} + \text{Int 2 IOA} + \text{Int n IOA}}{n \text{ intervals}} \times 100$$

EXACT COUNT-PER-INTERVAL IOA

In cases where a mean percentage of agreement is not sufficiently specific for the practitioner's purposes, exact count-per-interval IOA can be used to calculate the agreement within each interval (rather than using an evaluation of the mean agreement). Essentially, this calculation provides practitioners the percentage of total intervals in which two observers recorded the same frequency of the behavior's occurrence and is calculated using the following formula:

$$\frac{\text{Number of intervals of 100\% IOA}}{n \text{ intervals}} \times 100$$

TRIAL-BY-TRIAL IOA

At times, practitioners also need to measure whether a behavior occurred, or the occurrence or non-occurrence of a behavior within an interval. This sort of data collection often results in recording binary data (a "zero" or "one"), and each trial, when the behavior is expected to occur, is evaluated for agreement across the two observers. To calculate agreement for these data, one could use the following formula:

$$\frac{\text{Number of trials agreement}}{\text{Total number of trials}} \times 100$$

TOTAL DURATION IOA

Thus far, we have discussed options for calculating IOA for data obtained through event recording. Duration data require different calculations, though they follow the same principles outlined previously. The most straightforward approach to calculating IOA for duration data uses this formula:

$$\frac{\text{Shorter duration}}{\text{Longer duration}} \times 100$$

This formula, though helpful when specifically working with duration data, presents the same weakness as total count IOA, as it may have the potential to overestimate the agreement across observers. Due to this weakness, the duration-per-occurrence calculation can be much more specific.

MEAN DURATION-PER-OCCURRENCE

This calculation is reminiscent of the mean-count-per-occurrence IOA formula mentioned previously, as it focuses the calculation of the specific intervals of agreement instead of focusing on a longer period of observation. The following formula is used to calculate Mean Duration-Per-Occurrence:

$$\frac{\text{Dur IOA R1} + \text{Dur IOA R2} + \text{Dur IOA Rn}}{\text{n responses with Dur IOA}} \times 100$$

INTERVAL-BY-INTERVAL IOA

When it is necessary to compare two observers' recordings of interval data, in the case of time sampling data collection procedures for example, the following calculation can be used:

$$\frac{\text{Number of intervals agreed}}{\text{Total number of intervals}} \times 100$$

Validity

Aside from needing to be reliable, it is critical that a scientific measure is also valid. Validity is the extent to which a measurement tool captures the information that the tool is intended to capture. To use the example explored previously, if one wished to record their weight, the most valid—or appropriate—measurement tool would be a scale. A tape measurer, however, would not be a valid measurement of one's weight. A tape measurer is helpful for many applications, for instance, in recording a person's height, or a person's waistline, but not for measuring a person's weight. With respect to behavior measurement in ABA, validity is improved as the behavioral definition is written to closely capture the behavior of concern and an appropriate tool is selected to measure the desired dimension of the behavior. This is accomplished by following the guidelines outlined in Chapter 4 in the development of a well-crafted behavior definition well-crafted behavior definition and selection of the best measurement tool to capture the occurrence of the behavior.

Behavioral Measurement in FBA

FBA is a procedure intended to identify the function or purpose a behavior serves. As was explored in Chapter 4, there are several dimensional qualities of behavior and each can be measured using specific procedures. Although FBA involves the use of only a few types measurement procedures, it is necessary that those undertaking the task of completing FBA remain aware of the various dimensions of behavior and the potential applications of measurement procedures in the context of their assessment processes. As was discussed in Chapter 1, there are phases of data collection that must occur in a FBA, indirect and direct assessment.

INDIRECT ASSESSMENT

Often, at the start of an FBA, information regarding the extent of a behavior's occurrence across environments or the environmental events that typically evoke the behavior is either unclear or has not been systematically explored. An indirect assessment allows for information to be collected from individuals who have observed that behavior taking place. Because this stage in the assessment process does not include direct observation of the behavior, and instead relies on the report of others through the use of interviews and questionnaires, the assessment process is considered indirect.

If you have carefully reviewed the section of this chapter covering reliable and valid scientific measurement, it might strike you that interviewing others regarding a behavior's occurrence has the potential to lack some degree of objectivity, and, therefore, to potentially weaken reliability. However, indirect assessment serves both a scientific and practical purpose in the FBA process. Indirect assessment serves the scientific purpose in allowing practitioners to commence the FBA by comprehensively collecting as much "surface" information about the behavior's occurrence prior to allowing their own hypotheses to narrow the focus of the investigation too early in the process. An indirect assessment can therefore be considered similar to the approach a detective takes in "canvassing the area" and interviewing witnesses following the occurrence of a crime. In other words, it would be inappropriate for a detective to arrive at a crime scene and determine not to interview witnesses because the perceived criminal had been apprehended; doing so would skip the empirical process of identifying what took place using a variety of sources of data to confirm and verify events.

Indirect assessment also serves a practical purpose of allowing practitioners to determine where to focus their efforts. Direct observation of a behavior's occurrence requires a great deal of practitioner time and energy. If, for instance, a behavior occurs in a learner's school environment, the practitioner must physically go to the learner's classroom—which often involves layers of permission from parents/ guardians, school administrators and educators, as well as coordination of those logistics. Even when practitioners show up for such carefully arranged observation periods, it is not guaranteed that the learner will emit the target behavior within the observation session and additional observations need to be scheduled. Behaviors are also dependent on other physical or biological factors—such as a learner's consumption of certain food or medication, or exercise level. By carefully interviewing those who observe the behavior (and the learner him or herself, when possible), it is possible for the practitioner to obtain a clearer picture of the variables involved in the behavior's occurrence so that direct observation can occur at a time and location where the learner is experiencing the conditions that are most conducive to the behavior's occurrence.

When it comes to assessing the validity of indirect assessment tools, it is important to evaluate the published literature for studies evaluating the validity of each instrument. For example, the Functional Analysis Screening Tool (FAST; Iwata, DeLeon, & Roscoe, 2013) is a sixteen-item interview tool that is commonly used to gain background information on a learner as well as the target behavior. Iwata, DeLeon, and Roscoe (2013) evaluated the validity of the FAST by comparing the results of sixty-nine functional analysis procedures (a procedure wherein the assumed function of the behavior is tested by systematically manipulating the learner's environmental conditions to determine which condition is most likely to evoke the behavior) with the results of the FAST. The FAST results were compared against the results of the functional analysis, as that is the best practice method for evaluating the FAST specifically. The results from the FAST were consistent with the results of the functional analysis condition for the target behavior to occur in 63.8 percent of cases. These results suggest that although the FAST can be helpful toward gaining more information regarding the hypothesized function of behavior, it is necessary not to rely on this tool alone in the FBA process. This comparison of the results of the indirect assessment, as a component part of the FBA procedure, with the outcomes of the functional analysis assessment as a whole, is very helpful for determining validity of the tool.

Another tool commonly used in the indirect assessment stage of an FBA is the Motivation Assessment Scale (MAS; Durand & Crimmins, 1988). This brief, sixteen-item questionnaire focuses on four subscales, representing possible functions of behavior (escape, attention, access to tangibles, and sensory/automatic reinforcement). This questionnaire provides response options on a seven-point likert scale indicating the frequency of the behavior's occurrence (0 = never, 1 = almost never, 2 = seldom, 3 = half the time, 4 = usually, 5 = almost always, 6 = always). This tool is relatively simple to use as it is intended for the respondent to complete the questionnaire independently of an interviewer.

When the MAS was introduced by Durand and Crimmins (1998) it was reported to have strong inter-rater reliability, as different teachers were able to observe the same behavior and arrive at the same conclusion; and, it was shown to have strong test-retest reliability because those same teachers remained in agreement upon re-testing 30 days later. Durand and Crimmins (1998) also asserted that the MAS strongly predicted student behavior in analogue situations for eight students with self-injurious behavior, which indicates the tool's validity. Bihm and colleagues (1991) subsequently confirmed these findings via a factor analysis.

Despite this evidence, later evaluations of this instrument have not always consistently replicated these positive findings about the MAS's reliability and validity (Zarcone et al., 1991). This was specifically the case when the MAS was evaluated across topographies of behavior (Duker & Sigafoos, 1998) and when used to identify the function of aggressive behavior (Sigafoos, Kerr, & Roberts, 1994). This further indicates that practitioners should remain discerning about the tools used within their indirect assessment battery and that a variety of tools should be explored to supplement and confirm findings. There are many indirect assessment tools available, including interviews, questionnaires, and worksheets. These will be discussed in greater detail in Chapter 7 when the focus will be on indirect assessment and you will have the opportunity to review examples of these tools.

DIRECT ASSESSMENT

Specifically in the context of FBA, practitioners take care to collect data on the events, stimuli, or conditions occurring before and after the occurrence of the behavior. Collection of that type of data usually involves the recording of the antecedents, behaviors, and consequences that occur in an immediate temporal sequence. Specifically, there are two types of direct observation approaches used: **anecdotal observation** and **ABC recording**.

Anecdotal observation essentially consists of the observer recording a descriptive account of all the events occurring in temporal sequence during the period of observation. This would include a written account of all of the behaviors, as well as their antecedents and consequences, and all stimuli that could seem relevant to describing those variables. This approach to data collection provides what is essentially a broad brush stroke to gain a general and overall assessment of the learner's behavior, their interaction with the environment in which the behavior occurs, and the scope of target behaviors to more closely assess.

ABC recording consists of a more specific recording of the target behaviors and consists of recording the frequency and duration of the behavior. It is recorded using the framework of the antecedent-behavior-consequence contingency, with recording sheets that include separate columns for data to be recorded according to those classifications within the temporal sequence. Two examples are provided in the tables that follow, one with blank spaces for observers to record information in narrative format and the second with the opportunity to use a pre-populated checklist of frequent antecedents, behaviors, and consequences. This process is called "structured A-B-C data collection". The process of direct assessment data collection and examples will be described and explored in Chapter 7.

Computer-Assisted Data Collection Tools

No matter the skill and experience of a trained observer to collect data, there are inherent challenges when it comes to the reliability, validity, and practical ease of collecting data on target behaviors. Fortunately, technology designed specifically to collect, record, store, graph, and even analyze and present data has been created and is constantly evolving. Although practitioners must train themselves to be careful and vigilant observers, the use of computer-assisted data collection tools can assist in providing additional assurance that data were collected accurately and with precision. The table below outlines several popular tools for the purposes of data collection in functional behavior assessment, specifically. It is recommended that you review this list (Kelly & Connor, 2015) for options that may be appropriate for your future work.

Table 5.2 Software Applications for Data Collection in Functional Behavior Assessment

Application	Developer	Purpose	Cost
ABA1 Program	Estuary Consulting	Collects data on discrete trial programs (for iPhone or iPod only)	$9.99
ABC Behavior Assessment	Reticent Arts	Guides you through the process of developing hypotheses about the functional relationships among antecedents, behaviors, and consequences.	Free
ABC Data Tracker	Christopher Olstad	Behavior tracking and graphing. Can export files to Excel.	$3.99
ABC Video Pro	Raymond Romanczyk, BCBA-D, and Jennifer Gillis BCBA-D	Analysis of video recordings and live in vivo observations. Can export to free Web tools.	$49.99; free lite version
Autism Tracker Pro	Track and Share Apps, LLC	Tracks mood, behavior, food, and health for several learners. Comes with a visual calendar and multi-item graphs. Can communicate with team members using Dropbox, e-mail, or Twitter.	Cost: $9.99, free lite version
Behavior Snap-Behavior Observations at Your Fingertips	SuperPsyched, LLC	Multimodal behavior observation tool to identify the frequency, duration, and function of behavior in school. Records intervals, ABC, duration, and frequency data.	$9.99
Behavior Tracker	Troy Ochowicz	Collects data to use in your favorite spreadsheet application. Simple charting application within the program and can e-mail PDFs to parents.	$0.99
Behavior Tracker Pro	Marz Consulting Inc.	Allows tracking of behaviors and automatic graphing. Can export data to off-line manipulations in Excel, record video, and is customizable.	$29.99
Behaviour Observations	Cluster 8 Nga Manu Awhina	Tool for gathering baseline data about learner's on/off task behavior.	free

(continued)

Application	Developer	Purpose	Cost
Catalyst Client	DataFinch Technologies, Inc.	Comprehensive data collection and graphing system. Collect data offline that automatically syncs when an Internet connection is available.	Free to download, but need an account: $9-$39
D.A.T.A	Behavior Science.org, LLC	Direct assessment tracking application (DATA) measures how often and how long events occur overtime (iPhone only).	Free
Data Analysis	Data Evaluation Systems	General purpose iPad app for plotting data on x and y pairs. Variety of options for customizing graphs. Can enter or import data.	Free
Functional Behavior Assessment Wizard	WhizzWatt Software	Paperless conditions for taking data during an FBA. Default conditions of alone, attention, play, demand, and control. Conditions can be customized. Assists in identifying behavior function and generates graphs and reports.	$9.99
Intervals	elocinSoft	Used to record whole and partial intervals as well as momentary time sampling. Results can be saved in a format read by Excel and most other spreadsheet and database programs (iPhone only).	$4.99
iObserve	Prospect Training Services (Gloucester) Ltd	Audio and video recording app that allows you to time stamp criteria, give feedback, upload and review recordings, and create a signed declaration.	$74.99
On Task	Ryan Peters Productions	Behavior data collection and presentation tool.	$9.99
Rethink Behavior Tracking	Rethink Autism	Assesses and tracks the behavior of multiple individuals with a checklist format and customizable behaviors.	free to download, but need an account: $59-$89
SymTrend	SymTrend, Inc.	Electronic data collection and analysis system for a variety of symptom patterns. Assists in determining triggers and assessing whether treatments are working.	Free
Tantrum Tracker	Scott Grant	Tracks tantrums and outbursts of children and organizes data on charts and graphs.	$0.99
Teacher's Assistant Pro: Track Student Behavior	Lesson Portal, LLC	Tracks learner's actions, behavior, and achievements in the classroom. Communicates with parents via iPhone and iPad.	$5.99

Summary

This chapter provided an overview of the definition and purpose of measurement in the context of ABA as well as FBA. Additionally, the principles of appropriate scientific measurement, reliability, and validity were introduced and discussed. The role and purpose of indirect and direct assessment practices and processes were also explored.

Definition of Key Terms

- **reliability:** the extent to which consistent measures/values are reported
- **validity:** the extent to which a measurement tool captures the information that the tool is intended to capture
- **measurement:** the process of assigning numbers to the dimensional qualities of an observed behavior
- **Inter-observer Agreement (IOA):** the degree of agreement between two independent observers of the same target behavior
- **observer drift:** unintentional changes in the way data is collected that could impact the accuracy of measurement
- **anecdotal observation:** narrative recording of what occurs during the behavioral observation
- **ABC recording:** narrative or checklist recording of the events that occur and the stimuli that is present within the temporal sequence of the antecedent-behavior-consequence contingency upon the occurrence of a target behavior

Test Your Understanding

Level 1: Knowledge

1. True or False: Reliability is the consistency of measurement.
2. True or False: Validity is the extent to which a measure captures what it is intended to measure.
3. True or False: Inter-observer agreement is the degree to which the same observer measures the same behavior two different times.
4. True or False: Asking a learner to identify antecedents leading to their behavior is an acceptable indirect assessment measure.
5. True or False: Indirect assessment includes direct observation of a behavior's occurrence.

Level 2: Comprehension

1. Which of the following is a function of measurement?
   a. Optimizes effectiveness
   b. Enables accountability to learners, clients, consumers, employers, and society
   c. Allows for the development of function-based intervention
   d. All of the above
2. Identify the antecedent in this situation: Jeremy's sister, Sarah, takes Jeremy's Batman action figure from him. Jeremy grabs a block and throws it at her. Both children are sent to time out by their mother.
   a. Sarah takes Jeremy's Batman action figure from him.
   b. Jeremy grabs a block and throws it at her.
   c. Both children are sent to time out.
   d. None of the above.

3. Identify the consequence in this situation: Maddie has not eaten in a few hours and while walking home from the park, she and her father pass a bakery. Maddie begins screaming and crying out, requesting a cookie. Maddie's father initially resists and then takes her into the bakery to purchase a cookie for Maddie to eat.
   a. Maddie has not eaten in a few hours.
   b. Maddie and her father pass a bakery.
   c. Maddie's father takes her into the bakery to purchase a cookie for Maddie to eat.
   d. None of the above.

Level 3: Application

1. Eli is an eight-year-old who engages in repetitive non-functional vocalizations in the community. To collect direct assessment data, his practitioner and his mother observed his behavior while on a trip to the mall. Below, the data is displayed on a chart. Please do the following:
   - Calculate the IOA for the observations.
   - Does the IOA calculation indicate an acceptable degree of reliability? Why or why not?
   - What are some practices that could be considered that might improve the reliability of the observations?

One-minute period	Observer 1	Observer 2	Agree/Disagree
1	No	No	Agree
2	Yes	Yes	Agree
3	No	Yes	Disagree
4	Yes	No	Disagree
5	No	No	Agree

2. Consider the issue of observer drift. Define this term in your own words and provide three examples of ways in which it could be demonstrated and how it could be mitigated or corrected.
3. Examine Table 5.2's list of computer-assisted data collection tools and the descriptions of the tool's purpose. Imagine a scenario when you might use one of these tools and describe why it may be useful as a primary data collection method.
4. Examine Table 5.2's list of computer-assisted data collection tools and the descriptions of the tool's purpose. Imagine a scenario when you might use one of these tools and describe why it may be useful as a secondary data collection method while using your direct observation as the primary data collection approach.
5. Make a video recording of the oral explanation of any data collection process you wish to discuss and submit this recording for review. General tips: Students should address the camera as though they are speaking with either a consumer of ABA services or a supervisee (imagine

that the camera is the individual with whom you would be speaking). Students may elect to use props to demonstrate the way in which data should be collected or use other materials relating to how the behavior change procedure should be implemented. In the event that these props or data collection sheets are referenced in the video, these items should be made visible on camera.

In-Class Small Group Discussion Questions/Exercises

Create small groups (perhaps four or five students) and discuss the following topics, allowing 10 to 15 minutes to complete the response.

1. Within your small group, consider a scenario where an indirect assessment might reveal valuable information about a target behavior. Compose a brief case study identifying specific variables that would be identified through an indirect assessment that would shape your plan for direct observation opportunities.
2. Consider the role of direct assessment in the FBA process. Discuss why it is critical to conduct direct observations. Identify three logistical challenges to the direct assessment process. Identify three ways in which computer-assisted technology may be helpful in mitigating those challenges.
3. Data collection presents valuable information to clinicians for the purpose of assessment and progress monitoring; however, it also introduces ethical concerns. What are some ethical considerations you would need to account for throughout the indirect and direct assessment processes as well as with data storage and the management of data access? How would you address these considerations in your practice?

References

Bihm, E.M., Kienlen, T.L., Ness, M.E., and Poindexter, A.R. (1991). Factor structure of the Motivation Assessment Scale for persons with mental retardation. *Psychological Reports, 68*, 1235–1238.

Cooper J.O, Heron T.E, Heward W.L. *Applied behavior analysis* (2nd ed.) Upper Saddle River, NJ: Pearson; 2007.

Duker, P.C., and Sigafoos, J. (1998). The Motivation Assessment Scale: Reliability and construct validity across three topographies of behavior. *Research on Developmental Disabilities, 19*, 131–141.

Durand, M.V., and Crimmins, D.B. (1988). Identifying the variables maintaining self-injurious behavior. *Journal of Autism and Developmental Disorders, 1,* 99–117.

Iwata, B.A., DeLeon, I.G., & Roscoe, E.M. (2013). Reliability and validity of the functional analysis screening tool. *Journal of Applied Behavior Analysis, 46*(1), 271–284.

Johnston, J.M., & Pennypacker, H.S. (1993). *Strategies and tactics for human behavioral research* (2nd ed.). Hillsdale, NJ: Earlbaum.

Kelly, K.M., & Connor, J. (2015). Apps for behavior analysis. Behavior analysis and technology: A special interest group of the Association for Behavior Analysis International. Retrieved from: https://batechsig.com/2015/03/09/apps-for-behavior-analysts/.

Sigafoos, J., Kerr, M., and Roberts, D. (1994). Interrater reliability of the Motivation Assessment Scale: Failure to replicate with aggressive behavior. *Research on Developmental Disabilities, 15,* 333–342.

Zarcone, J.A., Rodgers, T.A., Iwata, B.A., Rourke, D.A., and Dorsey, M.F. (1991). Reliability analysis of the Motivation Assessment Scale: A failure to replicate. *Research on Developmental Disabilities, 12,* 349–360.

CHAPTER 6

Indirect Assessment

U p to this point, this book has been focused on the theoretical underpinnings, ethical considerations, and basic framework of conducting a functional behavior assessment (FBA). Now that
that groundwork has been laid, it is necessary that we begin a deeper focus on the mechanics
of the indirect assessment process.

Indirect assessment is the process of gathering information about a learner's behavior from indirect
sources, not from direct observation. Although different texts may call this process "informant methods"
or "indirect methods of assessment," the basic approach and purpose is the same. Indirect assessment
consists of either self-report (where the individual learner themselves provides anecdotal information
on their behavior, when possible) and informant report (where others who have observed the behavior remark on its occurrence). This systematic gathering of information from other sources allows for
the behavior analyst to review all the necessary background information coming in the form of school
and medical records, interviews with those who have observed the behavior, and, in cases where the
individual is able to communicate information about the behavior, the individual learner themselves.
Essentially, before directly observing the behavior, it is best to pull information from various sources to
better contextualize the behavior and the patterns of behavior in various environments, times of day, or
the individual's specific physiological circumstances that may be evoking the behavior.

Indirect assessments also provide valuable information on **setting events**, which are those events that
occur long before the problem behavior and the immediate events or stimuli that trigger the behavior.
Examples of setting events may be lack of sleep, illness, injury, or other events or physiological circumstances that increase the likelihood that if specific stimuli or events are present in the environment, the
behavior will occur. Identifying setting events and creating a plan to manage, or at least predict them,
may assist with prevention of the problem behavior in the first place.

This chapter will briefly review selected evidence-based tools available for behavior analysts to use to
conduct the indirect assessment phase of the FBA, including rating scales, questionnaires, interviews, and
surveys. The main purpose and objective of this chapter, however, is to more closely examine the indirect
assessment process so that the practice of carrying out the indirect assessment and composing a narrative
report of those results will be clear and effective. Because the specific indirect assessment tools may change

slightly over time due to new items being added on to certain tools or entirely new tools being developed, it is most useful for student practitioners (i.e., future educators and behavior analysts) to focus on the general process and bear in mind the specific considerations of carrying out an assessment of this sort.

Due to the importance of the indirect assessment step of the FBA, it is important that clinicians conducting FBAs become fluent in the process. For that reason, the format of this chapter will follow the "See one, do one, teach one" model, wherein, you will be shown a completed indirect assessment ("see one"), you will be asked to complete an indirect assessment ("do one"), and, finally, you will be asked to teach someone else to conduct an indirect assessment ("teach one"). Upon finishing this chapter, you will have a better understanding of which indirect assessment tools to use in various scenarios and how to conduct an indirect assessment.

LEARNING OBJECTIVES

After completing the chapter's activities, learners should be able to do the following:

- Describe and evaluate various indirect assessment tools

- Evaluate the format and basic features of each indirect assessment tool

- Describe and evaluate interviewer practices and considerations to increase validity and reliability of the assessment

- Analyze key elements to include in a narrative report of the indirect assessment

- Apply formatting requirements for a narrative report of indirect assessment results

---

Indirect Assessment Tools

An indirect assessment can take many forms and consist of different methods that are used to gather information about the behavior without directly observing it. The primary methods of indirect assessment consist of **structured interviews, questionnaires, rating scales, self-report instruments**, and **checklists**. As the research evaluating these tools continues and practices evolve, revisions to these tools and methods will emerge. At this time, however, there are a handful of different tools commonly used by behavior analysts to indirectly assess behavior. Selecting the best tool for the indirect assessment process is largely a matter of first identifying tools that have empirical evidence to support their reliability and validity. Once the pool of options is narrowed to include only those with empirical support, it is necessary to consider the following variables:

- The purpose for the indirect assessment (e.g., assist in formulating a hypothesis about the function of the behavior(s), guide/structure the direct assessment process, gain global information about the behavior's occurrence, etc.)
- The individual to be completing the assessment, as each assessment may require specific individuals (e.g., a teacher, parent, or learner themselves, etc.) serve as informants
- Practical variables:
  - How much time it takes to complete the assessment
  - Whether you have training completing the administration and scoring processes

Below, in Table 6.1, a non-exhaustive sample of a few of these commonly used assessment tools are listed along with the information about the tool's publisher or developer, format, and general features. It is important to note that each of these tools present similar concerns regarding potential reporting bias and variable validity due to the nature of informant reporting. Therefore, it is recommended one carefully examine the research regarding the reliability and validity of each tool prior to use.

Table 6.1 Indirect Assessment Tools

Indirect Assessment Tool	Publisher/ Developer	Format	Features	Advantages	Disadvantages
Functional Assessment Interview (FAI)	O'Neill, Horner, Albin, Sprague, Storey, & Newton (1997)	Interview (typically conducted with caregiver or teacher) to develop functional hypothesis	• Ten sections of items • Explores nature of problem behavior, relevant aspects of current social and adaptive skill level, environmental and setting events, functional alternative behaviors, past and present reinforcers, and worksheets to formulate functional hypotheses	• Identifies information regarding the learner's skills • Provides valuable information about reinforcers • Allows for more data to be captured as questions are open-ended	• Open-ended structure can cause it to be more time-consuming than other tools
Functional Analysis Screening Tool (FAST)	DeLeon & Iwata (1996)	Informant- or self-report checklist for initial screening	• Four sections of items • Intended as initial screening tool to provide to multiple informants • Intended to guide/ inform direct assessment process • Intended to identify the function(s) of a target behavior	• Brief • Efficient and objective scoring process	• Additional open-ended interview generally required to capture all indirect assessment data
Motivation Assessment Scale (MAS)	Durand & Crimmins (1988)	Informant- or self-report questionnaire to identify where and when the behavior occurs	• Brief (Sixteen items) • User-friendly (informant circles on a Likert scale "never" to "always") • Purpose is to identify the function(s) of a target behavior	• Likert scale allows for variation in responses • User-friendly scoring system	• Additional open-ended interview generally required to capture all indirect assessment data
Motivation Assessment Scale II (MAS-II)	Durand (2002)	Informant- or self-report questionnaire to identify where and when the behavior occurs	• More comprehensive than first edition (15 additional items) • User-friendly (informant circles on a Likert scale "never" to "always") • Purpose is to identify the function(s) of a target behavior	• Likert scale allows for variation in responses • User-friendly scoring system	• More time-consuming than first edition of MAS

Indirect Assessment Tool	Publisher/ Developer	Format	Features	Advantages	Disadvantages
Functional Assessment Checklist for Teachers and Staff (FACTS)	March, Horner, Lewis-Palmer, Brown, Crone, Todd, & Carr (2000)	Informant- or self-report interview for initial screening and to guide FBA and BIP process	• Brief (takes five to fifteen minutes to complete) • Various response options (narrative, checklist, Likert scale)	• Brief • Likert scale allows for variation in responses	• Used to guide direct assessment process but does not specifically identify function
Problem Behavior Questionnaire (PBQ)	Lewis, Scott, & Sugai (1994)	Informant- or self-report questionnaire for initial screening	• Responses provided by circling frequency of occurrence on Likert scale • Purpose is to identify the function(s) of a target behavior	• Brief • Likert scale allows for variation in responses • User-friendly scoring system	• Additional open-ended interview generally required to capture all indirect assessment data

Interviewer Practices and Considerations

One of the "soft skills" required of any assessor, including practitioners conducting an indirect assessment for an FBA, is the ability to interview informants in a manner that results in information that is reliable and valid. One way to control the variable of the role of the interviewer is to ensure those conducting indirect assessments must be cognizant of their own behavior in the process of conducting an interview. This is an important consideration, as indirect assessments often vacillate between an informal, conversational tone and more structured formality, and an assessor should be aware of when their approach influences more or less information sharing. There are several important interviewer practices and considerations that will need to be reviewed prior to conducting an indirect assessment.

As the individual seeking information, the assessor conducting the interview will first need to determine the credibility and reliability of the informant (the individual reporting about the learner's behavior). It is important to identify bias in an informant and consider whether the informant is being overly critical of the behavior or is minimizing the effects of the behavior due to an alternate motivation or concern about the implications of accurate reporting (e.g., to solicit additional support when caring for or working with the individual, or, conversely, to decrease the involvement of others, etc.). Credible and reliable informants are those who have observed the behavior recently, frequently, and closely and are willing to report on what occurred. To explain this further, it is critical that an informant has observed the behavior recently because it will be necessary that they report on the most recent topography or form that the behavior has taken. Behaviors have the potential to change form over time, and if an informant has not recently observed the behavior, it is possible that they will report on a previous iteration of the behavior or a different behavior altogether. Also, behaviors have the potential to change their function over time, or to take on multiple functions. For instance, a behavior that began to serve the function of escape may, over time, also serve the function of obtaining attention. Also, the more recently one observes a behavior, the more reliable they will be in reporting the behavior's occurrence with accuracy.

In addition to the need for recent observations, it is also very important that the informant reporting on the behavior has observed the behavior with relative frequency. When an informant is reporting on a behavior that happens multiple times per day, every day, it is important they have observed the behavior happening across multiple, different days to be sure that the informant is providing information based on a representative sample of observations. If not, it is possible that the informant would be reporting information about the behavior based on a few random occurrences and may not be providing the information needed to determine the behavior's function(s).

Additionally, though this may seem obvious, it is often important to inquire and assess the informant's proximity during their observation of the behavior. If the informant observed the behavior during most occurrences, but was across the room or in a different room only overhearing the behavior's occurrence, then the informant's report should be weighted with some skepticism. A proximally close and unobstructed visual and auditory observation of the behavior will yield more reliable information than an observation conducted from afar.

An additional concern for the behavior analyst is whether the informant is willing to provide detailed information about their observation. In other words, might the informant's motivations (or other cognitive limitations) lead him or her to convey information in a less-than-accurate way? At times, for example, informants who are interviewed for an FBA may be inclined to modify their reports of certain behaviors due to the nature of the behavior itself (i.e., masturbation, public urination, disrobing, etc.). The choice to modify reports of the behavior may stem from the informants' concerns about embarrassing themselves or the learner by reporting what they observed in detail, or from other similar reasons. However, if it is apparent that the informant is not sharing key information in the indirect interview, it is important to note that possibility when evaluating the weight of the informant's report.

In addition to evaluating the credibility and reliability of an informant, a practitioner must consider the format of their indirect interview. Some of the indirect interview tools explored in this chapter do not have specific instructions regarding the recommended or required format for which the interview should be conducted. Many tools indicate specifically in their instructions that an interview must be conducted with the assessor asking questions and recording responses, whereas other tools do not specifically state that this format should be used, and it is possible that the specific tool (perhaps more so in the case of a rating scale or checklist) can be completed entirely by the informant themselves. It is best to examine and follow the recommendations for each tool prior to conducting the interview.

Although the term "active listening" has most often been used in counseling and social work professions and less so in the field of Applied Behavior Analysis, there are aspects to the approach that bear discussion when considering one's interview skills and style. Active listening is used most often to demonstrate to a conversational partner, or interviewee, that you are listening to and understand what they are saying (Lang, Floyd, & Beine, 2000). The most basic technique in the active listening strategy is to mirror what the other person says after a period of listening to their responses.

For instance, imagine you are interviewing a parent of a child who is engaging in loud screaming when they would like to access a preferred toy. Perhaps the parent says, "It is a major issue in the home because it is very stressful to hear that sound frequently. However, it is even more difficult to be out shopping and have him scream like that. Other people turn and look and it makes me just want to get in the car and head home." An example of active listening would be when the behavior analyst responds, "Okay, I believe I follow what you are saying. Essentially, yes, his screaming is a challenging issue in the home because it is loud and causes stress. But out in the community, when you're in a store, it is not only stressful, but it is a bit embarrassing, too?" This statement by the behavior analyst will serve to demonstrate to the parent that his or her response was heard and that those details are relevant to the discussion of the problem behavior. Using active listening will assist in ensuring that the informant of the problem behavior will continue to share information in the course of the interview.

Writing the Narrative Report

Once the behavior analyst has carefully gathered information from credible sources using indirect assessment methods, a narrative report will need to be written that aggregates the information across multiple sources of information. This narrative report will form the initial section of the FBA report and will be shared with all members of the treatment team. For these reasons, it is important to consider sharing only information that is useful about the problem behavior (i.e., the report should be written concisely), but it should also provide sufficient detail regarding the background information about the learner so that any reader of the report will be able to follow along with relative ease. For this reason, it is important to ensure that the following information is included at the beginning of the report, in addition to the aggregated results of the completed indirect assessments:

- Learner's name (to safeguard confidentiality, you might want to use the first name and first letter of last name only)
- Learner's biographical information
    - With whom does the learner reside?
    - Where does the learner attend school/work?
    - What is the learner's typical daily schedule (e.g., in school full-time or working part-time)?
    - Other relevant details about the environments in which the learner spends time
    - Explanation of the purpose of the assessment
- Medical history
    - History of medical problems
    - Medication use (medication name, indication, doses, and schedules)
- Developmental history
    - Diagnostic information/reports
    - Results from a recent skills assessment
- Reports from school or work (e.g., individualized education plans, vocational training plans, supervisor evaluations, etc.)
- Information about informants who completed indirect assessments
    - For each informant, provide a brief rationale for why they were selected to report on the behavior (e.g., the learner's mother interacts with him daily and observes the behavior for several hours each day; the learner's co-worker is present when the behavior is most likely to occur at work and has observed the behavior multiple times per week for several months)
- Results of the indirect assessments conducted

In addition to considering the content of the indirect assessment report, the format of the report should be carefully determined as well. First, it is important to consider the audience for any clinical report that is written. In the case of an FBA, the audience will vary somewhat depending on the composition of the assessment team and on whether a recipient of the final report is an administrator for a school, vocational or employment program, inpatient rehabilitation or hospital facility, correctional facility, or health insurance company to bill for services. For that reason, prior to starting the process of writing a narrative report of any FBA data, it is important to consider whether a specific format or template should be followed in order for the final report to include all required elements in a specific manner.

Once the template and general format is determined, the next consideration in the process of writing the narrative report will consist of considering the style in reporting on the behavior itself. Below, in Table 6.2, a checklist for report writing is provided. In general, following these guidelines when writing any document that is intended to come from a clinical professional will be useful in ensuring that nearly any reader of your report will perceive your writing to be respectful, informed, and professional.

Table 6.2 Checklist for Professional Writing

Guideline	Example	Problem with the Example	Try This Instead. ...
Use observable and measurable terms	"He was being disruptive and aggressive."	The words "disruptive" and "aggressive" are not sufficiently specific and do not convey objective information about the specific behaviors that occurred (two observers may have differing perspectives on what constitutes "disruptive" or "aggressive" behavior).	"He threw three books at the wall with sufficient force to make a loud sound and a dent in the wall. He also used his open hand to make contact with the job coach's back, causing her to fall forward."
Avoid using "mentalistic" language	"I feel/believe/think the behavior is serving the function to escape."	Your emotions, beliefs, or thoughts are not relevant. Let the data speak for itself and focus on reporting observations and facts, not emotions, beliefs, or thoughts.	You could write, "According to all four indirect assessment reports, the behavior occurs when a demand is placed on the learner and once he engages in the behavior, the demand is removed relatively quickly."
Avoid using excessive adjectives	Try to avoid any use of the words "very," "extremely," "profound," "impressive," "disappointing," etc.	These words add very little, if anything, to your report and may cause the reader to question or lose trust in your objective reporting of events.	Focus on the aspect of the data that strike you as warranting the use of an excessive adjective. If the reason you are wishing to use the words "impressively frequent" is because the behavior occurs 40 times in one minute, focus on that dimension of the data in your report (perhaps also provide the reader with a value that would demonstrate what an "unimpressive frequency" would be for comparison). The reader will then interpret the behavior's frequency as impressive without you, as the report writer, telling them your inference about the impressiveness of the frequency.
If you are referring to a child's family member, use that person's name whenever possible	"John's mom reported the behavior occurs twice per day." OR "Mom reported the behavior occurs twice per day."	Using appropriate language sets a professional tone with parents and shows other professionals that you recognize the learner's family members to be equal team members.	Use real names of individuals (e.g., Mr. Henry Clark, or Ms. Moore, or Dr. Sarah Decker), or pseudonyms that are stated as pseudonyms. Never write, "Mom," "Dad," "Grandma," etc. to continuously refer to an individual informant in a formal report except to initially state the relationship of the informant to the learner (e.g., Mr. Henry Clark, John's biological father, completed the FAST. Mr. Clark reported ...").

Although the checklist in Table 6.2 is not exhaustive, it does provide a focused set of guidelines most often observed as problematic in narrative reports from novice clinicians. Tuning into these considerations will ensure that your narrative reports will be well received by all team-members and administrators.

Beyond considering the indirect assessment summary report's basic contents and the style in which it will be written, it is important to also consider how all of this information should be integrated and analyzed. Recall that the role of the indirect assessment is to primarily contextualize the occurrence of the behavior and guide the direct assessment process by allowing a framework for a preliminary hypothesis about the function of the behavior. Although the indirect assessment process is critical in the completion of an FBA, it does not stand as an independent source of information for drawing definitive conclusions about the function of the behavior. It is a critical initial step of a multi-stage process. It is possible, therefore, that the initial conclusions drawn from the indirect assessment process will be proven inaccurate or "off base" once a direct assessment is conducted and/or the functional analysis is conducted. Therefore, it is important to always work carefully to gather complete and, to the best of one's ability, reliable and valid indirect assessment data; however, it is important to not commit fully to the conclusions found through this single stage of the process, as the subsequent stages of the assessment process must be completed prior to reaching a conclusion as to the behavior's function.

Completed Indirect Assessment Example

FUNCTIONAL ANALYSIS SCREENING TOOL (FAST) COVERING ADAM'S LOUD VOCALIZATIONS BEHAVIOR.

Adam Wexler is a six-year-old boy with autism spectrum disorder. He engages in a behavior his parents call "loud vocalizations" where he opens his mouth and makes vowel sounds that do not resemble words (e.g., "oooh", "eeee", "ahhh", "ayyy", and "uhhh") repeatedly for durations for up to one minute (60s) per episode. The audible volume of these sounds varies from being loud enough that an observer would need to cover their ears (to avoid discomfort) if he were engaging in the behavior from 10 feet away. When Adam is engaging in this behavior, he appears to use all of his lung capacity to expel breath to emit the vocalization, the veins in his neck become visible, and his face is apparently flushed during and following an episode of this type of vocalization. This behavior is concerning from a health perspective for Adam, as emitting these vocalizations appears to cause strain to his body and he frequently displays a raspy voice following an episode. This behavior is also concerning in the way that it causes disruption to others (e.g. it distracts other students in his classroom, causes alarm for bystanders when he is out in the community, etc.).

His parents, Dr. and Mr. Wexler, contact Ms. Hewson, a Behavior Analyst who works at the agency providing home-based ABA services for Adam. Ms. Hewson holds a preliminary phone discussion with the Wexlers to gain some basic background information. This information is then the basis of the beginning of the indirect assessment report, shown in Table 6.3.

Table 6.3 Indirect Assessment Report

Adam W. resides with his mother and father, Dr. and Mr. Wexler, and attends a special education classroom specialized for children with autism at Beethoven Elementary school five days per week. When Adam is not in school he spends time at home with his parents, a gymnastics program for children with special needs, at speech therapy, or at a social skills group for children with autism.

Adam was diagnosed with autism at twenty-six months of age by a developmental pediatrician at an interdisciplinary clinic. Dr. and Dr. Wexler report that Adam does not have any additional diagnoses or medical concerns, and does not take any medication. A recent developmental assessment showed that Adam shows delays in the areas of speech and language, social and adaptive skill development. Nevertheless, his teachers report he makes consistent progress on a monthly basis in the areas of functional communication using sign language.

The Functional Analysis Screening Tool (FAST) was conducted with Mrs. and Mr. Wexler as they are the most frequent observers of Adam's loud vocalization behavior in the home and community. The results of that interview are shown in Figure 6.1.

FAST

Functional Analysis Screening Tool

Client: Adam Wexler   Date: 01/09/2018

Informant: Dr. Sally Wexler   Interviewer: Amy Hewson, BCBA

To the Interviewer: The FAST identifies factors that may influence problem behaviors. Use it only for screening as part of a comprehensive functional analysis of the behavior. Administer the FAST to several individuals who interact with the client frequently. Then use the results to guide direct observation in several different situations to verify suspected behavioral functions and to identify other factors that may influence the problem behavior.

To the Informant: Complete the sections below. Then read each question carefully and answer it by circling "Yes" or "No." If you are uncertain about an answer, circle "N/A."

Informant-Client Relationship

1. Indicate your relationship to the person: _X_ Parent _____ Instructor _____ Therapist/Residential Staff _____ (Other)
2. How long have you known the person? _6_ Years _5_ Months
3. Do you interact with the person daily? _X_ Yes _____ No
4. In what situations do you usually interact with the person?
   _X_ Meals   _X_ Academic training
   _X_ Leisure   _X_ Work or vocational training
   _X_ Self-care _____ (Other)

Problem Behavior Information

1. Problem behavior (check and describe):
   _____ Aggression _____
   _____ Self-Injury _____
   _X_ Stereotypy _Loud vocalizations_
   _____ Property destruction _____
   _____ Other _____
2. Frequency: _X_ Hourly _____ Daily _____ Weekly _____ Less often
3. Severity: _____ Mild: Disruptive but little risk to property or health
   _X_ Moderate: Property damage or minor injury
   _____ Severe: Significant threat to health or safety
4. Situations in which the problem behavior is <u>most</u> likely to occur:
   Days/Times _Daily / Any time of day_
   Settings/Activities _Any location_
   Persons present _Anyone_
5. Situations in which the problem behavior is <u>least</u> likely to occur:
   Days/Times _Variable_
   Settings/Activities _When food is in his mouth, sleeping_
   Persons present _Variable_
6. What is usually happening to the person right <u>before</u> the problem behavior occurs? _Variable. It can happen at any time, anywhere, with anyone present._
7. What usually happens to the person right <u>after</u> the problem behavior occurs? _At times we will ignore it and at times we will try to redirect._
8. Current treatments _We have tried using gum or chew toys to occupy his mouth. These approaches have not been consistently effective. We do not have a treatment we regularly practice._

1. Does the problem behavior occur when the person is not receiving attention or when caregivers are paying attention to someone else? **(Yes)** No N/A
2. Does the problem behavior occur when the person's requests for preferred items or activities are denied or when these are taken away? Yes **(No)** N/A
3. When the problem behavior occurs, do caregivers usually try to calm the person down or involve the person in preferred activities? Yes **(No)** N/A
4. Is the person usually well behaved when (s)he is getting lots of attention or when preferred activities are freely available? Yes **(No)** N/A
5. Does the person usually fuss or resist when (s)he is asked to perform a task or to participate in activities? Yes **(No)** N/A
6. Does the problem behavior occur when the person is asked to perform a task or to participate in activities? **(Yes)** No N/A
7. If the problem behavior occurs while tasks are being presented, is the person usually given a "break" from tasks? Yes **(No)** N/A
8. Is the person usually well behaved when (s)he is not required to do anything? Yes **(No)** N/A
9. Does the problem behavior occur even when no one is nearby or watching? **(Yes)** No N/A
10. Does the person engage in the problem behavior even when leisure activities are available? **(Yes)** No N/A
11. Does the problem behavior appear to be a form of "self-stimulation?" **(Yes)** No N/A
12. Is the problem behavior <u>less</u> likely to occur when sensory stimulating activities are presented? **(Yes)** No N/A
13. Is the problem behavior cyclical, occurring for several days and then stopping? Yes **(No)** N/A
14. Does the person have recurring painful conditions such as ear infections or allergies? Yes **(No)** N/A
    If so, list: _____
15. Is the problem behavior <u>more</u> likely to occur when the person is ill? Yes **(No)** N/A
16. If the person is experiencing physical problems, and these are treated, does the problem behavior usually go away? Yes **(No)** N/A

Scoring Summary

Circle the number of each question that was answered "Yes" and enter the number of items that were circled in the "Total" column.

Items Circled "Yes"				Total	Potential Source of Reinforcement
(1)	2	3	4	1	Social (attention/preferred items)
5	**(6)**	7	8	1	Social (escape from tasks/activities)
(9)	**(10)**	**(11)**	**(12)**	4	Automatic (sensory stimulation)
13	14	15	16	0	Automatic (pain attenuation)

The Functional Analysis Screening Tool (FAST) was conducted with Mr. Chang, Adam's Special Education teacher, as he spends 90% of the school day with Adam and is able to report on the behavior at school. The results of that interview are shown in Figure 6.2:

FAST

Functional Analysis Screening Tool

Client: <u>Adam Wexler</u>   Date: <u>01/11/2018</u>

Informant: <u>Mr. Benjamin Chang</u>   Interviewer: <u>Amy Hewson, BCBA</u>

To the Interviewer: The FAST identifies factors that may influence problem behaviors. Use it only for screening as part of a comprehensive functional analysis of the behavior. Administer the FAST to several individuals who interact with the client frequently. Then use the results to guide direct observation in several different situations to verify suspected behavioral functions and to identify other factors that may influence the problem behavior.

To the Informant: Complete the sections below. Then read each question carefully and answer it by circling "Yes" or "No." If you are uncertain about an answer, circle "N/A."

Informant-Client Relationship

1. Indicate your relationship to the person: _____ Parent __X__ Instructor _____ Therapist/Residential Staff _____ (Other)

2. How long have you known the person? __0__ Years __3__ Months

3. Do you interact with the person daily? __X__ Yes _____ No

4. In what situations do you usually interact with the person?
   __X__ Meals   __X__ Academic training
   __X__ Leisure   _____ Work or vocational training
   __X__ Self-care   <u>Adam attends school five days per week</u> (Other)

Problem Behavior Information

1. Problem behavior (check and describe):
   ____ Aggression _____
   ____ Self-Injury _____
   __X__ Stereotypy <u>Loud vocalizations, not functional</u>
   ____ Property destruction _____
   ____ Other _____

2. Frequency: __X__ Hourly ____ Daily ____ Weekly ____ Less often

3. Severity: _____ Mild: Disruptive but little risk to property or health
   __X__ Moderate: Property damage or minor injury
   _____ Severe: Significant threat to health or safety

4. Situations in which the problem behavior is <u>most</u> likely to occur:
   Days/Times <u>Behavior occurs throughout the day, every day</u>
   Settings/Activities <u>Behavior occurs across all activities and settings</u>
   Persons present <u>Anyone</u>

5. Situations in which the problem behavior is <u>least</u> likely to occur:
   Days/Times <u>Naptime</u>
   Settings/Activities <u>When food is in the mouth or when napping</u>
   Persons present <u>Anyone</u>

6. What is usually happening to the person right <u>before</u> the problem behavior occurs? <u>There does not seem to be a consistent antecedent</u>

7. What usually happens to the person right <u>after</u> the problem behavior occurs? <u>This is highly variable; there does not seem to be a consistent consequence following the behaviour.</u>

8. Current treatments <u>We do not have a protocol in place except to ignore the behavior</u>

---

1. Does the problem behavior occur when the person is not receiving attention or when caregivers are paying attention to someone else? **(Yes)** No N/A

2. Does the problem behavior occur when the person's requests for preferred items or activities are denied or when these are taken away? Yes **(No)** N/A

3. When the problem behavior occurs, do caregivers usually try to calm the person down or involve the person in preferred activities? Yes **(No)** N/A

4. Is the person usually well behaved when (s)he is getting lots of attention or when preferred activities are freely available? Yes **(No)** N/A

5. Does the person usually fuss or resist when (s)he is asked to perform a task or to participate in activities? Yes **(No)** N/A

6. Does the problem behavior occur when the person is asked to perform a task or to participate in activities? Yes **(No)** N/A

7. If the problem behavior occurs while tasks are being presented, is the person usually given a "break" from tasks? Yes **(No)** N/A

8. Is the person usually well behaved when (s)he is not required to do anything? Yes **(No)** N/A

9. Does the problem behavior occur even when no one is nearby or watching? **(Yes)** No N/A

10. Does the person engage in the problem behavior even when leisure activities are available? **(Yes)** No N/A

11. Does the problem behavior appear to be a form of "self-stimulation?" **(Yes)** No N/A

12. Is the problem behavior <u>less</u> likely to occur when sensory stimulating activities are presented? **(Yes)** No N/A

13. Is the problem behavior cyclical, occurring for several days and then stopping? Yes **(No)** N/A

14. Does the person have recurring painful conditions such as ear infections or allergies? Yes **(No)** N/A
    If so, list:_____

15. Is the problem behavior <u>more</u> likely to occur when the person is ill? Yes **(No)** N/A

16. If the person is experiencing physical problems, and these are treated, does the problem behavior usually go away? Yes **(No)** N/A

Scoring Summary

Circle the number of each question that was answered "Yes" and enter the number of items that were circled in the "Total" column.

Items Circled "Yes"				Total	Potential Source of Reinforcement
①	2	3	4	1	Social (attention/preferred items)
5	6	7	8	0	Social (escape from tasks/activities)
⑨	**⑩**	**⑪**	**⑫**	4	Automatic (sensory stimulation)
13	14	15	16	0	Automatic (pain attenuation)

Dr. Brian Iwata, "Functional Analysis Screening Tool" Copyright © 2005 by The Florida Center on Self-Injury. Reprinted with permission.

Summary

The goal of this chapter was to explore the indirect assessment process by exploring specific methods and tools, considerations while conducting interviews, and report writing. Additionally, since the most effective manner of learning clinical skills is often to see examples of practices being carried out, an example of a completed FAST was provided.

In order to make the most out of the training offered in this chapter, please complete the review activities at the end of this chapter. In those application exercises, you will be able to conduct a FAST and also teach someone how to conduct the FAST. Preparing yourself to complete an indirect assessment carefully and completely will perfectly position you to plan and complete the direct assessment process in Chapter 7.

Definition of Key Terms

- **indirect assessment:** the stage in the functional behavior assessment process where information is gathered from individuals who observe the behavior as well as from the individual learner themselves. This stage does not include directly observing the behavior
- **setting events:** events or physiological circumstances that occur before the immediate precursor to the behavior that increase the likelihood that the behavior will occur
- **structured interviews:** an interview tool consisting of a series of questions asked of individuals reporting on the target behavior
- **questionnaires:** an interview tool consisting of a series of questions posed to an individual reporting on the target behavior that the individual fills out himself or herself
- **rating scales:** an interview tool asking respondents to rate dimensions of a target behavior (e.g., frequency, magnitude, duration, etc.) or circumstances surrounding the behavior
- **checklists:** an interview tool providing respondents with potential responses regarding the nature of the target problem and requiring that they affirmatively respond to responses that are accurate

Test Your Understanding

Level 1: Knowledge

1. True or False: The Functional Assessment Interview (FAI) is a rating scale that the assessor provides to an informant and then scores.
2. True or False: The Functional Analysis Screening Tool (FAST) requires respondents to answer a lengthy series of questions and conduct a direct assessment.
3. True or False: The following statement contains mentalistic language, "The behavior occurs between seven to nine times per day and is most likely to occur when a task demand is presented to the individual."

4. True or False: As long as previous reports from school are included in an indirect assessment summary, it is not necessary to include more current reports from the employment/vocational setting.

Level 2: Comprehension

1. Credible and reliable informants are those who have observed the behavior recently. Why is this important?
    a. The topography of behaviors may change over time
    b. The function of the behavior may change over time
    c. Informants may forget key information regarding their observations
    d. All of the above
2. Reliable informants are those who have observed the behavior frequently. Why is this important?
    a. Unless one is constantly observing the behavior, that individual is not a reliable nor a credible source.
    b. Informants who are vigilantly observing others are most likely to be reliable.
    c. A large, representative sample of observations will be most likely to be reliable.
    d. None of the above

Level 3: Application

1. This first exercise will focus on completing an indirect assessment. You and a classmate will work to complete this assignment together. Use the Functional Analysis Screening Tool (FAST) to conduct an interview with a classmate, who will provide information on a fictional learner to inform the assessment. During the meeting, your partner will serve as the interviewee (using information provided to them regarding a fictional learner) and will respond to questions posed on the FAST. In the same meeting, you will then switch roles with your partner and you will serve as the interviewee as they conduct the FAST with you. Once both interviews have been completed, students will independently compose a brief narrative summary of the indirect assessment results.
2. This exercise focuses on teaching someone to complete an indirect assessment. The purpose of this assignment is to develop students' ability to explain behavior analytic principles, concepts, tasks, and procedures in a clear and professional manner, while tailoring language to specific audiences. Providing oral explanation of a behavior analytic principle, concept, task, or procedure is an important skill for a behavior analyst who has attained mastery in the field. Complete the following steps:
    a. Identify an indirect assessment tool to be conducted with a hypothetical informant of a behavior for a specific learner. Imagine you are a supervisor or an instructor of Applied Behavior Analysis. Develop an explanation (that you would hypothetically provide to your supervisee or student) of how to conduct the indirect assessment process
    b. Make a video recording of the oral explanation of the process and submit this recording for review. General tips: Students should address the camera as though they are speaking with either a consumer of ABA services or a supervisee (imagine that the camera is the individual with whom you would be speaking). Students may elect to use props to demonstrate the way in which data should be collected or use other materials relating to how the behavior-change procedure should be implemented. In the event that these props or data collection sheets are referenced in the video, these items should be made visible on camera.

In-Class Small Group Discussion Questions/Exercises

Create small groups (perhaps four or five students) and discuss the following topics, allowing 10 to 15 minutes to complete the response.

1. Each member of your team should identify a different indirect assessment tool to explore. To initially identify the tool, you may access the research literature to review which tools are most commonly used in experiments, search the Web, or ask colleagues what is commonly used in your place of work. Use the information provided in this chapter to obtain a copy of the tool online and explore it. In your team meeting, describe to your team members the basic features of the tool and your impressions. Specifically, what are some considerations about the tool's instructions (if there are any) and scoring process (if there is one) that should be taken into account. As a team, discuss whether you would use each tool in practice. Why or why not? Which tools stand out to you to be the most efficient? Which tools stand out to you to be the most comprehensive? Are there weaknesses about the tools that should be considered when using them in practice?

2. Carefully review the content in this chapter that focused on interviewer practices and considerations. In your team, discuss these considerations. Are any of them surprising? Are there more considerations you believe should be added?

3. Carefully review the content in this chapter that focused on narrative report writing. In your team, discuss the various content and formatting elements that were recommended to be included. Which do you believe were the most critical elements and why? Are there any elements that you believe would not be as important to include? Why?

References

DeLeon, I.G., & Iwata, B.A. (1996). Evaluation of multiple-stimulus presentation format for assessing reinforcer preferences. *Journal of Applied Behavior Analysis, 29*, 519–533.

Durand, V.M., & Crimmins, D.B. (1988). Identifying the variables maintaining self-injurious behavior. *Journal of Autism and Developmental Disorders, 18*, 99–117.

Lang, F., Floyd, M.R., & Beine, K.L. (2000). Clues to patients' explanations and concerns about their illnesses: A call for active listening. *Archives of family medicine, 9*(3), 222.

Lewis, T.J., Scott, M., & Sugai, E. (1994). The problem behavior questionnaire: A teacher-based instrument to develop functional hypotheses of problem behavior in general education classrooms. *Assessment for Effective Intervention, 19*, 2–3.

March, R.E., Horner, R.H., Lewis-Palmer, T., Brown, D., Crone, D., Todd, A.W., & Carr, E.G. (2000). *Functional assessment checklist for teachers and staff (FACTS)*. Eugene, OR: Educational and Community Supports.

O'Neill, R.E., Horner, R.H., Albin, R.W., Sprague, J.R., Storey, K., & Newton, J.S. (1997). *Functional assessment and program development for problem behavior*. Pacific Grove, CA: Brooks/Cole Publishing.

CHAPTER 7

Direct Assessment

Whereas indirect assessment serves the role of gathering background information and reports from those who have observed the behavior, the direct assessment stage focuses on observing the behavior in real time and collecting data on its occurrence. Direct assessment can include direct observation (observing the behavior in vivo), analog observation (observing the behavior in a contrived setting, such as a clinic or hospital), and self-monitoring (wherein the individual directly record occurrences of their own behavior as it is occurring). This chapter will touch upon the logistical and ethical considerations of direct assessment in various environments through the use of case studies and examples. At the end of this chapter, you will be able to select the direct assessment tools most appropriate for a given target behavior and environmental situation, as well as discuss the ethical considerations involved. In doing so, we will continue to employ the "See one, do one, teach one" process of exploring examples, practicing creating examples and teaching others about this stage of FBA.

LEARNING OBJECTIVES

After completing the chapter's activities, learners should be able to do the following:

- Describe the types of data collected through direct assessment observations

- Analyze various direct assessment tools

- Evaluate the format and basic principles of each direct assessment tool

- Analyze observer practices and considerations to increase validity and reliability of the assessment

- Evaluate observer practices and considerations to ensure ethical observation

- Identify and describe key elements to include in a narrative report of the direct assessment
- Apply formatting requirements for a narrative report of direct assessment results

Data Obtained through Direct Assessment Observations

There are a variety of formats used for collecting data during a direct assessment. Regardless of the approach used, they all aim to reach the same general objective and set of data. During a direct assessment, the primary goal is to observe the target behavior and take note of the environmental events surrounding each occurrence of the behavior. The temporal sequence of events, known as the **Antecedent-Behavior-Consequence (A-B-C) sequence**, or the **three-term contingency** in other ABA textbooks, is critical in determining the function of the behavior.

Before discussing the way in which those environmental events are catalogued, it is necessary to briefly focus on the development of the behavior definition, as the behavior itself is the fulcrum on which the direct assessment observation is balanced (the observer notices the occurrence of the target behavior and then asks, "What happened immediately prior to the behavior?" And, "What happened immediately following the behavior?"). Therefore, the observation is primarily focused on directly viewing the target behavior and systematically recording the antecedents and consequences to it. Since the target behavior's occurrence dictates what is recorded during direct assessment observations, it is always best to begin an observation with a clear, objective, and measurable definition of the behavior, as this will allow for the most reliable and valid data to be collected. However, sometimes the purpose of the initial observation is to further refine that definition, so a general label for the behavior is provided until the more specific and refined definition is formulated.

For example, instead of clearly stating what constitutes an occurrence of Carlos's kicking behavior with an objective and measurable description with examples of the behavior and non-examples (behaviors that do not match the description), it is possible to commence the direct assessment observation with simply the label of "kicking" and, during the observation, note what the various forms of kicking appear to be. Following that initial observation with the general label, the behavior analyst can examine the various forms of kicking that were observed in order to more carefully compose the behavior definition that will be the focus of the direct assessment.

Additionally, there are times when different challenging behaviors occur together (for example, in a "tantrum" episode when kicking is accompanied by screaming, hitting, and biting). In those cases, the initial observation will involve clearly identifying which behavior is the highest priority, in terms of social significance, to address, or, whether an entire episode with one or more challenging behaviors should be recorded. In other words, while starting a direct assessment observation with an objective and measurable behavior definition is always ideal, in practice, the definition may only achieve the most clarity when the behavior analyst can directly observe repeated instances of the behavior before formulating that definition.

Now that it is clear the state of the behavior definition may vary somewhat in terms of completeness at the start of a direct assessment, it is important to discuss the types of environmental data we need to collect during the direct assessment observation. The primary data to obtain through a direct assessment observation are the information regarding the occurrence of the target behavior, primarily a) what happened directly prior to the behavior, and b) what happened directly following the behavior.

This relatively rapid temporal sequence is discussed at length in many textbooks focusing on the theoretical foundations of ABA; however, for the purposes of this text, we will briefly review these terms.

All events and stimuli present immediately prior to (within one to three seconds) the occurrence of the target behavior are considered **antecedent** events and/or stimuli. It is critical to systematically record all antecedents for each occurrence of the behavior, as these "set the stage for" or "occasion" the occurrence of the behavior. Examples of antecedents to certain behaviors include those listed in Table 7.1.

Table 7.1 Examples of Antecedents to Specific Behaviors

Antecedent (event or stimuli immediately preceding behavior)	Behavior (action taken by the person)
Your phone rings	You answer the phone
Parent offers child a cookie	Child reaches out hand to take cookie
It begins to rain while you drive your car	You turn on your windshield wipers
Your friend turns on the television and the volume is loud	Your friend searches for the volume control on the remote to lower the volume
Your alarm clock buzzes	You turn it off

As you can see in these examples, antecedents are nearly constantly occurring because they are simply events or stimuli that are present in one's environment immediately prior to a behavior. In fact, if you think back to the last five behaviors (actions) you performed, there was an antecedent to each one (because something will always precede your action, as these are simply events in time and stimuli that are present).

It is important also to note that some antecedents are planned, while many are not. For instance, no one plans for it to rain; weather events just happen. But, as a response to the occurrence of rain falling, it is typical for one (who is a safe driver wishing to protect themselves and others on the road) to activate their vehicle's windshield wipers. It would be relatively odd for one to use windshield wipers in the absence of rain; therefore, rain is typically an antecedent to using one's windshield wipers.

Also, some antecedents very commonly precede certain behaviors, and we can usually accurately predict the antecedent to those behaviors. Consider, for example, a bout of sneezing followed by the response of reaching for a tissue. That said, attempting to identify the antecedents to the behaviors shown by individuals with developmental disabilities or other challenges that cannot or do not reliably report the reasons underlying their behavior, can be much more difficult. It should also be noted that the antecedents pinpointed may or may not be the one(s) that control behavior, but finding the specific pattern of antecedents will allow for the specific discriminative stimulus (i.e. the stimulus signalling access to the reinforcer) to be identified. It is for this very reason that we need to use the FBA process to determine the underlying reasons, or **functions**, of a behavior.

Often, when analyzing a target behavior during an indirect assessment interview, a person who has observed the behavior in the past will often report that the target behavior "simply occurs out of the blue," with no clear explanation. In those cases, the task of identifying the antecedent that maintains the behavior, or the **maintaining antecedent** that reliably occurs before the behavior, is particularly challenging. Therefore, carefully recording all antecedents prior to each occurrence of the behavior can be incredibly useful at determining whether there is one or a few antecedents that consistently occur prior to the behavior. The purpose of identifying the maintaining antecedent(s) is to be able to a) more accurately predict the occurrence of the behavior, and b) potentially modify the antecedent events or stimuli so that they are no longer present or they are modified so that the behavior occurs less frequently.

Just as it is critical for behavior analysts to know what occurred before a behavior, it is also necessary for us to know what happened directly following the occurrence of the behavior (within one to three seconds), or the **consequence** events and/or stimuli. When observers systematically record the antecedents and consequences immediately surrounding consecutive instances of a behavior over time, a wealth of important data are collected, and patterns can be identified. Examples of consequences to the behaviors shown in Table 7.1 are presented in Table 7.2.

Table 7.2 Examples of Consequences to Certain Behaviors

Antecedent (event or stimuli immediately preceding behavior)	Behavior (action taken by the person)	Consequence (event or stimuli immediately following behavior)
Your phone rings	You answer the phone	You hear a voice on the other end of the line
Parent offers child a cookie	Child reaches out hand to take cookie	Child eats cookie
It begins to rain while you drive your car	You turn on your windshield wipers	You can see outside of your vehicle
Your friend turns on the television and the volume is loud	Your friend searches for the volume control on the remote to lower the volume	The television's volume is lowered
Your alarm clock buzzes	You turn it off	You no longer hear the alarm buzzing

Once again, these examples of consequences clearly show that, for the purposes of the FBA direct assessment observation, the consequences needing to be examined are simply the immediate effects of the behavior on the individual's environment. Often, the word "consequence" is used in a colloquial sense, wherein a punitive action or circumstance is imposed that is intended to have a resulting effect on a person's behavior. In the science and practice of ABA, however, the word "consequence" is a much less loaded term and is focused on the temporal sequence of events. In other words, there is not an evaluative or subjective judgment or inference that takes place as to the individual's feelings, thoughts, or beliefs about what took place when the observer is recording the ABC data. Rather, a consequence is best defined as simply the events that occur, or stimuli that are present, immediately following the behavior. Collecting many consecutive instances of ABC data allows for us to determine a pattern of occurrences and, just as we aim to identify maintaining antecedents, we also aim to identify **maintaining consequences**.

Direct Assessment Tools

Anecdotal A-B-C recording

By now, it should be clear that the primary data one seeks to obtain through direct assessment is related to environmental events and stimuli. A frequently used tool when beginning the process of direct assessment is **anecdotal A-B-C recording**. Anecdotal A-B-C recording is used when conducting direct and continuous observation by writing direct statements in an A-B-C chart, like the one provided in Table 7.3. The general rule of thumb with respect to anecdotal A-B-C recording is to ensure you write down everything the learner says and does, as well as what happens to them during the observation. Note, it is best practice to record 10–12 different behavior instances of the behavior on different days to reliably capture the maintaining antecedents and consequences; the examples in this chapter are abbreviated.

Table 7.3 A-B-C Chart

Date	Time	Antecedent	Behavior	Consequence
June 7	4:33 p.m.	Parent told child she could not have snack before dinner	Spitting	Parent verbal reprimand "Stop that"; one minute later provided cereal bar
	5:11 p.m.	Parent told child to eat all carrots on plate	Spitting	Parent verbal reprimand for spitting
	5:13 p.m.	Parent told child to stop singing and eat bread on plate	Hitting, spitting	Parent verbal reprimand "Stop that" and "Don't hit"; sent to room alone for five minutes.
	5:27 p.m.	Parent told child she could not have ice cream	Spitting	Parent verbal reprimand "Stop that"
	5:43 p.m.	Parent told child "No, you cannot watch a movie; you didn't eat your dinner"	Hitting, spitting, screaming	Parent verbal reprimand "Stop that" and sent to room alone for five minutes.

Anecdotal A-B-C recording provides a direct and temporal account of what took place across each occurrence of the behavior. Using a blank form to manually record the direct accounts of what occurred can be especially helpful when the common antecedents and consequences have yet to be clearly identified. However, once those behaviors are identified, a checklist form to record these same data can be useful. See an example of a checklist A-B-C recording form in Table 7.4.

Table 7.4 Checklist A-B-C Recording Form

Date	Time	Antecedent	Behavior	Consequence
June 7	4:33 p.m.	✓ Wanted something	✓ Spitting	✓ Reprimand
		✓ Told "No"	Hitting	✓ Got something
		✓ Demand Placed	Screaming	Sent to room alone
	5:11 p.m.	Wanted something	✓ Spitting	✓ Reprimand
		Told "No"	Hitting	Got something
		✓ Demand placed	Screaming	Sent to room alone
	5:13 p.m.	Wanted something	✓ Spitting	✓ Reprimand
		Told "No"	Hitting	Got something
		✓ Demand placed	✓ Screaming	✓ Sent to room alone
	5:27 p.m.	Wanted something	✓ Spitting	✓ Reprimand
		✓ Told "No"	Hitting	Got something
		Demand placed	Screaming	Sent to room alone
	5:43 p.m.	✓ Wanted something	✓ Spitting	✓ Reprimand
		✓ Told "No"	✓ Hitting	✓ Got something
		Demand placed	Screaming	✓ Sent to room alone

The checklist in Table 7.4 illustrates an efficient way to collect anecdotal A-B-C data. Essentially, after the behavior analyst has listed the most common antecedents, behaviors, and consequences observed, the process of collecting data can be made more efficient by simply placing a checkmark by the events that were observed.

SCATTERPLOTS

The scatterplot is an additional tool in the direct assessment data arsenal (Touchette, MacDonald, & Langer, 1985). Data from scatterplots are particularly useful in the analysis of the relationship between certain environmental variables and the target behavior. (The process of creating scatterplots will be covered in Chapter 8 when graphing procedures are discussed.) Once the A-B-C chart is completed and anecdotal A-B-C data are collected in real-time, it is possible to transfer these data to a scatterplot in order to evaluate the relationship between the behavior's occurrence and the setting in which the behavior occurs. Scatterplots are particularly useful when a specific, predictable schedule can be used as the framework for the analysis, such as the school schedule or a vocational work schedule. Having specified times of day and locations that certain activities take place can make the process of aligning and analyzing the relationship between the environmental stimuli and the behavior more straightforward. When there is high variability across activities throughout the day or week, the creation of a matrix to evaluate the alignment of occurrences of the behavior with specific activities may be difficult to create and analyze. For an example of a completed scatterplot, please review Table 8.4 in Chapter 8. Typically, it is best to collect the A-B-C and anecdotal observation data first and then determine whether the environment(s) in which the behavior occurs would lend themselves well to a scatterplot analysis.

DURATION

At times, the principal dimension of a behavior that is the focus of behavior change is the behavior's duration, or the length of time it occurs. Behaviors like screaming or time spent on a task would be useful durations to record. Most observers will plan to use a digital stopwatch to time the duration of a behavior, by starting the stopwatch at the onset of the behavior and stopping the stopwatch when the behavior ends. It would then be possible for the observer to record the duration using a pencil and paper, re-setting the stopwatch to zero and recording the next occurrence of the behavior if they were interested in examining discrete instances of the behavior. However, it may also be useful to consider re-cording cumulative duration: simply stopping and starting the stopwatch each time the behavior begins and ends. Once the cumulative duration is recorded using the stopwatch, the observer can calculate the percentage of that duration using this formula:

$$\frac{\text{Cumulative duration (seconds)}}{\text{Total observation period (seconds)}} \times 100$$

LATENCY RECORDING

When the behavior of concern has to do with the time it takes for a learner to respond to a particular discriminative stimulus (e.g., a task demand or prompt), the focus of the data recording should be on the response latency. Response latency is the duration of time from when a specific stimulus is presented and the learner responds. Common examples of measuring response latency center on the time it takes to complete task demands. Let's imagine a parent asks his or her child to take out the trash. If the time elapsed between the parent's request and the child's commencement of the steps required to complete taking out the trash is four minutes, then the four minutes would represent the response latency. Recording response latency allows practitioners to examine the variables that either increase or decrease it, and behaviors falling under the realm of non-compliance with task demands or weak stimulus control are likely to be the focus of FBA.

TIME SAMPLING

At times, a global picture of the occurrence of the behavior, such as what is provided through A-B-C recording, scatterplots, duration, and latency recording, is not sufficient in our understanding of the specific dimension of a behavior or the relation between the antecedents and consequences that surround it. **Time sampling** is a particularly useful set of methods of behavior observation within specific intervals of time. This approach allows observers to focus their observation period on shorter intervals of time to capture what is intended to be a representative sample of the frequency of the behavior. For instance, instead of observing and recording a behavior's frequency over an entire twenty-minute observation and arriving at a total at the end of that twenty-minute time period, time sampling allows observers to divide the observation period into many shorter time intervals to more precisely record when within that twenty-minute time period the behavior occurred. This is particularly useful when a behavior's frequency varies in that total observation period. For example, perhaps one is recording foot-stomping behavior in a twenty-minute period. When a total frequency is recorded, the frequency of the behavior is revealed to be thirty-two foot stomps. However, when the twenty-minute period is broken into ten-second increments, it becomes clear that twenty-eight of those foot stomps (the majority) occurred within the first five minutes of the twenty-minute observation, whereas the remaining four occurred later in the twenty-minute observation. By breaking the observation into shorter intervals, patterns regarding the intensity of the behavior or other environmental variables—within the larger time observation—can be analyzed. The three types of time sampling include whole-interval, partial-interval, and momentary time sampling. Regardless of the method of time sampling used, a percentage of intervals in which the behavior occurred is usually calculated and expressed in direct assessment reports. Given the need to mark the time intervals, many observers use discreet indicators, such as a stop watch, vibrating alarm, or data recording application on their phone or tablet to indicate when an interval has begun and ended.

Whole-interval time sampling. Whole-interval time sampling consists of dividing the total observation period into brief (generally five- to ten-second) time intervals and recording when the behavior occurs throughout the *entire* brief time interval. In other words, if the time interval is set for five seconds, at the end of the interval, the observer only records that the behavior occurred if the behavior lasted for the entire five-second period (i.e., if the behavior only occurs for the first two seconds, or last second of the interval, for example, the behavior will not count as having occurred for the entire interval). An important note about whole-interval time sampling is that it has a tendency to underestimate occurrences of the behavior, because even if a behavior occurs for four seconds of a five-second interval, the occurrence of the behavior will not be recorded. Nevertheless, whole-interval time sampling is incredibly useful in terms of capturing continuous behaviors, such as pretend play, or when behaviors occur at such high rates that it is challenging to differentiate discrete occurrences of the behavior, such as singing or on-task behavior.

To begin a whole-interval time sampling observation period, it is necessary to determine the appropriate time interval that will capture the occurrence of the behavior. Generally, starting with a five- to ten-second interval will allow the observer to determine if the resulting data are useful or if the interval should be extended to a longer period of time. Once the interval is determined, the observer will need to use or create a recording form with various intervals represented by boxes, such as what is shown in Table 7.5 regarding a child's instances of cooperative play with peers.

Table 7.5 Whole-Interval Recording Form

Cooperative Play

Five-second intervals	Did the behavior occur for the entire interval?	
1	(Yes)	No
2	(Yes)	No
3	(Yes)	No
4	(Yes)	No
5	Yes	(No)
6	Yes	(No)
7	Yes	(No)
8	(Yes)	No
9	Yes	(No)
10	(Yes)	No
11	(Yes)	No
12	(Yes)	No
13	(Yes)	No
14	Yes	(No)
15	(Yes)	No
Total	**10**	**5**
Percent Intervals Cooperative Play	**66%**	

The data recorded in Table 7.5 show that the learner engaged in brief, twenty- to twenty-five-second intervals of cooperative play. If this data on this observation session focused on cumulative total duration of the behavior's occurrence, the observer would only know that the behavior lasted for fifty seconds total. Here, using the whole-interval time sampling approach, observers can see that the behavior occurred in two bursts of twenty to twenty-five seconds at a time, which could be useful as the behavior continues to be monitored over time.

Partial-interval time sampling. The same principles explored in whole-interval time sampling apply to partial-interval time sampling. The process of dividing an observation period into brief five- to ten-second intervals and evaluating the occurrence of the behavior within those specific intervals applies. However, instead of asking oneself if the behavior occurs within the entire interval, partial-interval time sampling focuses on whether the behavior occurs *at any point* in the interval. This means that, if, within a ten-second interval the behavior occurs for two seconds (the sixth and seventh second in the interval, for example), the behavior would be recorded as having occurred. Changing the criterion of recording the interval from the entire interval to any point in the interval lowers the threshold for recording the behavior's occurrence. In so doing, this changes the implications of the collected data because more intervals will be recorded as a result of the lower threshold. It is therefore important to note that partial-interval recording has a tendency of over-estimating occurrences of the behavior. Table 7.6 shows the same target behavior as was recorded in Table 7.5, but using the partial-interval recording method.

Table 7.6 Partial-Interval Recording Form

Cooperative Play

Five-second intervals	Did the behavior occur at any point in the interval?	
1	(Yes)	No
2	(Yes)	No
3	(Yes)	No
4	(Yes)	No
5	(Yes)	No
6	(Yes)	No
7	(Yes)	No
8	(Yes)	No
9	(Yes)	No
10	(Yes)	No
11	(Yes)	No
12	(Yes)	No
13	(Yes)	No
14	(Yes)	No
15	(Yes)	No
Total	**15**	**0**
Percent Intervals Cooperative Play	**100%**	

Since partial-interval time sampling only requires that the behavior occurred at any point in the interval, more intervals are marked as having observed the behavior's occurrence.

Momentary time sampling. This final method of time sampling employs the same principles of whole- and partial-interval recording. The difference with momentary time sampling is that instead of recording only the intervals when the behavior occurs for the entire interval or just at any point during the interval, momentary time sampling focuses on whether the behavior was occurring at the end of the interval. Therefore, in a five-second interval, if the behavior was occurring in the fifth second of the interval, the behavior should be recorded to have occurred. This is a particularly useful method when an observer's constant attention cannot be focused on the behavior during the entire interval. Whereas whole-interval time sampling tends to underestimate the occurrence of the behavior and partial-interval time sampling tends to overestimate the behavior's occurrence, momentary time sampling has been shown to both under- and overestimate the behavior's occurrence when the time interval exceeds two minutes (Cooper, Heron, & Heward, 2007; Gunter, Venn, Patrick, Miller, & Kelly, 2003; Powell, Martindale, Kulp, Martindale, & Bauman, 1977; Powell, Martindale, & Kulp, 1975; Saudargas & Zanolli, 1990). Therefore, it is generally best, when using momentary time sampling, to use intervals that are less than two minutes. Table 7.7 shows what the data from the same observation explored in Tables 7.5 and 7.6 would appear to be if momentary time sampling were the method of observation.

Table 7.7 Momentary Time Sampling Recording Form

Cooperative Play

Five-second intervals	Did the behavior occur at the end of the interval?	
1	(Yes)	No
2	(Yes)	No
3	(Yes)	No
4	(Yes)	No
5	(Yes)	No
6	Yes	(No)
7	(Yes)	No
8	(Yes)	No
9	(Yes)	No
10	Yes	(No)
11	(Yes)	No
12	Yes	(No)
13	(Yes)	No
14	Yes	(No)
15	(Yes)	No
Total	**11**	**4**
Percent Intervals Cooperative Play	**73%**	

Observer Practices and Considerations

Directly observing a learner's behavior in the natural environment where the behavior typically occurs can present multiple types of challenges and may influence the results of the assessment. For this reason, it is important to recognize the potential threats to a valid and reliable direct assessment and to work to minimize them at all times to the greatest extent possible. For example, Kazdin (1979) wrote about the effects of **behavioral reactivity**, where the simple act of observation can change that which is being observed; in other words, simply having observers present having observers present may change learner's behavior.

The most ideal circumstance for direct observation would be to identify an observer already present in the environment in which the behavior often occurs. If the behavior occurs in a classroom, the most ideal observer and recorder of behavioral data would be the classroom teacher or an aide who is often in the classroom. In the learner's home, the observer would most ideally be a parent or a family member who is consistently present. However, at times, it is necessary for an outside observer to conduct the direct assessment—either to increase objectivity of the assessment by bringing in "fresh eyes," because there is a technical skill set needed, or due to practical limitations that prevent the naturally present observer from conducting the assessment properly. Often, behavior analysts are contracted to enter a new setting to conduct observations. As a newcomer to the learner's setting, there is an inherent obtrusiveness to their presence that needs to be acknowledged and minimized. In this situation, it can be helpful for the behavior analyst to visit the setting without the learner present (e.g., before the learner arrives in the setting) to determine where to position themselves to pose minimal distraction/disruption and still have the ability to see and hear what the learner is doing.

Cooper, Heron, and Heward (2007) provided several guidelines to follow when conducting the direct assessment process:

- Write down everything the learner does and says and everything that happens to the learner.
- Use homemade shorthand or abbreviations to make recording more efficient, but be sure the notes can be and are accurately expanded immediately after the observation session.
- Record only actions that are seen or heard, not interpretations of those actions.
- Record the temporal sequence of each response of interest by writing down what happened just before and just after it.
- Record the estimated duration of each instance of the learner's behavior. Mark the beginning and ending time of each behavioral episode.
- Be aware that continuous anecdotal observation is often an obtrusive recording method. Most people behave differently when they see someone with a pencil and clipboard staring at them. Knowing this, observers should be as unobtrusive as possible (e.g., stay a reasonable distance away from the subject).
- Carry out the observations over a period of several days so that the novelty of having someone observe the learner will lessen and the repeated observations can produce a valid picture of day-to-day behavior.
- If it is possible to video record the occurrence of the behavior, doing so will provide a permanent product for further review and more reliable data collection and analysis.

Writing the Narrative Report

After the behavior analyst has carefully conducted multiple direct assessment observations and has systematically collected A-B-C data, a narrative report will need to be written that aggregates the information in a manner so that the behavioral patterns can be clearly understood. This narrative report will form the subsequent section of the FBA report (following the indirect assessment narrative) and will be shared with all members of the treatment team. Once again, it is important to consider sharing only information that is useful about the problem behavior and ensure conciseness in your writing, but also to provide sufficient detail regarding the background information about the specific observations so that readers of all backgrounds can contextualize the findings of the report. For this reason, it is important to ensure that the following information is included at the beginning of the report, in addition to the aggregated results of the completed indirect assessments:

- Date
- Time
- Duration of observation (e.g., "one hour") for each observation conducted
- Activities observed (e.g., structured art activity, leisure time—television, playground—swings, etc.)
- A detailed, objective report of exactly what was seen and heard. It is best to take the shorthand reports obtained through anecdotal A-B-C recording and flesh out this information into complete sentences and paragraphs.

Again, in addition to considering the content of the direct assessment report, the format of the report should be carefully determined as well. Please review the formatting guidelines discussed in Chapter 6 to ensure your writing is accessible as well as professional in tone and style for all treatment team members to read and understand.

Completed Direct Assessment Example

A-B-C chart and Anecdotal A-B-C Recordings of Adam's loud vocalization behavior (Case Study Continued from Chapter 6). As you'll recall, Adam Wexler is a six-year-old boy with autism spectrum disorder. He engages in a behavior his parents call "loud vocalizations" where he opens his mouth and makes vowel sounds that do not resemble words (e.g., "oooh", "eeee", "ahhh", "ayyy", and "uhhh") repeatedly for durations for up to one minute (60s) per episode. The audible volume of these sounds varies from being loud enough that an observer would need to cover their ears (to avoid discomfort) if he were engaging in the behavior from 10 feet away. When Adam is engaging in this behavior, he appears to use all of his lung capacity to expel breath to emit the vocalization, the veins in his neck become visible, and his face is apparently flushed during and following an episode of this type of vocalization. This behavior is concerning from a health perspective for Adam, as emitting these vocalizations appears to cause strain to his body and he frequently displays a raspy voice following an episode. This behavior is also concerning in the way that it causes disruption to others (e.g. it distracts other students in his classroom, causes alarm for bystanders when he is out in the community, etc.).

His parents, Dr. and Mr. Wexler, invited Ms. Hewson, a Behavior Analyst who works at the agency providing home-based ABA services for Adam, to their home to observe Adam's loud vocalizations and to conduct a series of direct assessment observations. The results of those observations are recorded in Table 7.8 (note, for this example, the indirect assessment narrative report provided in Chapter 6 would precede the direct assessment narrative report):

Table 7.8 Completed A-B-C Recording Form: Adam Wexler

Date	Time	Setting	Antecedent	Behavior	Consequence
June 7	4:06–4:07 p.m.	Adam's home (living room)	Watching television	Stands on tip-toes, face ten inches from television, loudly vocalizes "eeee" and "ahhh" repeatedly	Dr. Wexler prompts Adam to "move away from TV"
	4:09–4:11 p.m.	Adam's home (living room)	Leaning on living room couch, ten feet from Television	Walks slowly to television, stands on tip-toes, loudly vocalizes "ahhh" and "eeee" repeatedly	Dr. Wexler prompts Adam to "move away from TV"
	4:12–4:13 p.m.	Adam's home (living room)	Leaning on living room couch, ten feet from Television	Walks slowly to television, stands on tip-toes, loudly vocalizes "oooh" and "ahhh" repeatedly"	Dr. Wexler prompts Adam to "move away from TV"

(continued)

	4:14–4:15 p.m.	Adam's home (living room)	Leaning on living room couch, ten feet from Television	Walks slowly to television, stands on tip-toes, loudly vocalizes "eeee" and "ayyy" repeatedly	Dr. Wexler prompts Adam to "move away from TV"
	4:16–5:07 p.m.	Adam's home (living room)	Dr. Wexler leaves room to take a phone call	Stands on tip-toes, faces ten inches from television, loudly vocalizes "ayyy" and "oooh" repeatedly, occasionally jumping, bumps into observer two times	Dr. Wexler turns off television
June 11	12:13–12:14 p.m.	Adam's school classroom	Sitting at table with six other children, teacher opening lunch boxes	Loudly vocalizes "ayyy" and "eeee" repeatedly	Teacher did not say anything, gently placed hand on his spoon in applesauce container
	12:15–12:16 p.m.	Adam's school classroom	Took bite of applesauce	Loudly vocalizes "ahhh" and "oooh" repeatedly	Teacher did not say anything, gently placed hand on his spoon in applesauce container
	12:17–12:18 p.m.	Adam's school classroom	Took bite of applesauce	Loudly vocalizes various sounds	Teacher did not say anything, gently placed hand on his spoon in applesauce container
	12:19–12:20 p.m.	Adam's school classroom	Took bite of applesauce	Loudly vocalizes "eeee" and "ayyy" repeatedly	Teacher did not say anything, gently placed hand on his spoon in applesauce container
	12:24–12:25 p.m.	Adam's school classroom	Took bite of applesauce	Loudly vocalizes various sounds repeatedly	Teacher did not say anything, gently placed hand on his spoon in applesauce container
	12:29–12:30 p.m.	Adam's school classroom	Took bite of applesauce	Loudly vocalizes "ayyy" and "uhhh" repeatedly	Teacher did not say anything, gently placed hand on his spoon in applesauce container
	12:32–12:33 p.m.	Adam's school classroom	Washed hands, remained in bathroom after teacher and other children left	Loudly vocalizes various sounds	Teacher located him in bathroom and prompted him to join structured art activity at table
	12:45–12:46 p.m.	Adam's school classroom	Prompted to glue paper plates together	Loudly vocalizes "eeee" and "ayyy"	Teacher silently and physically prompted him to complete next step
	12:49–12:50 p.m.	Adam's school classroom	Prompted to glue plastic eyes on plate	Loudly vocalizes "oooh" and "eeee"	Teacher silently and physically prompted him to complete next step
	12:55–12:56 p.m.	Adam's school classroom	Prompted to color plates using markers	Loudly vocalizes "eeee" and "ayyy" repeatedly	Teacher silently and physically prompted him to complete next step
	1:01–1:02 p.m.	Adam's school classroom	Prompted to glue on caterpillar legs	Loudly vocalizes various sounds repeatedly	Teacher silently and physically prompted him to complete next step

(continued)

June 14	8:04–8:05 a.m.	Adam's home (kitchen)	Adam eating cereal	Loudly vocalizes various sounds repeatedly	Mr. Wexler says, "Stop, Adam. Eat please"
	8:07–8:08 a.m.	Adam's home (kitchen)	Adam eating cereal	Loudly vocalizes "oooh" and "ahhh"	Mr. Wexler says, "Stop, Adam. Eat please."
	8:12–8:13 a.m.	Adam's home (kitchen)	Adam eating cereal	Loudly vocalizes various sounds repeatedly.	Mr. Wexler says, "Stop, Adam. Eat please."
	8:15–8:16 a.m.	Adam's home (kitchen)	Adam eating cereal	Loudly vocalizes "eeee" and "ayyy"	Mr. Wexler says, "Stop, Adam. Eat please."
	8:17–8:18 a.m.	Adam's home (kitchen and bathroom)	Mr. Wexler says, "Let's go upstairs and brush your teeth"	Loudly vocalizes various sounds while walking up the stairs	Mr. Wexler places Adam's hand on his toothbrush
	8:20–8:21 a.m.	Adam's home (bedroom)	Mr. Wexler says, "Put on your shoes"	Adam loudly vocalizes "eeee" and "ooh" repeatedly	Mr. Wexler silently places Adam's hand on the velcro strap of his right shoe and places it on the Velcro strap of his right shoe
	8:34–8:35 a.m.	Adam's home (foyer)	Has shoes and backpack on, standing by front door while Mr. Wexler is in another room	Adam loudly vocalizes "ayyy" and "eeee" for one minute"	Mr. Wexler says, "Quiet now, buddy. Too loud." Takes Adam's hand and walks to bus stop
June 15	11:00–11:01 a.m.	Adam's family car	Adam is in car seat, listening to his preferred music.	Rocking in seat, smiling, singing, and loudly vocalizing various sounds when not singing	Behavior is ignored (except on two occasions when Dr. Wexler told observer, "I see he is doing it now. I can't really stop the behavior"
	11:10–11:11 a.m.	Playground	Adam climbs on top of the play structure	Loudly vocalizing "oooh" repeatedly	Behavior is ignored

OBSERVATION 1: JUNE 7, 4:06 P.M., ONE HOUR, HOME, WATCHING TELEVISION

Adam was first observed standing on his tip-toes, with his face positioned approximately ten inches from the television. Dr. Wexler asked Adam to "move away from the TV" approximately four times within the first ten minutes of the observation. Adam would briefly move away and walk ten feet to lean on the living room couch, but after approximately one minute, slowly walked back to the television to stand close to it. Following the first ten minutes of the observation, Dr. Wexler left the room to take a work phone call and only the observer and Adam were in the living room together while Adam walked around the room on his tip-toes, watching television and occasionally jumping. Adam did not make eye contact with the observer and on two occasions bumped into the observer as he was staring at the television and walking around. A cumulative timer (stopwatch) recorded Adam engaging in loud vocalization behavior intermittently for 47:37 minutes of the 60 minutes of the observation.

OBSERVATION 2: JUNE 11, 12:13 P.M., ONE HOUR, SCHOOL CLASSROOM, EATING LUNCH, STRUCTURED ACTIVITY

Adam was seated at a table with six other classmates and was heard to be loudly vocalizing while his teacher opened his classmates' lunch boxes for them. When his teacher observed he was loudly vocalizing, he did not say anything and gently placed Adam's hand on his spoon, which was already in his applesauce container. Adam swallowed one bite of applesauce and immediately began loudly vocalizing. A cumulative timer (stopwatch) recorded Adam engaging in Loud vocalizations behavior intermittently for seventeen minutes of the twenty-five-minute lunch-time observation. After lunch, Adam followed instructions to put away his lunchbox and wash his hands in the bathroom. After he finished washing his hands, he remained in the bathroom and engaged in loud vocalizations behavior for approximately four minutes until his teacher located him and prompted him to join the rest of the class at the table for a structured art activity. Adam was hand-over-hand prompted to glue paper to a series of plates to make a caterpillar. He followed brief one-step instructions, but once he completed each instruction, he would engage in loud vocalizations. A cumulative timer (stopwatch) recorded Adam engaging in loud vocalization behavior intermittently for five minutes of the twelve-minute activity.

OBSERVATION 3: JUNE 14, 8:04 AM, 30-MINUTES, HOME, PREPARING FOR SCHOOL

Adam was sitting at his family's kitchen table finishing his cereal at the start of the observation. Mr. Wexler was sitting next to him, praising Adam for taking bites of his cereal. When Adam would stop eating and engage in loud vocalizations, his father would say, "Stop, Adam. Eat, please." And Adam would comply. After approximately 10 minutes, Adam had finished eating his cereal and Mr. Wexler prompted him to follow him upstairs to brush his teeth. Adam engaged in loud vocalizations behavior as he walked up the stairs and only stopped when Mr. Wexler placed the toothbrush in his hand. After brushing his teeth, Adam was instructed to put on his shoes. Adam sat down and put his right foot inside of his shoe, but did not attempt to secure the Velcro straps and instead began to engage in loud vocalization behavior. Dr. Wexler entered the room and sat down, silently placed Adam's hand on the strap. Adam then secured the straps to his shoe and began to put his left foot into the shoe. After he had his shoes on, Adam went downstairs and independently put on his backpack and stood by the front door. He engaged in loud vocalizations intermittently for a full five minutes until Mr. Wexler came to him, told him to quiet down now, buddy, and walked with him to the bus stop.

OBSERVATION 4: JUNE 15, 11AM, 20 MINUTES, CAR, DRIVING TO THE PARK

Adam was seated in his car seat in the rear of the car. Dr. Wexler drove the car and had turned on Adam's preferred playlist of songs. Adam rocked in his seat, smiling and singing. He engaged in loud vocalizations for the entire duration of the ride, only stopping for up to five seconds at a time to sing a lyric or verse of the song. Dr. Wexler observed Adam engaging in loud vocalizations, but did not say anything to Adam as she was driving. She did state on two occasions "I hear he is doing it now. I can't really stop the behavior." Once at the park, Adam yelled the park, Adam yelled "Yay! Park!" and waited to be taken out of his car seat. Once he was let out of the car, he ran to the playground and climbed to the top platform, sat down, and engaged in a loud vocalization.

SUMMARY OF CASE STUDY

The completed A-B-C chart and anecdotal A-B-C recordings indicate that Adam's loud vocalizations to occur regardless of the antecedents or consequences (i.e., there is no clear maintaining antecedent or maintaining consequence). These results are consistent with the results of the indirect assessment interview (FAST) completed in Chapter 6 that indicate regardless of whether Adam is obtaining attention, preferred tangible objects or activities, or is escaping demands, he engages in the behavior at a consistent frequency. This set of circumstances most commonly indicates that the individual being assessed is engaging in loud vocalizations in order to receive automatic, or sensory, reinforcement. As always, functional analysis should be conducted to confirm this is the maintaining function of the behavior.

Summary

This chapter focused on the direct assessment stage of the FBA and the need to observe target behaviors in real time and collect data on its occurrence. In this chapter, we explored two types of anecdotal A-B-C recording tools and the logistical and ethical considerations of direct assessment in various environments. We also explored the process for composing a narrative summary of direct assessment data and a completed narrative summary. In order to make the most out of the training offered in this chapter, please complete the review activities at the end of this chapter. In those application exercises, you will be able to conduct a direct assessment observation and also teach someone how to conduct direct assessment.

Definition of Key Terms

- **Antecedent-Behavior-Consequence (A-B-C) sequence:** the temporal sequence of environmental events surrounding the occurrence of a behavior, also known as the Three-Term Contingency. This sequence is used to predict future occurrences of behavior
- **Three-Term Contingency:** see A-B-C sequence
- **antecedent:** environmental events, conditions, or stimuli that occur prior to the occurrence of the behavior
- **consequence:** environmental events, conditions, or stimuli that occur following the occurrence of the behavior
- **functions:** a behavior's purpose for the individual
- **maintaining antecedent:** the most common antecedent to precede a behavior
- **maintaining consequence:** the most common consequence to precede a behavior
- **anecdotal A-B-C recording:** collection of A-B-C data on a written record
- **behavioral reactivity:** a phenomenon wherein the behavior of an individual changes when they are being observed

Test Your Understanding

Level 1: Knowledge

1. True or False: When completing an anecdotal A-B-C recording, it is important to write down everything the learner says and does as well as what happens to them.

2. True or False: An antecedent is any event that occurs or any stimulus present following the occurrence of a behavior.
3. True or False: Consequences can be planned or unplanned.
4. True or False: As long as your descriptions in an anecdotal A-B-C recording are detailed, you can collect just one hour's worth of data.
5. True or False: It is important to include subjective, inferential information to supplement your direct observation recordings of the behavior.

Level 2: Comprehension

1. Jackson hits Ella after she takes his cracker from his plate at lunch and is reprimanded by the teacher. Identify the antecedent.
   a. Ella took the cracker from Jackson's plate.
   b. Jackson hits Ella.
   c. Jackson is reprimanded by the teacher.
   d. None of the above.
2. Kelly is placed in time out when her mother observed she bit her brother, Stephen. Identify the consequence.
   a. Kelly bit Stephen.
   b. Kelly was placed in time out.
   c. Kelly's mother observed her bite her brother.
   d. None of the above.
3. Liam cries and whines loudly when at home with his father. Upon completion of anecdotal A-B-C recording, the maintaining antecedent appears to be any occasion when his father stops playing with him or interacting with him to complete another task (e.g., answer his phone or complete household chores). The maintaining consequence appears to be that Liam's father stops what he is doing to interact with Liam. The likely function of the behavior is
   a. to access tangible objects
   b. to obtain attention
   c. automatic reinforcement
   d. escape

Level 3: Application

1. This first exercise will focus on completing a direct assessment. Pair yourself with a classmate to complete this assignment. Use the blank anecdotal A-B-C recording form to conduct an observation with a classmate, who will perform a behavior. During the meeting, your partner will serve as the learner (using information provided regarding a fictional learner) and you will record the behavior. In the same meeting, you will then switch roles with your partner and you will serve as the learner as your partner conducts an observation of your behavior. Once both observations have been completed, you will independently compose a brief narrative summary of the direct assessment results.
2. This exercise focuses on teaching another person to complete a direct assessment. The purpose of this assignment is to develop your ability to explain behavior analytic principles, concepts, tasks,

and procedures in a clear and professional manner, while tailoring language to specific audiences. Providing oral explanation of a behavior analytic principle, concept, task, or procedure is an important skill for a behavior analyst who has attained mastery in the field. Complete the following steps:

a. Identify a direct assessment tool to be conducted with a hypothetical learner. Imagine you are a supervisor or an instructor of Applied Behavior Analysis. Develop an explanation (that you would hypothetically provide to your supervisee or student) of how to conduct the direct assessment process.

b. Make a video recording of the oral explanation of the process and submit this recording for review. General tips: Students should take care to address the camera as though they are speaking with either a consumer of ABA services or a supervisee (imagine that the camera is the individual with whom you would be speaking). Students may elect to use props to demonstrate the way in which data should be collected or use other materials relating to how the behavior change procedure should be implemented. In the event that these props or data collection sheets are referenced in the video, these items should be made visible on camera.

In-Class Small Group Discussion Questions/Exercises

Create small groups (perhaps four or five students) and discuss the following topics, allowing 10 to 15 minutes to complete the response.

1. Carefully review the content in this chapter that focused on observer practices and considerations. In your team, discuss these considerations. Are any of them surprising? Are there more considerations you believe should be added?

2. Carefully review the content in this chapter that focused on narrative report writing. In your team, discuss the various content and formatting elements that were recommended. Which do you believe were the most critical elements and why? Are there any elements that you believe would not be as important to include? Why?

References

Cooper J.O., Heron, T.E, and Heward, W.L. (2007). *Applied behavior analysis* (2nd ed.). Upper Saddle River, NJ: Pearson.

Gunter, P.L., Venn, M.L., Patrick, J., Miller, K.A., & Kelly, L. (2003). Efficacy of using momentary time samples to determine on-task behavior of students with emotional-behavioral disorders. *Education and Treatment of Children, 26*, 400–412.

Kazdin, Alan E. (1979, Winter). Unobtrusive measures in behavioral assessment. *Journal of Applied Behavior Analysis, 12*(4), 713–724.

Powell, J., Martindale, B., Kulp, S., Martindale, A., & Bauman, R. (1977). Taking a closer look: Time sampling and measurement error. *Journal of Applied Behavior Analysis, 10*, 325–332.

Powell, J., Martindale, B., & Kulp, S. (1975). An evaluation of time-sample measures of behavior. *Journal of Applied Behavior Analysis, 8*, 463–469.

Saudargas, R.A., & Zanolli, K. (1990). Momentary time sampling as an estimate of percentage time. A field validation. *Journal of Applied Behavior Analysis, 23*, 533–537.

Touchette, P.E., MacDonald, R.F., & Langer, S.N. (1985). A scatter plot for identifying stimulus control of problem behavior. *Journal of applied behavior analysis, 18*(4), 343–351.

CHAPTER 8

Graphing Data

Since FBA data are focused on the behavior of one individual, a graph of the data can be created to allow for a **visual analysis** to draw interpretations about the relationship between the behavior's occurrence and the antecedent and consequence variables that occur before and after it. Visual analysis is a form of examination that is systematic and often addresses the questions of whether a behavior change has occurred and, if so, to what extent. In the context of the FBA process, the primary data obtained are plotted in a **scatterplot** and/or a **bar graph** and require visual analysis to be interpreted. In this chapter, we will be focusing on the process of constructing these graphical displays for visual analysis in the sections that follow. Later in the FBA process, once the FBA is completed and a behavior intervention plan (BIP) is created based upon the function identified in the FBA, a **line graph** is created as baseline and intervention data are collected. Because a line graph is very commonly used in the behavior-change process, it is useful to explore its basic construction as well.

Selecting, designing, and formatting a graphical display of data are critical aspects to allow for proper visual analysis. Specifically, this chapter will provide you with guidance to competently construct and interpret a scatterplot, bar graph, and line graph. After finishing reading this chapter and completing the end-of-chapter activities, you will have completed each step of the "See one, do one, teach one" model for mastery, putting you one step closer to independent construction of FBA graphs.

LEARNING OBJECTIVES

After completing the chapter's activities, learners should be able to do the following:

- Briefly define visual analysis
- Explain why visual analysis is the primary method used to analyze data in Applied Behavior Analysis
- Identify graphing conventions and best practices
- Identify and construct a scatterplot
- Identify and construct a bar graph
- Identify and construct a line graph

Graphing Conventions and Best Practices

It should be clear by now that behavior analysts strive to work exclusively with objective, quantifiable data. Because graphs provide a relatively easy way to visually display relationships among and between different variables or sets of data, they are ideal in our work to identify the function of a behavior and determine behavior change. Graphs are helpful for organizing and storing data in a manner that allows for reliable interpretation of the data. In short, graphs help us "make sense" of the information we obtain through our countless data collection methods and measurement opportunities.

Since graphs are our primary method of coherently representing the relationships between quantitative variables, it is critical that we follow some basic conventions when constructing them. First, it should be the goal of anyone constructing a graph to make it simple and clean and make sure it accurately tells the story of the data (Stoelb & Gage, 2013). Additionally, in our construction of graphs, we need to ensure that the focus remains on the data and not extraneous information that may be distracting or that may bias one's interpretation of the data. For example, the use of colors on a graph, though visually appealing, can be distracting to those analyzing the data or may bias one's interpretation of the data in some way. Additionally, scaling the graph in such a manner that does not exaggerate or minimize effects is important as well. Following certain conventions in the construction of any graph (such as ensuring that graphs are printed in black and white only) assist in providing a consistent framework for all behavior analysts to "read" the information provided in the graph accurately and without ambiguity. The following sections discuss the various graphical displays used in FBA and provide basic steps and "rules" to follow when constructing graphs to ensure others who engage in visual analysis of your data interpret it accurately.

Scatterplot

A scatterplot is a graphical display that presents the relative distribution in a data set across two variables, represented respectively on an x and y axis. When conducting the FBA, a scatterplot allows the analyst to graphically display the occurrence of a behavior with the time of day and activity or environment in which the behavior is taking place. Such information is especially useful in narrowing the focus for further assessment and observation to take place.

Scatterplots are incredibly useful for identifying the **temporal distribution** of a target behavior, which allows for the interpretation of the function of a behavior. Touchette, MacDonald, and Langer (1985) published a procedure for the use of a scatterplot specifically applicable to the FBA process. This practice is outlined in this chapter and graphically demonstrates whether a certain target behavior is associated with specific time periods of the day. Let's take a look at an example to see how a scatterplot is constructed and how it may be useful. The steps to constructing a scatterplot are provided as follows:

1   **Create a chart and begin with the information provided.** (Note: This chart can be created in Microsoft Word by creating a custom table, or in Microsoft Excel by entering the information outlined below in various cells to create specific columns and rows of data. The application used is not of significant importance, but the arrangement of the data should resemble what is outlined in the example in Table 8.1.)

Table 8.1 Creating Scatterplot Chart

Activity	Time		Total
Total			

2 **Divide the day into blocks of time** (e.g., a series of twenty-minute segments or naturally occurring class/activity periods).

Table 8.2 Dividing the Scatterplot Chart into Time Segments

Activity	Time	Day					Total
		Monday	Tuesday	Wednesday	Thursday	Friday	
English	8:00–9:15 a.m.						
Music	9:15–10:30 a.m.						
Lunch	10:30 a.m.–11:45 p.m.						
Free Period	11:45 a.m.–1:15 p.m.						
Math	1:15–2:30 p.m.						
Art	2:30–3:45 p.m.						
Total							

3 **For each block of time, an observer uses a different symbol to indicate the occurrence of the behavior** (e.g., a circle to indicate the behavior did not occur, a triangle to indicate it occurred occasionally, or a square to indicate it occurred with high frequency; or a tally mark indicating frequency). In the example below, tally marks are used to indicate the behavior's occurrence.

Table 8.3 Adding Frequency of Behavior to the Scatterplot Chart

Activity	Time	Day					Total
		Monday	Tuesday	Wednesday	Thursday	Friday	
English	**8:00–9:15 a.m.**	I	I	I	0	I	7
Music	**9:15–10:30 a.m.**	IIII	III	V	VI	IIII	22
Lunch	**10:30 a.m.–11:45 p.m.**	0	0	0	0	0	0
Free Period	**11:45 a.m.–1:15 p.m.**	0	0	0	0	0	0

(continued)

Math	1:15–2:30 p.m.	I	0	II	II	I	6
Art	2:30–3:45 p.m.	VI	VIII	V	VIII	VII	35
Total		12	12	13	16	13	

4   **Repeat data collection for several days, weeks, or months.**

5   **Analyze the scatterplot data by highlighting the rows in the "Total" column and rows that have the highest frequency.** (In the following example, the behavior occurs much more frequently during Music and Art classes at school, but there is not significant variation across days of the week as the range is between twelve and sixteen occurrences per day.)

Table 8.4 Analyzing Scatterplot Data

Activity	Time	Day					Total
		Monday	Tuesday	Wednesday	Thursday	Friday	
English	8:00–9:15 a.m.	I	I	I	0	I	7
Music	9:15–10:30 a.m.	IIII	III	V	VI	IIII	22
Lunch	10:30 a.m.–11:45 p.m.	0	0	0	0	0	0
Free Period	11:45 a.m.–1:15 p.m.	0	0	0	0	0	0
Math	1:15–2:30 p.m.	I	0	II	II	I	6
Art	2:30–3:45 p.m.	VI	VIII	V	VIII	VII	35
Total		12	12	13	16	13	

Scatterplots can be very useful for identifying recurring response patterns and determining if they are related to certain environmental events or conditions. In the case of the example above, it is evident that the target behavior is being observed at a disproportionately high rate when the learner is attending both Music and Art class, and at significantly lower rates during English, Lunch, Free Period, and Math. It is also clear that these behaviors seem to occur with relatively consistent frequency across the course of the five weekdays that were observed.

It would therefore be important for behavior analysts to focus their attention and observation of the environmental stimuli and events that occur in Music and Art class. It is possible that the demands being placed on the learner in that environment are challenging the learner, and they could be modified. Or, perhaps there are other stimuli in both environments that serve as antecedents to the behavior. For example, it is possible that the instructors or classmates present in those environments have an effect on the learner's behavior. A scatterplot does not necessarily indicate the information needed to respond to these hypotheses, but it does allow for the behavior analyst to identify the times and locations in which the behavior occurs to further focus direct observation and analysis to identify those critical variables.

Bar Graph

A bar graph, also called a histogram, is commonly used in the FBA process to clearly summarize behavioral data. A bar graph is constructed on the x-y axis. Most often, a bar graph is used to display the relationship between one quantitative and one categorical variable. In the case of behavioral data, usually the quantitative variable is a dimension of behavior, such as frequency or duration. A **categorical variable** may take a variety of forms, such as in the case of a preference assessment, when a behavior analyst identifies the number of times a potential reinforcer is selected and the categories include the names of the different reinforcers (e.g., apple, chip, banana, or donut).

Figure 8.1 Bar Graph Depicting Frequency of Stimulus Selection

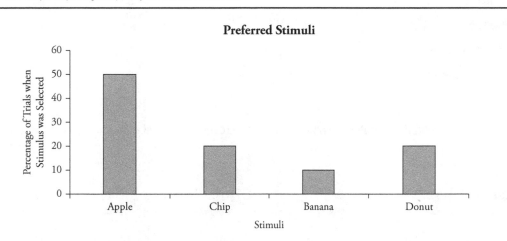

Because the focus of this text is on the FBA process, it is important to consider the ways in which a bar graph can be used as a tool for us to better interpret ABC recording data. The steps for constructing a bar graph to demonstrate the frequency of identified antecedents across a FBA are as follows:

1   **Review ABC recording data and make a table of the antecedents identified most frequently.** For example, let's imagine a learner who engages in self-injurious scratching behavior in school. After carefully collecting ABC recordings across ten school days, it is clear that a pattern has emerged in the data. There are four antecedents that have been identified across the multiple occasions of self-injurious scratching. These antecedents are the presentation of a task demand (an instruction by a teacher), being told "no" she cannot access a desired item or activity, being deprived of peer or adult attention for longer than five minutes, and the occurrence of a loud auditory stimulus (construction is taking place at the school). Once these antecedents are identified, the following table is created:

Table 8.5 Frequency of Antecedents

Antecedent	Frequency of Scratching
Task demand	40
Told "no"	16
Attention deprivation	8
Loud auditory stimulus	16

2   Using that table, the frequency data are converted to percentages (using the total number of occurrences of scratching behavior, eighty).

Table 8.6 Percentages for Antecedents

Antecedent	Frequency of Scratching	Percentage of Total
Task demand	40	50
Told "no"	16	20
Attention deprivation	8	10
Loud auditory stimulus	16	20

3   Using Microsoft Excel, enter the antecedent and percentage of total data into two adjacent columns.

4   Then, using your cursor, highlight the data (limit the highlighted area to the four rows and two columns depicted in the graphic below).

	A	B	C	D	E	F
1	Task Demand	50				
2	Told "No"	20				
3	Attention Deprivation	10				
4	Loud Auditory Stimulus	20				
5						
6						
7						
8						
9						
10						
11						
12						
13						
14						

5   Using the tools in your version of Microsoft Excel, create a bar graph using the selected data (see Recommended Resources List in Appendix A).

6   Format the graph with a chart title and axis labels. Additionally, ensure that the bars of the graph are filled in black.

Figure 8.2 Bar Graph of Antecedents

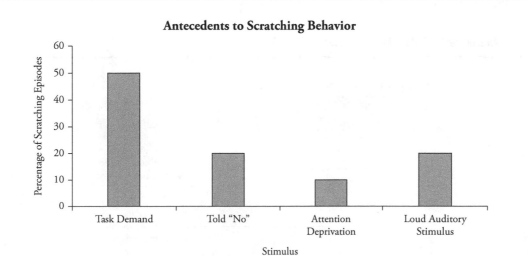

Now that the final graph of the antecedents to the self-injurious scratching behavior has been created, it is evident that the most common antecedent is the presentation of a task demand. Once the corresponding data revealing the frequency of consequences to the scratching behavior are graphed, it will be possible to analyze whether escape from task demands has been reinforced, and, if so, escape will likely be a hypothesized function for this behavior.

Like any analytical device or tool, a bar graph presents advantages and disadvantages. Bar graphs are remarkably efficient in providing a summary of data while also allowing for large amounts of data to be compared easily (one could imagine graphing ten or more possible stimuli or antecedents in the bar graph examples previously discussed, without the graph appearing overcrowded or confusing to interpret). However, this ease of use also presents a sacrifice in the form of a lack of variability that can be provided in a line graph. For this reason, it is important to consider a bar graph as being helpful when attempting to communicate or determine measures of central tendency (mean or median) instead of data with more precise or nuanced differences.

Line Graph

A line graph is the final graphing device in the FBA tool chest. Details about how and when to use line graphs are presented in most basic statistics texts, as well as in the *Publication Manual of the American Psychological Association* (see current edition), so we will not cover that information here. In general, the analyst should be aware that although bar graphs are considered preferable for understanding an individual's behavior *within a segment of time*, line graphs can be a useful ancillary source of information for depicting changes in that behavior *over a period of time.* In the context of the FBA process, line graphs are used most frequently when evaluating the change in behavior from baseline (pre-intervention) through the introduction of the intervention. In the section that follows, a basic set of steps are provided to prepare the data to be graphed and to format the line graph itself.

1   **Enter the baseline and intervention data into Microsoft Excel by listing the baseline data in one column and the intervention data in the second column directly after.** (Note: The data must be entered such that the two sets of data are staggered across the columns and that no two data points occupy the same row.)

Figure 8.3 Arrangement of Data in Microsoft Excel

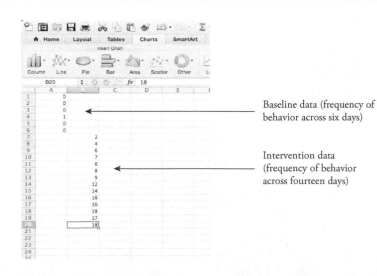

2   Create graph.

Figure 8.4 Initial Appearance of Graph in Microsoft Excel.

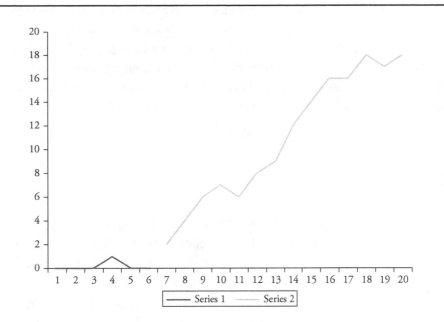

Initially, the graph that is produced in Microsoft Excel may not contain all the required formatting require-ments according to APA style conventions or the specifications of an FBA report. For this reason, it is important that one carefully review those style conventions so that the final graph is not only simple and clean in its display, but also meets the expectations of those who will conduct visual analysis.

3   Format graph according to APA style conventions.

Figure 8.5 Graph Formatted According to APA Style Conventions

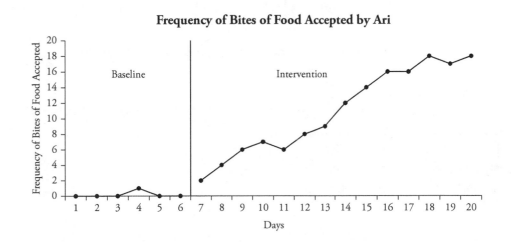

The final graph depicted in Figure 8.5 contains all the required elements of APA style conventions. It is free of horizontal grid lines, contains clear axis titles for both the x and y axes, is clearly labeled with "Baseline" and "Intervention," and includes a chart title. Most importantly, the vertical line that was added to differentiate between the baseline and intervention phases allows those analyzing the data to clearly and efficiently evaluate the change in behavior from the six days during baseline and the fourteen days of intervention. In this example, the learner (Ari) accepted very few bites of food during baseline, but once intervention was introduced on day seven, it is clear that the frequency of bites of food increased steadily over time. This is a pattern that would clearly indicate to practitioners that the behavior change intervention was effective and that it should continue to be implemented with ongoing progress monitoring.

Summary

This chapter provided an overview of the basic concepts underlying the application of visual analysis and graphical displays of data specific to the process of completing an FBA. The most commonly used graphical displays in the FBA are the scatterplot and the bar graph, as both provide a summary of data that assist in pinpointing times of day, activities, or antecedents or consequences that are likely to evoke and reinforce the target behavior. Along with the scatterplot and bar graph, a line graph is often used in the BIP stage of the intervention process that occurs after the FBA is complete. Even though the BIP process follows the FBA, it is occasionally the case that part of the way through implementation of the BIP, the FBA process needs to be revisited. For this reason, it is important to consider the assessment and intervention process as occurring in a cycle, and an awareness of the graphing skills needed at that point should be practiced. Through the use of the suggested resources provided at the end of this chapter, the process of creating and interpreting scatterplots, bar graphs, and line graphs should be more clear. You are encouraged to apply these concepts and procedures in the activities that follow.

Reviewing the Concepts

After completing the learning activities in this chapter, take a moment to confirm that you are able to do the following:
- Briefly define visual analysis
- Explain why visual analysis is the primary method used to analyze data in Applied Behavior Analysis
- Identify graphing conventions and best practices
- Identify and construct a scatterplot
- Identify and construct a bar graph
- Identify and construct a line graph

Definition of Key Terms

- **bar graph:** graphical display that is most often used to display the relationship between one quantitative and one categorical variable

- **categorical variable:** a variable that can take on one of a limited, and usually fixed, number of possible values; assigned to a particular group or nominal category on the basis of some qualitative property
- **line graph:** a graphical display that depicts the value of a quantitative variable over time
- **temporal distribution:** pattern of a behavior's frequency over time
- **visual analysis:** a form of systematic examination that occurs by visually inspecting data on a graphical display
- **scatterplot:** graphical display that presents the relative distribution in a data set across two variables, represented respectively on an x and y axis

Test Your Understanding

Level 1: Knowledge

1. True or False: Visual analysis of the data is the primary data analysis method used in ABA.
2. True or False: Scatterplots and bar graphs are the most common graphical displays used in an FBA.
3. True or False: Bar graphs are best for graphing data that have high variability.
4. True or False: Temporal distribution pertains to the duration of a behavior's occurrence within the time frame of a day.
5. True or False: Colorful graphs are the most visually appealing, making visual analysis of the data more accurate.

Level 2: Comprehension

1. A bar graph depicts _____.
   a. the relationship between two quantitative variables
   b. the relationship between two categorical variables
   c. the relationship between one categorical and one quantitative variable
   d. the data collected from an indirect assessment
2. A scatterplot depicts _____.
   a. the temporal distribution of a dimension of a behavior across a day
   b. the temporal distribution of a dimension of a behavior across a month
   c. the temporal distribution of a behavior's duration
   d. the temporary occurrence of a behavior
3. A line graph depicts _____.
   a. the value of a quantitative variable over time
   b. the frequency, duration, or magnitude of a behavior across baseline and intervention phases
   c. the value of a categorical variable over time
   d. both A and B.

Level 3: Application

1. Jessica engages in high rates of non-compliance. She generally ignores any requests made by her parents or teachers to complete non-preferred tasks. Although she does not engage in tantrums, when she is not complying, she will not complete the task and will move away from the individual making the request and sit in a chair or lie on the floor. Most often, she will not engage in the task unless she is physically forced to do so. As she is approaching seven years of age, it is becoming challenging to force her to engage in non-preferred activities. Her treatment team has determined that implementing a reinforcement system is the best approach to motivate Jessica to begin to comply with such tasks. First, the team must identify the most potent reinforcers. They therefore interview her parents and teachers to identify possible reinforcers and then systematically present them to her to identify which items or activities are selected most frequently. The following is the data they collected during the preference assessment. Construct an APA formatted bar graph displaying this data.

Potential Reinforcer	Frequency Item/Activity was Selected
Elmo toy	5
Troll doll	12
Slinky	1
Panda bear stickers	7
Princess stickers	20
Trampoline	29
Water play (sink)	28
Bubbles	10

2. Emilio is displaying aggressive tantrums throughout the day. The daycare he attends full time has warned his parents that if an effective behavior plan is not developed and his behavior does not improve within the next month, he will need to attend a different program. The chart below provides the initial step to creating a scatterplot. Fill in data to indicate what the scatterplot data would appear to be if the tantrums were occurring in a specific recurring pattern. Once the data is filled in, provide an explanation of your analysis of the data.

Activity	Time	Day					Total
		Monday	Tuesday	Wednesday	Thursday	Friday	
Breakfast	8:00–8:20 a.m.						
Free Play	8:20–8:50 a.m.						
Circle	8:50–9:10 a.m.						
Art Activity	9:10–9:40 a.m.						
Free Play/Potty	9:40–10:10 a.m.						
Playground	10:10–10:40 a.m.						

(continued)

Snack	10:40–11a.m.
Math Activity	1:00–11:20 a.m.
Free Play	11:20–11:40 a.m.
Story Time	11:40 a.m.–12:00 p.m.
Lunch	12:00–12:20 p.m.
Nap	12:20–3:00 p.m.
Potty	3:00–3:10 p.m.
Playground	3:10–4:00 p.m.
Circle	4:00–4:20 p.m.

3. Samuel engages in calling out behavior in his academic classes at school (Language Arts, Spanish, Social Studies, Science, and Math). His teachers have arranged to implement an extinction procedure during each course wherein they ignore his calling out behavior and provide him reinforcement when he raises his hand appropriately. The following is the data they collected across the school day. Construct an APA formatted line graph displaying this data.

Day	Frequency of Occurrences of Calling Out Across School Day
1 (baseline)	48
2 (baseline)	55
3 (baseline)	52
4 (baseline)	50
5 (baseline)	49
6 (intervention)	30
7 (intervention)	28
8 (intervention)	72
9 (intervention)	25
10 (intervention)	15
11 (intervention)	10
12 (intervention)	1
13 (intervention)	1
14 (intervention)	0

4. Select one of the case studies explored in questions 1–3. Make a video recording of the oral explanation of the process you employed to create your graph and submit this recording for review. General tips: Students should take care to address the camera as though they are speaking with either a consumer of ABA services or a supervisee (imagine that the camera is the individual with who, you would be speaking). Students may elect to use props to demonstrate the way in which

data should be collected or use other materials relating to how the behavior change procedure should be implemented. In the event that these props or data collection sheets are referenced in the video, these items should be made visible on camera.

In-Class Small Group Discussion Questions/Exercises

Create small groups (perhaps four or five students) and discuss the following topics, allowing 10 to 15 minutes to complete the response.

1. Independently complete the activity described in Application Exercise 1 to share with your small group. Within your small group, discuss the data collected and the bar graphs created. Respond to the following questions:
   a. Are each of the graphs constructed the same? Which elements were similar or different? If there were formatting differences, identify those differences and work together to correctly format according to APA style guidelines.
   b. Visually inspect and analyze the data on the graph. What does the graph convey? What does the data indicate in terms of next steps for intervention regarding Jessica's non-compliance?
2. Independently complete the activity described in Application Exercise 2 to share with your small group. Within your small group, discuss the data collected and the scatterplots created. Respond to the following questions:
   a. Briefly review each group member's scatterplot and description of their visual analysis. Are the analyses accurate and do they represent the data? Why or why not? Work together to refine your analyses and descriptions of the data's findings.
   b. What does the data indicate in terms of next steps for intervention regarding Emilio's tantrums?
3. Independently complete the activity described in Application Exercise 3 to share with your small group. Within your small group, discuss the data collected and the line graphs created. Respond to the following questions:
   a. Are each of the graphs constructed the same? Which elements were similar or different? If there were formatting differences, identify those differences and work together to correctly format according to APA style guidelines.
   b. Visually inspect and analyze the data on the graph. What does the graph convey? What does the data indicate in terms of the effectiveness of the intervention to address Samuel's calling out behavior? If you were working on Samuel's treatment team, what would your recommendation be regarding continuing the intervention? Why?

References

Stoelb, M., & Gage, N. (2013). *Handbook: Creating graphs in Microsoft Excel*. Columbia, MO: Thompson Center for Autism, University of Missouri.

Touchette, P.E., MacDonald, R.F., & Langer, S.N. (1985). A scatter plot for identifying stimulus control of problem behavior. *Journal of Applied Behavior Analysis, 18*(4), 343–351.

Appendix A

Recommended Resource List for Graph Construction and Formatting

- American Psychological Association Manual
- Online Tutorials for Microsoft Excel
    - https://support.office.com/en-us/article/Excel-training-9bc05390-e94c-46af-a5b3-d7c22f6990bb
    - http://spreadsheeto.com/
    - http://www.excel-easy.com/

Credits

- Fig. 8.1b: Copyright © by Microsoft.
- Fig. 8.1c: Copyright © by Microsoft.
- Fig. 8.3: Copyright © by Microsoft.

CHAPTER 9

Functional Hypotheses

T hroughout the last few chapters of this text, we have moved through the general chronological sequence of conducting an FBA. At this point, it may seem as though you have done quite a lot in the FBA process—from carefully identifying the target behavior for change, conducting multiple levels of assessment with various informants and through direct observations, to composing most of a report summarizing these findings. You should nearly be finished! However, all of that leg work and amassed data only bring us to the point where we are able to make an educated guess about what function the behavior could serve the individual. This educated guess, or hypothesis, comes from carefully and objectively reviewing the data collected thus far. Often, the indirect assessment data will give us a rough idea of what the function may be, but direct observation is needed to more directly collect data on antecedents and consequences and the general behavior pattern. At this point, it is necessary to consider those data and formulate the hypothesized function by creating a **functional hypothesis statement**.

A functional hypothesis statement concisely and objectively describes the data-driven assumption about the purpose or function of the behavior. This chapter will review the process for developing the functional hypothesis statement and will briefly discuss the four possible functions of behavior (attention, escape, access to tangible, and automatic reinforcement) once again. This will occur through the provision of multiple case studies with completed data sheets on target behaviors. Be sure to complete the exercises included at the end of the chapter to practice the process of formulating a functional hypothesis and of composing the functional hypothesis statement. Throughout this chapter and the end-of-chapter activities, we will follow the now familiar "See one, do one, teach one" model of practicing these important concepts and skills to ensure mastery of the functional hypothesis formulation process.

Arriving at a Functional Hypothesis

The functional hypothesis statement achieves the goal of concisely stating the purpose of the behavior for the individual. In other words, it informs readers of a treatment plan or Individualized Education Plan (IEP): what the collected data indicate is the reason why the behavior is occurring. However, before one begins to compose this statement, it is necessary to carefully review the data at hand to determine the possible function. As was discussed in Chapter 3, there are four possible functions (or purposes) that a behavior might serve; although, at times it is possible that a behavior is multiply controlled (serves multiple functions at once):

1 Attention
2 Escape
3 Access to Tangible (items or activities)
4 Automatic Reinforcement/Sensory

Most indirect assessment tools (as were reviewed in Chapter 6) allow the behavior analyst to tentatively identify possible functions of behavior after they are scored. Direct assessment data, such as anecdotal A-B-C recording, requires an analysis of the occurrences of the behavior for patterns.

Essentially, if the maintaining antecedents and maintaining consequences continue to occur across the data collected in a similar sequence before and after the behavior, it is possible that the function will be identified in those particular sequences. In other words, the behavior analyst asks, "When a particular antecedent occurs, is the behavior likely to occur?" And "When the behavior occurs, does a particular consequence follow?" If the responses to those questions seem to be consistent, it is possible to hypothesize that the antecedents, behaviors, and consequences occur together frequently enough to explain the purpose the behavior serves. For instance, if the antecedent is consistently marked by an absence of attention, and after the behavior occurs the individual receives attention, a hypothesis of the function for the behavior could be attention. Or, let's imagine the antecedents listed routinely indicate the presence of a preferred object, and the consequences are typically indicated to be that the individual receives access to the item; then, the behavior could be serving the purpose of obtaining the tangible item. The function can also be that the person is attempting to escape (or "get out of") a task or non-preferred activity or simply trying to receive sensory reinforcement.

Writing the Functional Hypothesis Statement

The functional hypothesis statement can be written using a very brief template comprised of three main parts or the three primary events that occur: the antecedent, behavior, and consequence. This can be written using the following general template:

> "When [ANTECEDENT] occurs, [LEARNER] engages in [BEHAVIOR(s)], and this results in [CONSEQUENCE]. It is hypothesized that [LEARNER] engages in [BEHAVIOR(S)] to serve the function of [HYPOTHESIZED FUNCTION]."

Of course, more can be written with the hypothesis statement to further qualify or "flesh out" the statement, but the basic essence of the functional hypothesis statement is captured in that brief template. To illustrate this further, please review the following four case studies and continued case study from Chapters 6 and 7. In doing so, you will have several examples of how functional hypotheses should be formed, completing the "see one" stage of the model for mastering this process.

Identifying the Function: Silvia's Aggressive Behavior

Silvia is a four-year-old girl with Down Syndrome. She is very social and particularly enjoys interacting with peers in her inclusive preschool program. Silvia has a vocabulary of approximately five intelligible words and imitates play with peers. Lately, Silvia has been engaging in aggressive behavior such as slapping with an open palm and with enough force to leave a red mark on the skin of the other individual. She also will occasionally throw objects. The behavior analyst at Silvia's preschool conducted two indirect assessment interviews with the preschool teacher and one of the paraprofessionals who commonly work with Silvia in the classroom. The results of those indirect assessments suggested that Silvia's behavior was most likely serving the function of obtaining social attention but could also be serving the function of obtaining a tangible. The behavior analyst then collected the following aggregated direct assessment data (note, direct assessment data should consist of at least 10–12 behavior observations but the data that follow were aggregated for brevity within the case studies in this chapter), focusing on all occasions when Silvia had the opportunity to engage in aggression (was in close physical proximity to another individual) across three different school days and at different times of day.

Table 9.1 Examples of Antecedents, Behaviors, and Consequences to Seek Attention

Antecedent	Behavior	Consequence
Silvia waves at Marcus when she arrives at school, but Marcus does not see her.	Silvia runs up to Marcus and slaps him in the arm and laughs.	Marcus screams, "Hey! Silvia! Don't hit me!" and walks away, rubbing his arm.
Silvia approaches some children playing in the sand in the sand box at recess.	Silvia throws sand at them while smiling.	They scream, "Stop! That hurts."

(continued)

Silvia approaches two children playing a game during free play.	Silvia slaps them and smiles.	Both children scream and cry. One child says "Why did you do that, Silvia? You're so mean!"
Silvia approaches a child playing on a playground climber and extends her hand to slap the child. But, the child says "Hi Silvia!"	Silvia smiles and waves, then climbs up the climber.	Silvia imitates the other child's pretend game of being on a pirate ship.
Silvia's teacher is talking to the school nurse and Silvia approaches them.	Silvia slaps the teacher.	Silvia's teacher yells out "Stop, Silvia! No hitting." Then asks more calmly "What did you need?"

The anecdotal A-B-C recording indicated that Silvia engaged in slapping three times and threw sand one time. Just as important in the analysis is that Silvia did not engage in aggression when another child greeted her. Additionally, three of the four instances of aggression were toward peers. In all four instances of the behavior, Silvia approached others who did not immediately greet her. A clear and consistent pattern is shown when one reads down the "consequence" column, as each of the four instances demonstrates a social response was emitted by the other person. Obviously, these responses were not entirely positive, but Silvia was clearly able to obtain the other individual's attention immediately following the behavior. The functional hypothesis for this behavior would be that Silvia is engaging in these behaviors to obtain attention from her peers and teacher. To fully construct the functional hypothesis statement, you would use the template provided previously and fill in the information in brackets:

> *"When in the presence of others and she is not immediately greeted, Silvia engages in slapping or throwing behavior, and receives immediate attention from her peers or teacher. It is hypothesized that Silvia engages in slapping or throwing to obtain attention."*

This statement concisely informs readers of the common antecedents and consequences of the behavior as well as the hypothesized function. Readers of this statement will then be able to use this critical information about the hypothesized function to consider potential interventions to address a behavior that is maintained by attention.

Identifying the Function: Peter's Screaming Behavior

Peter is an eight-year-old boy with a diagnosis of Oppositional Defiant Disorder. He is known as a "bully" at school. He has a history of non-compliance when it comes to demands to complete household chores, but over the last two months, his non-compliance has been accompanied by screaming and, when fully escalated, property destruction. His screaming behavior is particularly troublesome, because it is very high-pitched, and he will scream until he is out of breath, and, after taking a breath, will begin screaming again. When he screams, his face turns red and veins are visible in his neck. He also breathes heavily at the end of one of his screaming episodes and has lost his voice. The in-home behavior analyst conducted an indirect assessment interview with Peter's father. The results of that indirect assessment suggested that Peter's screaming behavior was most likely serving the function of escaping task demands. The behavior analyst then collected the following aggregated direct assessment data, focusing on all occasions when Peter screamed, across four different days at home.

Table 9.2 Antecedents, Behaviors and Consequences for Avoiding Task Demands

Antecedent	Behavior	Consequence
Peter's dad tells him, "Please wash your plate."	Peter screams very loudly and lifts the plate over his head.	Peter's dad tells him to leave the dinner table.
Peter's mom tells him, "Put away your action figures."	Peter screams and throws a toy at his mother.	Peter's mother tells him to "sit on the step" and "calm down."
Peter's dad says, "Turn off the TV; it's bedtime."	Peter screams and runs to hit his dad with his open hand.	Peter's dad shouts, "Fine. Stop getting so upset. Five more minutes and then you need to go to bed!"
Peter's dad says, "Get in the car, we have to go to the store."	Peter runs away screaming.	Peter's dad tells him he needs to sit in his room until he is calm. After one hour, and another three requests by Peter's dad, Peter slowly walked to the car and went to the store.

These brief anecdotal A-B-C recordings show that Peter engaged in screaming episodes four times across the observations, and that the antecedent was consistently the presentation of a non-preferred task demand (usually to clean in some fashion). In three of the occasions, Peter was screaming in response to his father and once in response to his mother placing a demand. Following each instance of screaming, it is clear Peter was consistently sent out of the environment where the task demand was placed and was not required to immediately engage in the task (only in the last occasion recorded did he actually complete the task—but he did so after one hour of the original request). The functional hypothesis for this behavior would be that Peter is engaging in screaming to escape non-preferred task demands placed on him. Below is the functional hypothesis statement that could be generated following analysis of these data:

"When provided a non-preferred task demand (e.g., to clean up toys), Peter screams and throws items and is not required to complete the task. It is hypothesized that Peter engages in screaming and/or throwing to escape non-preferred task demands."

Once again, this statement concisely informs readers of the common antecedents and consequences of the behavior as well as the hypothesized function. Those who read this statement will be able to confidently determine effective interventions to decrease these challenging behaviors and increase appropriate behaviors now that it is clear that the function of Peter's screaming and throwing is to escape task demands.

Identifying the Function: Ennis's Crying Behavior

Ennis is a ten-year-old boy with Autism Spectrum Disorder. He is currently non-verbal and rarely interacts with peers. He has an obsession with Batman and fixates on playing with a particular action figure. He seeks to have the action figure in his possession at all times (i.e., the bathtub, meals, in the car, out in the community, etc.). Ennis will cry loudly when he is unable to locate his action figure and is rarely able to be redirected when he does not have it in his possession. Ennis's mother and his teachers conducted two indirect assessment interviews regarding the occurrence of this behavior. The results of those indirect assessments suggested that Ennis's behavior was most likely serving the function of obtaining a tangible. The behavior analyst then collected the following aggregated direct assessment data, focusing on all occasions when Ennis engaged in crying behavior during four different days and times of day.

Table 9.3 Examples of Antecedents, Behaviors, and Consequences for Obtaining a Tangible

Antecedent	Behavior	Consequence
Ennis's mother tells him he cannot bring his Batman action figure to school.	Ennis cries for twenty-two minutes.	Ennis brings the Batman action figure with him to school and stops crying.
Ennis sees another child playing with his Batman action figure.	Ennis cries and screams at the other child.	The other child immediately drops the action figure and runs to another area of the classroom. Ennis picks up the toy and stops crying.
The Batman action figure is missing and neither Ennis nor his mother can locate it.	Ennis cries for two hours and thirty-four minutes.	Ennis's older sister comes home from school and locates the toy. Ennis stops crying.
Ennis's mother tells him to put the Batman action figure away and get ready to sit down for dinner.	Ennis cries for nine minutes.	Ennis's mother tells him he can bring the Batman action figure with him to the dinner table. Ennis stops crying and brings the toy to the dinner table.

It should be clear from the anecdotal A-B-C recordings of Ennis's crying behavior that the antecedent in each case had to do with him not having access to the Batman action figure. Consistently, once access to the object could be provided, he was given access following the occurrence of his crying episode. The hypothesized function in this case would be that Ennis is engaging in screaming to obtain access to the Batman action figure. Below is the functional hypothesis statement that could be written following analysis of these data:

> "When he does not have access to the Batman action figure, Ennis screams and is provided access to the action figure. It is hypothesized that Ennis engages in crying to access the Batman action figure."

This hypothesis statement communicates the maintaining antecedents and consequences of the behavior as well as the function. Those who read this statement will be able to confidently determine effective interventions to decrease these challenging behaviors and increase appropriate behaviors now that it is clear that the function of Ennis's screaming behavior is to obtain this toy.

Identifying the Function: Madison's Dangling Behavior

Madison is a six-year-old girl with Autism Spectrum Disorder. She does not vocally communicate, but uses over fifty signs to communicate her wants and needs. She engages in many repetitive and stereotyped behaviors. The most concerning behavior she engages in is visual stimulation from dangling objects in front of her face. This is particularly problematic because she will invade the personal space of others (including strangers) to touch and move their hair, earrings, or other belongings. She will engage in this behavior until she is redirected to another activity.

At times, her parents have been concerned about her safety (given her invasion of other's personal space) and also the social stigma and impact on her learning other skills. She is described as being "absorbed" in the visual inspection of dangling objects and will not respond to redirection without physical prompting. Madison's parents and her teachers conducted two indirect assessment interviews regarding the occurrence of this behavior. The results of those indirect assessments suggested that Madison's behavior was most likely serving the function of automatic/ sensory reinforcement. The behavior analyst then collected the following aggregated direct assessment data, focusing on all occasions when Madison engaged in dangling behavior across two different days and times of day.

Table 9.4 Examples of Behaviors, Antecedents, and Consequences for Automatic/Sensory Stimulation

Antecedent	Behavior	Consequence
Madison finds a string on the floor.	She picks up the string and moves it in front of her face, staring at it. This occurs for twenty-three minutes	Madison's father comes into the room and prompts her to play on the slide in the backyard.
Madison accompanies her grandmother to an errand at the bank. While waiting, she sees a woman seated who is wearing dangling earrings.	Madison approaches the woman, stands closely in front of her, and visually inspects her earrings, reaching her hand up to touch them.	The woman pulls her face away and Madison's grandmother picks up Madison, tells the woman sorry, and carries Madison back to the line for the bank teller.
Madison sits next to her sister, whose long hair is not in a ponytail.	Madison picks up a lock of her sister's hair and gently moves it in front of her eyes for forty-five seconds.	Madison plays with her hair until her sister turns around, tells her to stop, and moves across the room from Madison.
Madison sees a cellular phone charger cord.	Madison picks up the cord, disconnects it from the electrical outlet, and dangles it in front of her line of sight.	Madison plays with the cord until her father asks her to stop.

These A-B-C data demonstrate that Madison engaged in dangling behavior four times across two-day observations. Each time, the antecedent was consistently the presence of an object that could be dangled in front of her visual field. It is clear that the behavior occurred across different settings and circumstances and did not reliably result in attention, access to tangibles, or escape from a task demand. The functional hypothesis for this behavior would be that Madison is engaging in dangling behavior to achieve automatic reinforcement. Below is the functional hypothesis statement that could be generated following analysis of these data:

> *"When in the presence of an object that can be dangled (e.g., a string, a phone cord, earrings, her sister's hair), Madison grasps the object and dangles it in front of her visual field until she is redirected. It is hypothesized that Madison engages in dangling behavior to achieve automatic reinforcement."*

This hypothesis statement concisely informs readers of the common antecedents and consequences of the behavior as well as the hypothesized function. Those who read this statement will be able to confidently determine effective interventions to decrease these challenging behaviors and increase appropriate behaviors now that it is clear that the function of Madison's dangling behavior for is automatic or sensory reinforcement.

Continued Case Study: Functional Hypothesis of Adam's Loud Vocalization Behavior

Now we will return to the case study introduced in Chapters 6 and 7. Recall that Adam is a six-year-old boy who is engaging in loud vocalization behavior. So far, his team has conducted an indirect assessment using the FAST and also collected direct assessment data in the form of A-B-C recordings, anecdotal observations, and duration data. At this point, the information indicates that Adam engages in loud vocalization behavior across all settings (his home, school, and community), and seemingly regardless of the antecedent or consequence of the behavior. Given the results of all these sources of data, it could be concluded that the function of this behavior is automatic reinforcement. The functional hypothesis is as follows:

> *"When his hands are not actively engaged to complete a task (e.g., brushing his teeth, completing a craft at school, putting on his shoes, etc.), Adam places his hand or other objects to his mouth, past his lips until he is redirected. It is hypothesized that Adam engages in loud vocalization behavior to achieve automatic reinforcement."*

Although one can be reasonably confident that the function of Adam's loud vocalization behavior has been identified, it is next the task of the practitioner to test this hypothesis by conducting a functional analysis. The process for conducting a functional analysis will be discussed in great detail in Chapter 10.

Summary

As has hopefully been made clear after reading this chapter, a functional hypothesis statement concisely and objectively describes the data-driven assumption about the purpose or function of the behavior. This chapter reviewed the process for developing the functional hypothesis statement and briefly reviewed the four possible functions of behavior (attention, escape, access to tangible, and automatic reinforcement) using detailed case studies. In order to compose the functional hypothesis statement, it is necessary to analyze and synthesize the indirect and direct assessment data using a general template. This template includes a statement of the common, or maintaining, antecedents and consequences, as well as directly stating the hypothesized function. Be sure to complete the exercises that follow in order to practice the process of formulating a functional hypothesis, compose the functional hypothesis statement ("do one"), and practice being a supervisor and "teach one."

Definition of Key Terms

- **functional hypothesis statement:** a statement clearly stating the maintaining antecedents and consequences for a target behavior, as well as the educated guess regarding the behavior's function

Test Your Knowledge

Level 1: Knowledge

1. True or False: The functional hypothesis is a definitive statement of the confirmed function of the behavior.
2. True or False: The functional hypothesis introduces just one possible function of the behavior.
3. True or False: The functional hypothesis should contain a behavior intervention plan or suggestions for intervention.

Level 2: Comprehension

1. The functional hypothesis statement should contain which of the following?
   a. The maintaining antecedent(s)
   b. The maintaining consequence(s)
   c. What the data indicate the function of the behavior to be
   d. All of the above
2. What is missing from the following functional hypothesis statement? *"After school, when he has not seen his mother for several hours, Malcolm whines. It is hypothesized that Malcolm engages in whining in order to gain his mother's attention."*
   a. The maintaining antecedent(s)
   b. The maintaining consequence(s)
   c. What the data indicate the function of the behavior to be
   d. All of the above
3. What is missing from the following functional hypothesis statement? *"When Malcolm whines, his mother sits down and plays with him. It is hypothesized that Malcolm engages in whining in order to gain his mother's attention."*
   a. The maintaining antecedent(s)
   b. The maintaining consequence(s)
   c. What the data indicate the function of the behavior to be
   d. All of the above
4. What is missing from the following functional hypothesis statement? *"After school, when he has not seen his mother for several hours, Malcolm whines and his mother sits down to play with him."*
   a. The maintaining antecedent(s)
   b. The maintaining consequence(s)
   c. What the data indicate the function of the behavior to be
   d. All of the above

Level 3: Application

1. Review the data that follow and construct a functional hypothesis statement.

Antecedent	Behavior	Consequence
Jackson and his mother visit the grocery store and pass through the freezer section. Jackson saw his favorite popsicles.	Jackson dropped to the floor and refused to stand up. He screamed, "Blue popsicle!" four times.	Jackson's mother placed a box of popsicles in the grocery cart. Jackson immediately stood up and walked with her to the next aisle.
Jackson's grandma took care of him at her house. Jackson saw the iPad he uses while he is at her house, just as his father arrived to take him back home.	Jackson screamed and cried and dropped to the floor. He refused to stand up and his father carried him to the car.	Jackson's grandma followed behind with the iPad and gave it to Jackson to take home with him for the night. Jackson immediately stopped crying and played on the iPad.
Jackson played at the sand table at recess during the school day. A timer went off and Jackson was told by his teacher to leave the table and come inside.	Jackson hid under the table and went "limp," refusing to come inside.	His teacher attempted to lift him and could not do so. Jackson was then permitted to remain outside for an additional five minutes to play with the sand table.
Jackson entered a restaurant with his parents and passed a bakery display case featuring a chocolate cake and immediately requested cake. His father told him he could not have any cake until after dinner.	Jackson immediately dropped to the floor and refused to walk to the table in the dining area.	Jackson's mother ordered a piece of cake and brought it with them to the table. Jackson stood up and followed his parents to the table. He then repeatedly asked (seventeen times) when he could eat the cake throughout the entire meal.

2. Review the functional hypothesis statement that follow and fill in the data one would expect to see recorded to arrive at the functional hypothesis statement provided.

   In art class, when Mrs. Jenkins's attention is focused on other children, Henry engages in property destruction, and this results in him immediately receiving a verbal reprimand from the teacher and laughter from other children. It is hypothesized that Henry engages in property destruction to serve the function of social attention.

Antecedent	Behavior	Consequence

3. Now it's time for you to practice teaching what you know. Use the recording form below to enter A-B-C data on a target behavior of either someone you know or a fictional learner. Then, use the data to formulate a functional hypothesis based on the direct assessment data.

Antecedent	Behavior	Consequence

Functional hypothesis: _____

_____

_____

_____

_____

CHAPTER 10

Functional Analysis and Hypothesis Testing

**Christina King, Ph.D., BCBA, LABA
and Kylan Turner, Ph.D., BCBA-D, LABA**

By now, you have completed most of the FBA process and have likely formulated a functional hypothesis for the target behavior. This stage in the FBA process is a bit like solving a mystery or a police investigation—after the indirect and direct assessments are conducted, the behavior analyst is left with different "threads" of data. These threads of information are pulled together into a concise statement that identifies the variables that are likely evoking the targeted behavior as well as the consequence variables that are maintaining the behavior—this is called a **hypothesis statement**. At times, it may be appropriate to design and implement an intervention matched to the function identified in the hypothesis statement and to closely measure the effectiveness of that treatment. However, when self-injurious or other dangerous behaviors are the focus, simply intervening based on the hypothesis statement would not be sufficient. In this case, the next step would be conducting experimental or **systematic manipulations** to identify a functional relation between environmental variables and the targeted behavior. There are two different types of experimental manipulations used in behavior assessment: 1) **structural analysis**, wherein the antecedents to a behavior are systematically manipulated while continuing to maintain the same consequences; and 2) **functional analysis**, which focuses on systematically manipulating consequence variables to identify the reinforcing stimuli maintaining behavior. It is important to note that both structural and functional analyses allow for a **functional relation** to be demonstrated.

Systematically manipulating antecedent variables may be less intrusive and lead to interventions that are preventative. Through structural analysis, you may identify specific antecedent variables that are evoking the targeted behavior. Interventions would then be developed that eliminate or alter those specific antecedent variables to decrease the undesired behavior. For example, if it is identified that the presentation of a demand is discriminative for verbal outbursts (e.g., screaming "No" or "I won't do it"), then altering the difficulty of the demand, the amount of work, or the length of the task may change the rate of the outbursts.

At times, it is not possible to identify, alter, or eliminate antecedent variables, and it is vital that a functional analysis or an analysis of the consequence variables be conducted. Functional analysis is not without risk; however, conducting this experiment will likely provide conclusive evidence of the maintaining function of the targeted behavior. For example, if it is hypothesized that attention is the maintaining function of shouting, a functional analysis condition could be implemented in which attention would be provided contingent on shouting. The experimenter would measure the change in the behavior to determine if attention is truly acting as a reinforcing stimulus, thereby increasing shouting when the condition is implemented.

In this chapter, a general overview of the functional analysis conditions will be explored, and you will revisit case studies with FBA data that were previously explored; you will also have the opportunity to again complete the process of the "See one, do one, teach one" model of mastery.

LEARNING OBJECTIVES

After completing the chapter's activities, learners should be able to do the following:

- Define structural analysis and functional analysis

- Define and describe various conditions of functional analysis, their purpose, and considerations for implementation

- Discuss the process for data collection and analysis following a structural or functional analysis

- Define and discuss the concept of multiple control and how it can be identified using visual analysis of graphical data

- Construct a plan to carry out a functional analysis, including detail regarding the various conditions and procedural safeguards

- Discuss modifications to traditional functional analysis procedures and identify rationale for implementation

- Discuss a rationale for conducting systematic manipulations and discuss limitations and strategies to address

Experimental Manipulations

Following the development of the hypothesis statement, the behavior analyst should evaluate the strength of that hypothesis and determine the need to demonstrate a functional relation. If indirect and direct assessment results all point to a specific variable that is evoking or maintaining the targeted behavior and that behavior is not dangerous to the learner or other individuals in the environment, it may be best to intervene with a treatment matched to that function. A limitation of intervening at this stage is that if the hypothesis statement is not correct, an intervention matched to that incorrect conclusion would be introduced, leading to ineffective treatment and potentially harmful outcomes for the learner. If a strong hypothesis statement is unable to be put forth or the behavior is unsafe, it is recommended that a structural and/or functional analysis be conducted to demonstrate a functional relation. The demonstration of a functional relation will increase the likelihood of selecting an intervention that is the least intrusive and most effective and that leads to generalized outcomes (Axelrod, 1987).

The formulation of a concise yet descriptive hypothesis statement allows the practitioner to develop conditions that test if there is a relation between those identified variables and the behavior. Conditions should be developed based on the hypothesis statement, and the learner should not be exposed to conditions that do not test for functions included in the hypothesis statement. For example, if a learner hits others when preferred items are removed and it is hypothesized that he is doing this to gain access to these items, then a test condition should be developed that assesses if providing access to the items contingent on hitting increases the behavior, but a test for escape, for example, should not be conducted.

Structural Analysis

The hypothesis statement that is developed at the conclusion of the indirect and direct assessment should outline the possible maintaining consequence variables as well as the antecedent stimuli that coincide with and may evoke the target behavior. Experimental manipulations may then be conducted that are focused on those antecedent variables. A structural analysis is an experiment in which antecedent variables are systemically introduced and removed to determine if there is a functional relation between those antecedents and the target behavior. Structural analyses may be focused on manipulating physical variables (e.g., lighting, temperature, noise), educational variables (e.g., difficulty level, number of demands, length of task), or biological variables (e.g. hunger, sleep) (Axelrod, 1987). The goal of a structural analysis is to identify a functional relation between a specific antecedent variable and the target behavior. Following the demonstration of a functional relation, an intervention that makes changes to the learner's environment or teaches the learner to engage in an alternative behavior in the presence of these specific antecedent variables can be developed and introduced. Examples may include changing elements of the learner's schedule, controlling for setting events like lack of sleep or hunger, or even changing the ways in which task demands are delivered or prompts are used.

Functional Analysis

A **functional analysis** is an experiment wherein behavior analysts attempt to evoke the target behavior by creating situations in which a possible function could be served. This is done by contriving different conditions (circumstances) in the environment that are specifically designed to result in a certain function of behavior and comparing those to a control condition. Conditions are counterbalanced to reduce sequence effects, and behavior data are collected across all conditions. As with structural analysis, it is best practice that only those conditions that are hypothesized to be maintaining the target behavior are introduced. Functional analysis may be conducted in the learner's natural environment (in-vivo functional analysis) or in a contrived setting (analog functional analysis). Functional analysis procedures may provide conclusive evidence of a functional relation between the behavior and tested environmental variables, but there are several inherent risks in the procedure. During at least one of the conditions, the target behavior will likely increase; therefore, it is best practice that each session is carried out as briefly as possible and procedural safeguards are in place.

In 1982, the seminal article on functional analysis was published. The article provided a methodology for identifying the function of self-injurious behavior (Iwata, Dorsey, Slifer, Bauman, & Richman, 1982/1994). Results empirically demonstrated that individuals may engage in the same topography of behavior as one another (e.g., self-injury) to gain access to different reinforcers or functions. These findings were instrumental in advancing the field of behavior analysis away from behavior modification and toward applied behavior analysis (ABA), which promotes the use of assessments to determine the function of behavior, thus allowing for individualized function-based treatments to be implemented. Since the original publication, the procedures have been replicated with different behaviors, populations, settings, and conditions.

Several conditions were outlined in the article that can be implemented as written. Again, only those conditions that are hypothesized to be altering the occurrence or nonoccurrence of the behavior should be tested; however, if the behavior analyst cannot put forth a hypothesis statement, it is best practice to implement those common test conditions outlined in the original publication. Each condition allows for a full behavioral contingency to be experienced by the learner and capitalizes on motivating operations, discriminative stimuli, and the actual delivery of the consequence stimuli (e.g., escape, attention, etc.).

Demand/Avoid Condition. This condition assesses if the individual is engaging in the behavior to escape a task, situation, or another aversive stimulus and tests for social negative reinforcement. In the **demand/avoid condition**, the individual is presented with a nonpreferred task (or multiple nonpreferred tasks) by someone who commonly presents task demands to the individual (e.g., parent, teacher, caregiver). It is important to note that the specific task or aversive stimulus presented should be individualized to the learner and should be based off the information obtained in the indirect and direct assessments. At the onset of the condition, the learner will be presented with the nonpreferred task or aversive stimulus; this may temporarily increase the value of escape as a reinforcer, thereby creating a condition in which the target behavior is more likely to be emitted if escape is a maintaining variable. The experimenter should prompt the learner to complete the task that is presented and praise instances in which it is completed correctly. If the individual engages in the target behavior following presentation of the nonpreferred task, the experimenter would allow the individual to escape or avoid the task. Escape from the nonpreferred task or stimulus should be brief (e.g., 5–30 seconds), and multiple presentations of the aversive stimulus or task should be conducted per session. The goal is to create a situation in which the individual experiences the full behavioral contingency of escape and then to record whether the behavior occurs again in the future (indicating that the task removal was reinforcing).

If the function of the behavior is escape, we would expect to see occurrences of the target behavior *continue* to occur when the task is presented because that behavior has led to the removal of the task. However, if the function of the behavior is something different and not related to escape or avoidance, we would likely see the individual complying with the task demand and perhaps not engaging in the target behavior very frequently.

We will talk more about the analysis of these data later in the chapter. For now, it is important simply to recognize the purpose of this condition in creating a scenario in which a demand is present and escape is permitted following the occurrence of the target behavior.

Attention/Social Condition. Similar to the escape/avoid condition, if there is a possibility that the individual is engaging in the behavior to obtain social positive reinforcement in the form of attention, it is necessary to create an **attention/social condition** to test that possible function. The onset of this condition will consist of creating a circumstance in which the individual is deprived of attention for a period. Perhaps the experimenter (e.g., parent, teacher, or other caregiver) is present in the room but is ostensibly busy reading a book, working on a computer, or clearly engaging in an activity other than providing attention to the learner. In this contrived situation, the experimenter would simply ignore the individual until the target behavior occurs. Contingent on the occurrence of the target behavior, the experimenter would provide attention to the learner in the form of eye contact, verbal responses, and other forms of attention that would typically occur following the target behavior (e.g., physical touch, redirection) for a designated brief period. The experimenter would then go back to what he or she was doing (i.e., removing attention) until the next occurrence of the target behavior.

If the target behavior continues to occur in the condition, it would be clear that experimenter attention was the maintaining variable and was reinforcing the target behavior. Similar to the escape/avoid condition, if the target behavior does not continue to be emitted under these circumstances, then attention is not a reinforcing function.

Tangible/Access Condition. Following the same theme as the other conditions, in the **tangible/access condition**, an experimenter tests for social positive reinforcement by contriving a situation in which highly preferred objects or activities are present in the environment but inaccessible to the individual. Prior to the onset of the condition, the learner typically has free access to these tangibles for a period, thereby creating a state of deprivation when they are removed at the beginning of the session. Periodically, the experimenter should point out the presence of these items, either by personally engaging with the objects or activities or simply telling the individual that the objects are present but not immediately available.

An example for an individual whose top-ranked reinforcer is a specific movie would be for the experimenter to have a portable DVD player present and play the individual's favorite movie but turn the screen away so the individual cannot view it. If the target behavior occurs in response to this antecedent, the experimenter would immediately provide access, allowing the individual to view the DVD player screen for a short duration. After repeated trials with various objects and activities being presented and only provided contingent upon the occurrence of the target behavior, the frequency of the behavior would be recorded to determine if access to those items and activities is, in fact, the function of the target behavior.

An important note on this condition is that it is inherently prone to false-positive results in that access to preferred stimuli contingent on target behavior may increase the behavior regardless of the maintaining function. Access to potent reinforcers is likely to increase behavior regardless of function; therefore, it is highly recommended that this condition is only run if the hypothesis statement and data suggest that it is a possible maintaining function.

Alone Condition. Although it is relatively simple to contrive environmental conditions and behavioral contingencies wherein the functions of escape, attention, and access to tangibles can be observed, the final function of behavior requires a slightly different approach. Automatic/sensory reinforcement is defined as the reinforcement one can provide for oneself. For many people, singing to themselves in the shower can be automatically reinforcing, as they gain reinforcement by hearing the sound of their singing voice and listening to the song itself. Singing alone in the shower would clearly *not* serve the function of attention, as being alone precludes the possibility that someone would provide attention as a consequence of the behavior. This behavior also could *not* serve the function of escape unless the individual is singing while also not engaging in the other typical actions of showering at the same time. Finally, singing in the shower does *not* result in any tangible gain for the individual. By ruling out all the other functions of behavior, one can determine that the function of that behavior is for automatic/sensory reinforcement. This example helps us only so far, though, as singing in the shower is rarely considered a problem behavior that is sufficiently socially significant to warrant a behavior analyst's services.

To fully test the functional hypothesis of automatic reinforcement, it is necessary to create a condition wherein the individual will not receive attention, the opportunity to escape, or access to tangibles or activities. For this reason, the condition created to test whether automatic/sensory reinforcement is the function of a behavior is also often called the alone condition. Simply put, the person is observed when they are alone or when the other environmental contingencies are not influencing the behavior. An ideal way to conduct an alone condition would be to place the individual in a room without stimulation (i.e., no toys or enriching materials) with a one-way mirror and observe the occurrences of the behavior from an observation area. If, when the individual is by themselves and has no task demands placed on them or has the opportunity to gain access to preferred tangibles or attention and the behavior still occurs, the function can clearly be determined to be automatic reinforcement.

Play Condition. The play condition serves as a control condition that counters the other common conditions utilized when conducting a functional analysis. In the control condition, the experimenter and learner are both present in the room, and the environment is "enriched" in that toys and preferred items are freely accessible. The experimenter does not place any demands or present any nonpreferred tasks to the learner but does periodically present toys and deliver praise and physical contact if the learner is engaging in appropriate behavior. Instances of the target behavior are ignored.

This condition controls for all conditions in that there is no experimenter consequence provided that is contingent on the emission of the target behavior. Escape should not be valuable as a reinforcer, as there are no nonpreferred stimuli or tasks being presented to the learner. Attention (in the form of physical and verbal attention is delivered as an antecedent, thereby abolishing the value of attention) is not delivered contingent upon the target behavior. Lastly, the learner is in an enriched environment, allowing access to activities they may compete with the motivation to engage in automatically maintained behavior.

The **play condition** as described above controls for the common conditions used in functional analysis procedures, but is not a control for all possible test conditions. Experimenters should take special care to ensure that if novel conditions are implemented with a learner, the control condition is altered accordingly. Additionally, if any of the conditions are modified or individualized, then the control should be altered in a similar fashion. For example, if, in the attention condition, tickles are delivered contingent on the target behavior being emitted, then tickles (instead of praise statements) should be proactively delivered in the control condition.

Condition	EO	Example Discriminative Stimulus	Consequence	Function
Demand	Present nonpreferred task or aversive stimulus	"Do the puzzle."	Escape provided	Social negative reinforcement
Attention	Experimenter in the same room but withholds attention (e.g., reads a magazine)	"I'm going to read while you X."	Attention provided (e.g., verbal statements, eye contact, physical attention)	Social positive reinforcement
Tangible	Materials within sight yet inaccessible	Item visible/within sight	Tangible provided	Social positive reinforcement
Alone	Alone	Impoverished environment	Ignore learner/no programmed experimenter consequence	Automatic reinforcement
Play	Play	Enriched environment	Ignore behavior/no contingency	Control

Considerations for Implementation of a Functional Analysis

Selecting Experimenter. It is best for the person who would normally work with or care for the learner to be the person who is serving as the experimenter during functional analysis conditions. Although all people involved in the design and implementation of the condition will be aware of the purpose of each condition and the overall goal of the functional analysis, the objective is to evoke natural behavioral responses from the individual despite the contrived circumstances. Someone who is typically around the learner will have a history of reinforcement under certain conditions that may aid in the differentiation of responding across conditions. However, the person running each condition must implement the condition with integrity. This means that the person who is implementing the condition should be trained to prepare the materials required, begin the condition with the specific discriminative stimulus, and deliver consequence stimuli as outlined in the protocol. If a familiar person is not available to implement the conditions, a novel experimenter may be trained, as this would be preferable to not completing the assessment.

Timing. The duration of a functional analysis can occur across several days or in a little as a couple of hours. Since each condition of the functional analysis will present different contingencies for the individual, it is possible to space the conditions over time. For example, one might conduct each condition on a different day and then continue to alternate the presentation of the conditions until sufficient data are collected on each condition for comparison. Alternatively, if there is a need to complete the functional analysis more rapidly, it would be possible for the conditions to be presented in 5- or 10-minute intervals and rapidly alternated, with a short break (5 minutes) in between each of the conditions. During the break, the learner should complete a neutral activity (e.g., go to the bathroom, go for a walk, get a drink of water) that is unrelated to any of the conditions. Functional analysis conditions vary in length and may be as short as 2 minutes or as long as 30 minutes. The length of conditions should be decided per learner, and multiple factors should be considered, including, but not limited to, the learner's discrimination skills and the frequency of the behavior.

Ecological Validity. When selecting the environment in which the functional analysis conditions will be implemented, there are two options: in-vivo or analog. In-vivo functional analyses (those that are conducted in the actual environment where the behavior occurs) may have greater ecological validity; however, it is important that the actual environment can be controlled and that no confounding variables are present. An analog environment is a controlled environment that is meant to replicate the actual environment in which the behavior occurs. Although there may be the possibility for greater control to be exerted in an analog environment, it is possible that variables from the natural environment will not be carried over into the analog environment and, therefore, the target behavior will not be assessed under the same environmental conditions. For example, if one is attempting to conduct a functional analysis to test the hypothesized function for aggression in the classroom, conducting the functional analysis conditions in an empty classroom will have less ecological validity because there are many variables present in the natural environment (e.g., peers, classroom materials, other classroom environmental variables) that are not present in the analog environment. Therefore, it is important to consider practical ways in which salient variables within the typical environment can be replicated, yet still controlled, within the various conditions of the functional analysis or to determine if it is possible to implement the functional analysis in the natural environment while still ensuring internal validity of the procedures.

Procedural Safeguards. Although functional analysis allows for the demonstration of a functional relation and the selection of an intervention that is more likely to be effective, the procedure is not without risk, and special attention should be paid to developing protocols that minimize these risks to the learner and to others in the environment. The goal of functional analysis is to identify the reinforcing variable; therefore, an increase in the target behavior should be expected in one, if not more than one, condition. Procedures for implementing the functional analysis should be considered carefully and, ideally, should be peer reviewed, with scheduled, frequent analysis of the data collected.

Prior to implementing a functional analysis for a target behavior that could lead to injury to the learner, a medical screening should be conducted to determine if the behavior can safely happen for short durations (i.e., the length of the condition). In the event that a functional analysis is being conducted on a behavior that can lead to injury to the learner or the experimenter, medical personnel should be present during the test conditions to determine if the session needs to be terminated. Termination criteria should be established prior to beginning to run experimental sessions. Terminating a session is not ideal and should not be taken lightly, as it will often result in the data from the session being thrown out due to a change in the length of that particular session relative to other sessions.

Signaling of Conditions. As outlined above, each condition of a functional analysis likely tests for a different function of the behavior, and the number of different conditions to be tested is a product of the hypothesis statement. However, the number of conditions should be evaluated prior to the outset of the experiment, and the learner's discrimination skills should be considered. Experimental functional analyses can have as few as two conditions (pairwise functional analysis), and it is recommended not to exceed five conditions within one analysis. The traditional protocol includes salient discriminative stimuli that should signal to the learner the contingency in any certain condition (e.g., escape condition begins with a demand presented). At times, however, learners may benefit from additional environmental signals that cue the contingency in place. For example, experimenters may wear different-colored shirts to signal each condition, or the experimenter may state a rule at the beginning of the condition to inform the learner of the contingency.

Variations in Traditional Conditions

As functional analysis technology has advanced, several variations that streamline procedures and reduce the risk to the learner and experimenter have been put forth. The following variations will be covered briefly; however, the reader is encouraged to review the literature prior to implementing any of these variations, as providing sufficient detail for replication is beyond the scope of this text.

Idiosyncratic Conditions. In designing experimental manipulations, the experimenter should take special care to determine individual variables that may be evoking or maintaining a target behavior. Idiosyncratic variables may develop from a reinforcement or punishment history with a certain stimulus or set of stimuli. For example, a learner is observed to engage in verbal protests when flash cards are presented. In this case, the experimenter may design a condition to present tasks via both flash cards and a computer-based presentation to determine if there is a functional relation demonstrated between the presentation of flash cards and verbal protests. In this example, if this structural analysis demonstrated a functional relation, an intervention could be designed to decrease the target behavior of verbal protests in the presence of flash cards.

Single-Function Test/Pairwise Functional Analysis. At times, the hypothesis statement is sufficiently strong but it is required that a functional relation be demonstrated. In this case, the experimenter may execute a single-function test, or pairwise functional analysis. In a pairwise functional analysis, one test condition is evaluated against a control. For example, if it is hypothesized that a learner is throwing items to gain attention, an attention test condition (i.e., attention is withheld and only delivered contingent on the behavior) could be compared to a control condition (i.e., attention is provided at a set rate as an antecedent and no attention is delivered contingent on the behavior). If the function of throwing items is maintained by attention, a clear differentiation in the two data paths would be demonstrated rapidly, with minimal sessions required.

Brief Functional Analysis (BFA). A BFA allows for multiple test conditions and can still demonstrate a functional relation, but it abbreviates the length of each session and requires only one or two data points per condition (Gardener, Spencer, Boelter, Dubard, & Jennet, 2012). The data are still visually analyzed, but instead of analyzing trends in the data, the analyst is simply identifying changes in level across the conditions. A BFA can show patterns similar to a full-length experimental functional analysis and may be more useful in natural settings because the experimenter does not need to maintain a controlled environment for as long as would be required in a full-length experimental functional analysis. Additionally, this assessment reduces risk to the learner and experimenter in that each condition is presented for a shorter duration than would occur in traditional procedures. A limitation of this procedure may be that there is not sufficient time for the learner to experience the full behavioral contingency of each condition; therefore, behavior may not be differentiated due to lack of discrimination of the contingencies.

Latency-Based Functional Analysis. Functional analyses that utilize latency as the measure of the dependent variable are referred to as latency-based functional analyses. In this variation, the duration of time between the onset of the condition and the first instance of the target behavior is measured (Neidert, Iwata, Dempsey, & Thomason-Sassi, 2013). Upon the target behavior occurring, the session is terminated. Data are analyzed to identify which condition has the shortest latency, indicating that the learner will more immediately engage in the behavior in the condition in which the maintaining reinforcer is provided. This assessment can be used when behavior is determined to be too dangerous to conduct full-length sessions or when the experimenter will need to intervene prior to the end of a condition. An example of a behavior that would be ideal for this type of assessment is elopement.

Branch Functional Analysis. A branch analysis is a specific type of functional analysis procedure that is used to identify the specific attribute or component of the consequence stimulus that is reinforcing. Systematic manipulations are conducted in a manner similar to other functional analysis procedures, but instead of attempting to identify the function, the experimenter is attempting to identify the reinforcing element. For example, if it is identified that the learner is engaging in swearing behavior to gain attention, a branch analysis could be conducted that evaluates the specific type(s) of attention that are maintaining the swearing. In this example, conditions may include 1) verbal disapproval, 2) eye contact, 3) laughter, and/or 4) physical touch (Kodak, Northup, & Kelley, 2007). In this branch analysis, the consequences would be systematically varied and delivered contingent on swearing. This type of analysis can be helpful in that it pinpoints the specific reinforcing consequence and may allow for more targeted interventions to be developed and implemented.

Data Analysis

A functional analysis results in data on the occurrence of the behavior being collected from each of the conditions employed. The objective in a functional analysis is to compare the frequency of the occurrence of the behavior across conditions to determine which condition evoked the most frequent occurrences of the behavior. As is commonly used in ABA, a visual analysis of the data is conducted to best determine the function of the behavior. The most common experimental designs utilized when analyzing functional analysis data are multi-element designs and reversal designs.

In the example in Figure 10.1, it is clear that over 16 sessions of alternating conditions, the frequency of hitting behavior was highest during the condition in which attention was contingently provided upon occurrence of the behavior. During the tangible, escape, and alone conditions, the behavior did not occur as frequently. This separation of the data path for the attention condition from the other conditions clearly indicates that the function is attention.

Figure 10.1 Graph of Functional Analysis of Self-Injurious Hitting

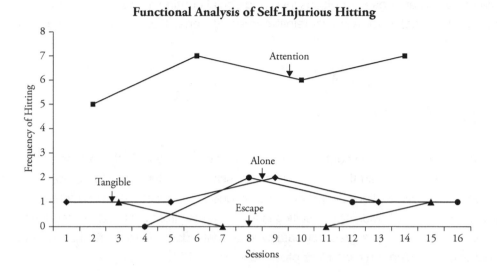

In Figure 10.2, the graph displays data from another 16-session functional analysis examining the function of screaming behavior. By conducting a visual analysis of the data, it is clear that the duration of screaming was highest during the condition in which escape was contingently provided upon occurrence of the behavior. The second condition that evoked the highest duration of screaming was the contingent attention condition, which suggests the behavior is possibly multiply controlled (e.g., more than one maintaining function) but primarily serves the function of escape. During the tangible and alone conditions, the behavior did not occur as frequently.

Figure 10.2 Graph of Functional Analysis of Screaming

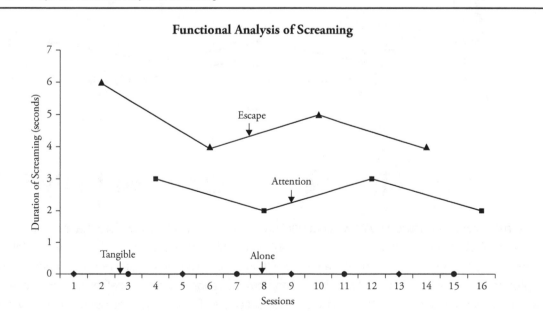

A behavior can be determined to be automatically maintained if the alone condition is the highest data path and is higher than the play/control condition or if all data paths are high and there is no differentiation between those conditions involving social contingencies (e.g., attention and escape) and those that do not involve social reinforcement (Roane, Fisher, Kelley, Mevers, & Bouxsein, 2013).

Multiple Control

It is possible for behaviors to be controlled by more than one function. In these cases, they are considered multiply controlled. When this occurs, it is necessary for all functions to be accounted for in the development of the intervention. Simply focusing on one of the functions will not result in a change in the behavior, since the behavior is still resulting in reinforcement from the unaddressed function. Multiple control is often observed in a graph of data wherein data paths from more than one condition are intertwined or overlapping. An example is provided in Figure 10.3.

Figure 10.3 Graph of Functional Analysis of Biting

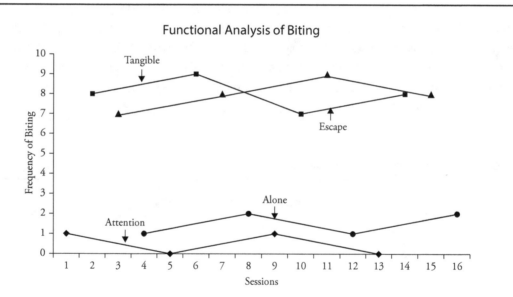

Overcoming Challenges of Functional Analysis

As you may have determined by now, functional analysis is a complex procedure that requires expertise in behavioral observations and experimental control, many resources, and a plan for the safety of the learners and personnel conducting the assessment. For these reasons, many behavior analysts may be tempted to implement an intervention without the demonstration of a functional relation. However, these challenges may be overcome by using the modifications in technology that were previously outlined (Hanley, 2012).

Although it is a requirement that an individual with substantial training in functional analysis be the person who designs the procedures, it is not required that the experimenter have this same training.

Implementing functional analysis conditions should be no different than implementing intervention plans, and it has been demonstrated that people with varying amounts of training can implement test conditions with high levels of procedural integrity (Hanley, 2012).

By using the variations of brief functional analysis and latency-based functional analysis, we can use fewer resources. In both analyses, the setting must be controlled for only short durations of time, making it possible for sessions to be interspersed throughout the day as needed based on the availability of a certain setting (e.g., classroom). Also, these two experimental procedures do not require personnel to be present to run sessions for long durations; in fact, it is possible that it may only require as little as 30 minutes for the total assessment and may occur across multiple days.

The last challenge that analysts often cite is that they are concerned with the safety of the learner. One could argue that the learner is at no more risk if we conduct a functional analysis than if we continued to allow the learner to engage in the target behavior without identifying the source of reinforcement. In the absence of intervention, it is likely the behavior would continue to increase.

Summary

This chapter defined and discussed the functional analysis process in detail, along with the various conditions and considerations for carrying out each step. Additionally, this chapter covered the process for implementing functional analysis to determine the function of the behavior as well as to explore the possibility that behaviors may be multiply controlled. Finally, the process of planning a functional analysis was discussed in terms of considering the timing of carrying out each condition over the course of days or rapidly conducted successive sessions.

Definition of Key Terms

- **hypothesis statement:** a statement that identifies the variables that are likely evoking the targeted behavior as well as the consequence variables that are maintaining the behavior.
- **systematic manipulation:** experimental procedure in which an independent variable is repeatedly introduced and removed to measure the effect on the dependent variable with the goal of demonstrating a functional relation.
- **structural analysis:** systematic manipulation of the antecedents to a behavior while maintaining the same consequences. The intent of a structural analysis is to identify the antecedents controlling the behavior to manipulate or modify them in order to prevent a behavior from occurring.
- **functional analysis:** a step in the functional-behavior-assessment process that includes systematically manipulating conditions to test the functional hypothesis and demonstrate a functional relation between the behavior and environmental variables.
- **functional relation:** is shown when a change in the behavior is demonstrated to be due to a systematic manipulation of the environmental variables preceding or following that behavior.
- **demand/avoid condition:** a planned environmental condition of a functional analysis to test whether a behavior is occurring to escape a task demand, stimulus, or environmental event. In this condition, a demand or aversive stimulus is presented and immediately removed upon occurrence of the target behavior.

- **attention/social condition:** a planned environmental condition of a functional analysis to test whether a behavior is occurring to obtain social attention. In this condition, attention is provided immediately upon occurrence of the target behavior.
- **tangible/access condition:** a planned environmental condition of a functional analysis to test whether a behavior is occurring to obtain a preferred tangible object or event. In this condition, the individual receives access to the object or is able to engage in the preferred activity immediately upon occurrence of the target behavior.
- **alone condition:** a planned environmental condition of a functional analysis to test whether a behavior is automatically maintained. In this condition, the environment is arranged such that attention, access to tangibles or preferred activities, and escape are not provided as a result of engaging in the target behavior. Most often, this condition is referred to as the "alone" condition, as the individual is left alone and observed from a distance or through a one-way mirror to properly assess whether the behavior is being maintained automatically.
- **play condition:** a control condition in which the experimenter and learner are both present in the room, the environment is "enriched" in that toys and preferred items are freely accessible, and instances of the target behavior are ignored.
- **ecological validity:** the extent to which the findings from an experiment (e.g., functional analysis) can be applied to a real-life setting.

Test Your Understanding

Level 1: Knowledge

1. True or False: The functional analysis has not been conducted properly if the results do not confirm the functional hypothesis.
2. True or False: Statistical analysis is the only way by which to analyze and interpret the results of a functional analysis.
3. True or False: The tangible/access condition involves providing the individual with access to an object or activity that he or she prefers upon the occurrence of the target behavior.
4. True or False: It is always necessary to conduct a functional analysis over the course of several days, with each condition occurring across a different day.
5. True or False: If the results of a functional analysis reveal that there is more than one function for the behavior, another functional analysis should be conducted to identify the true function.

Level 2: Comprehension

1. Which of the following situations would occur in a demand/avoid condition of a functional analysis?
    a. The individual would be provided with a nonpreferred task demand and, upon occurrence of the problem behavior, would be required to complete the task.
    b. The individual would be provided with a nonpreferred task demand and, upon occurrence of the problem behavior, would not be required to complete the task.

    c. The individual would be allowed to protest when presented with a nonpreferred task demand, but this would be ignored until they complete the task.

    d. None of the above.

2. Which of the following situations would occur in an attention/social condition of a functional analysis?

    a. The individual would initially be provided with high-quality attention and, upon occurrence of the problem behavior, would continue to be provided attention.

    b. The individual would initially be ignored and, upon occurrence of the problem behavior, would be provided attention.

    c. The individual would be ignored for the duration of the condition to determine the threshold of the target behavior's occurrence.

    d. None of the above.

3. Which of the following situations would occur in a tangible/access condition of a functional analysis?

    a. The individual would initially be shown a preferred object or activity and, upon occurrence of the problem behavior, would immediately be provided with access to the object or activity.

    b. The individual would be asked if he or she would like access to the preferred object or activity and, upon occurrence of the problem behavior, would not be provided with access to the object or activity.

    c. The individual would initially be shown a preferred object or activity and, upon occurrence of the problem behavior, would immediately be provided with access to the object or activity, but it would promptly be taken away again to evoke the occurrence of the target behavior.

    d. None of the above.

4. Which of the following situations would occur in an alone condition of a functional analysis?

    a. The individual would be left in a room with nonpreferred items and activities and observed from another location.

    b. The individual would be left alone in a room with free access to any toys or activities they prefer and observed from another location.

    c. The condition would be carried out in the same manner as an attention condition, but the attention provided would be minimized.

    d. None of the above.

Level 3: Application

1. Review the case study for Silvia from Chapter 9 and consider what the functional analysis for that behavior would require. How would each condition look? What would the confederate do, and how would the environment be arranged? Be specific in your description of what the different conditions would look like and what resources you would need in order to carry out the process. In lieu of being able to conduct this functional analysis yourself, consider this plan a way to imagine how you would practice *doing* the functional analysis yourself.

2. Review the case study for Peter from Chapter 9 and consider what the functional analysis for that behavior would require. How would each condition look? What would the confederate do, and how would the environment be arranged? Be specific in your description of what the different conditions would look like and what resources you would need in order to carry out the process. In lieu of being able to conduct this functional analysis yourself, consider this plan a way to imagine how you would practice *doing* the functional analysis yourself.

3. Review the case study for Ennis from Chapter 9 and consider what the functional analysis for that behavior would require. How would each condition look? What would the confederate do, and how would the environment be arranged? Be specific in your description of what the different conditions would look like and what resources you would need in order to carry out the process. In lieu of being able to conduct this functional analysis yourself, consider this plan a way to imagine how you would practice *doing* the functional analysis yourself.

4. Review the case study for Madison from Chapter 9 and consider what the functional analysis for that behavior would require. How would each condition look? What would the confederate do, and how would the environment be arranged? Be specific in your description of what the different conditions would look like and what resources you would need in order to carry out the process. In lieu of being able to conduct this functional analysis yourself, consider this plan a way to imagine how you would practice *doing* the functional analysis yourself.

In-Class Small-Group Discussion Questions/Exercises

Create small groups (perhaps four or five students) and discuss the following topics, allowing 10 to 15 minutes to complete the response.

1. Select one of the case studies from Chapter 9 as a focus for this exercise. Within your team, discuss how you would go about explaining the plan for completing a functional analysis for that individual to others. Specifically consider what instructions you would provide to the confederate as well as to the caregivers of the individual.

References

Axelrod, S. (1987). Functional and structural analyses of behavior: Approaches leading to reduced use of punishment procedures. *Research in developmental disabilities, 8,* 165–78. 10.1016/0891-4222(87)90001-1.

Gardener, A.W., Spencer, T.D., Boelter, E.W., Dubard, M., & Jennet, H.K. (2012). A systematic review of brief functional analysis methodology with typically developing children. *Education and Treatment of Children, 35*(2), 313–332. 10.1353/etc.2012.0014.

Hanley, G.P. (2012). Functional assessment of problem behavior: Dispelling myths, overcoming implementation obstacles, and developing new lore. *Behavior Analysis in Practice, 5*(1), 54–72. 10.1007/BF03391818.

Iwata, B.A., Dorsey, M.F., Slifer, K.J., Bauman, K.E., & Richman, G.S. (1982/1994). Toward a functional analysis of self-injury. *Journal of Applied Behavior Analysis, 27,* 197–209.

Kodak, T., Northup, J., & Kelley, M.E. (2007). An evaluation of the types of attention that maintain problem behavior. *Journal of Applied Behavior Analysis, 40*(1), 167–171. 10.1901/jaba.2007.43-06.

Neidert, P.L., Iwata, B.A., Dempsey, C.M., & Thomason-Sassi, J.L. (2013). Latency of response during the functional analysis of elopement. *Journal of Applied Behavior Analysis, 46*(1), 312–316. 10.1002/jaba.11.

Roane, H.S., Fisher, W.W., Kelley, M.E., Meyers, J.L., & Bouxsein, K.J. (2013). Using modified visual-inspection criteria to interpret functional analysis outcomes. *Journal of Applied Behavior Analysis, 46,* 130–146. 10.1002/jaba.13.

CHAPTER 11

Selecting Function-Based Interventions

As was covered in Chapter 3, the purpose of an FBA is to identify the function of a behavior to then be able to change the behavior. To effectively reduce a challenging behavior and promote an appropriate replacement behavior, it is necessary to design interventions that will result in the individual gaining the reinforcement he or she is seeking, using different behaviors, of course. Knowing the function of the behavior allows one to select and design intervention(s) based on the behavior's function or create a **function-based intervention**. Failure to design and implement an intervention based on the behavior's function will not necessarily result in behavior change and may only reinforce new functions of the behavior (Ingram, Lewis-Palmer, & Sugai, 2005). Additionally, failure to design function-based intervention will likely result in more intrusive interventions than are required and may lead to less generality.

This chapter will discuss the various considerations involved in selecting function-based interventions that are supported by the scientific literature and will explore exemplars and non-exemplars of function-based interventions. Additionally, partially completed FBA materials will be explored and analyzed. Be sure to complete the learning activities at the end of the chapter to properly test your knowledge and to design function-based intervention plans to best address a target behavior's function and complete all stages of the "See one, do one, teach one" model to master this important stage of the FBA process.

LEARNING OBJECTIVES

After completing the chapter's activities, learners should be able to do the following:

- Describe functional equivalence and provide examples

- Evaluate functional replacement behaviors and provide examples

- Create and evaluate plans for function-based interventions and provide examples

Functional Equivalence

At this point, it should be clear that all behaviors, whether they are socially appropriate or not, serve a particular function. Therefore, even when challenging behaviors occur, we can assume that they serve a purpose. This is good news for practitioners because it means that there are all sorts of behaviors that might serve the same function, and that many of those alternatives might be socially appropriate. When two different behaviors serve the same function, they are considered to be **functionally equivalent**. Once behavior analysts know the function of a challenging behavior, a more socially appropriate—functionally equivalent—behavior can be taught to replace the need for the challenging behavior to occur (Baer, Wolf, & Risley, 1968; Bijou & Baer, 1978; Carr, 1988; Horner & Day, 1991). After all, if the intended purpose of the behavior is being served, the outcome for the individual will be the same in terms of the reinforcement they receive. Table 11.1 outlines some examples of functionally equivalent behaviors by function.

Table 11.1 Examples of Functionally Equivalent Behaviors by Function

	Behaviors that are functionally equivalent	
Attention	Calling out in history class	Raising your hand
	Child screaming until her father comes to play with him	Child asking his father to play with him
Escape	Running away from a parent when told, "After dinner it will be time to take a bath"	Prolonging meal-time by eating slowly after being told, "It's time to take a bath"
	Screaming and throwing art supplies at school when the activity exceeds ten minutes in duration	Stating "I need a break from this activity. May I be excused for a few minutes?" and leaving the area once permission is provided
Access to Tangibles	Climbing on top of the kitchen counter and refrigerator to access a high cabinet containing cookies and other candy treats	Using sign language to request access to an item
	Grabbing the dice out of another person's hand while playing a board game	Extending an open hand to the other person and saying "Okay, it's my turn to roll"
Automatic/Sensory Reinforcement	Jumping on the couch	Jumping on a trampoline
	Dumping out water from a cup onto a table top and putting fingers in it	Playing at a water table

Functionally Equivalent Replacement Behaviors

The core principle underlying the selection of function-based interventions is that the reinforcement for the challenging behavior will be withdrawn while we simultaneously teach new behaviors that will address the function the individual was seeking. Functionally equivalent replacement behaviors to challenging behaviors are any behaviors that are considered to be more socially appropriate than the challenging behavior while still serving the same function. Some of the examples in Table 11.1 exemplify functional replacement behaviors that can be taught. For example, to teach a learner a more appropriate way to gain attention in history class, we could teach the learner to raise her or his hand in class. This would still address the fundamental purpose the original calling out behavior was serving, but would be much more socially appropriate (and less of a hindrance to other learners' learning).

Function-Based Interventions

The literature base of published studies evaluating the efficacy of behavioral interventions to address specific behaviors by function provides many options for practitioners to examine. Rather than searching scientific databases for studies evaluating interventions to address the topography of a behavior (e.g., "biting" or "spitting"), it could be more effective to search in terms of the function of the behavior (e.g., "aggression maintained by attention" or "escape-maintained property destruction"). Searching for interventions by function will allow for practitioners to develop a treatment package that will effectively reduce the occurrence of the challenging behavior and also teach functionally equivalent replacement behaviors. In the section that follows, some common intervention approaches for each function of behavior are outlined to provide a starting point for an intervention package. Note that this list is not exhaustive, but should provide sufficient examples of how interventions designed to specifically address the function of behavior can be identified and implemented. Please note that identification of empirically rigorous and well-controlled studies that closely align with the population characteristics of the individual learner—in other words, evidence-based practice to target behavior's function—will allow for the greatest potential for replication in your practice. In the sections that follow, various interventions will be explored based on the function of behavior they are designed to address. Note that the interventions listed may be used across functions with modifications. For example, functional communication training is an intervention that could be applied to address multiple functions.

INTERVENTIONS TO ADDRESS BEHAVIORS MAINTAINED BY ACCESS TO TANGIBLES

Behaviors maintained by access to tangibles should result in the tangible being removed or withdrawn following the occurrence of the behavior (extinction), but training of a functional replacement behavior should also occur.

INTERVENTIONS TO ADDRESS ATTENTION-MAINTAINED BEHAVIORS

Behaviors maintained by attention can be challenging to address because the sources of reinforcement can come from any individual in the person's environment and even low-quality attention (e.g., brief eye contact or a short vocal response) can be reinforcing for certain behaviors. For this reason, it is important, regardless of which intervention is selected for use, that all individuals on the team practice the same protocol as consistently as possible. Intermittent reinforcement (i.e., occasional occurrences of reinforcement) will result in the behavior maintaining over time. (Consider a highly motivated child crying for candy in the checkout line at the market. If crying works even once, that behavior will be harder to reduce!)

Additionally, all members of the team should follow strict parameters of how attention should be provided. In this section, we will explore several commonly used and effective interventions to address attention-maintained behaviors. Exploring these interventions in greater depth, or evaluating the use of additional interventions not listed here, is encouraged, as it would be helpful prior to crafting a behavior intervention plan. These examples are provided to walk you through some common options when behaviors are attention-maintained and will call your attention to the logic employed when designing interventions to address behaviors based on attention. Practitioners should also bear in mind the ethical considerations and codes that apply to behavior change intervention selection and implementation, as outlined in the BACB® Professional and Ethical Compliance Code (BACB®, 2014), as well as any other professional ethical conduct codes that may apply. Specifically, obtaining written consent from the learner and/or their caregiver(s)or guardians, providing a written explanation of the behavior change procedure, ensuring all parties are properly trained to implement the intervention, and collecting baseline and intervention data to monitor the effectiveness of the intervention are all critical considerations and practices to ensure ethical practice is being followed.

ATTENTION EXTINCTION AND DIFFERENTIAL REINFORCEMENT

Extinction consists of the withdrawal or removal of reinforcement following a particular behavior (Cooper, Heron, & Heward, 2007). It is a consequence-based intervention with the purpose of decreasing the target behavior. **Attention extinction** is, therefore, the withdrawal or removal of attention (as it was the identified reinforcer through the FBA process) following a target behavior, also known as *planned ignoring*. Over time, the individual engaging in the target behavior to obtain attention will stop engaging in the behavior because it no longer produces the desired result. Now that we have reviewed the basic principles of extinction, it is important to carefully discuss the more detailed considerations that should be addressed if attention extinction is to be used to address a target behavior.

Extinction results in well-documented effects on behavior. Initially, however, the behavior may increase significantly (either in frequency, magnitude, or duration—or, when applicable, all three dimensions of behavior). This significant but temporary increase is called an **extinction burst** (Lerman, Iwata, & Wallace, 1999). Although this is troublesome for many individuals addressing the behavior directly, it is actually good news for the behavioral treatment team, because the pattern makes it clear that the appropriate function was identified, triggering the predictable behavior pattern. When the extinction protocol is consistently held in place (and attention is not provided following any occurrences of the target behavior), even when this sharp increase in the behavior's amplitude is occurring, the behavior will eventually decrease through stability of the intervention over time (Iwata, Pace, Cowdery, & Miltenberger, 1994). Because this is a well-known effect when extinction is properly applied to any behavior, practitioners often prepare the treatment team for the occurrence of a burst and encourage them to continue the protocol in spite of this increase in the behavior.

As we explore the effect of extinction on behavior, it is also necessary to explore an event commonly observed, which is called **spontaneous recovery** (Cooper, Heron, & Heward, 2007). Spontaneous recovery occurs when, after a period of the behavior remaining eliminated or significantly decreased, the behavior spontaneously occurs again. This additional occurrence is usually less intense than the extinction burst or the typical intensity observed at baseline, but it is critical to consider because if the behavior is reinforced at that point with attention, it is possible the behavior will occur at high rates once again.

When using attention extinction, it is important to withdraw all sources of attention from the person's environment. If the behavior usually occurs when just one other person is present, carrying out attention extinction is relatively simple, because only one person needs to ignore the behavior. When the behavior occurs in a classroom, or a dinner table at home with younger siblings who laugh at the target behavior, for instance, the process of carrying out attention extinction can be more challenging.

Cooper, Heron, and Heward (2007) outlined ten considerations to use extinction effectively. Table 11.2 outlines those considerations briefly, though you are encouraged to explore these considerations through further reading, utilizing resources such as the Professional and Ethical Compliance Code for Behavior Analysts (BACB®, 2014), and through supervision by and consultation with a Board Certified Behavior Analyst® (BCBA) in good standing prior to using these interventions.

Table 11.2 Using Extinction Effectively (Cooper, Heron, & Heward, 2007)

General Guideline	Explanation
Withhold all reinforcers maintaining the problem behavior	Extinction will only be effective if all sources of reinforcement are withheld. If any amount of reinforcement is being provided from any source, the learner will continue to engage in the behavior.
Withhold reinforcement consistently	When reinforcement is not consistently withheld, the individual learns that *sometimes* the behavior will result in reinforcement. This results in an intermittent schedule of reinforcement going into effect, and therefore strengthens the behavior's resistance to extinction (achieving the opposite effect than what is desired).
Combine extinction with other procedures	There are two primary reasons why combining extinction with other procedures is important. 1) The effectiveness of extinction is increased when positive reinforcement is used, because those procedures focus on teaching the learner what *to engage in*, instead of simply withdrawing reinforcement for behaviors they are being taught *not* to engage in. 2) Combining extinction procedures with differential reinforcement and antecedent interventions has the potential to reduce unwanted effects of extinction (such as the extinction burst or aggression).
Use instructions	Even though an individual need not be informed that a behavioral intervention is being applied in order for it to be effective, providing instruction expressing to the learner that the target behavior will not result in reinforcement can be more effective than not informing them.
Plan for extinction-produced aggression	Once extinction is in effect, the individual may respond by engaging in a range of different behaviors to receive the previously obtained reinforcement. Aggression is an observed side effect of extinction in many cases (regardless of how infrequently it has occurred). Therefore, a plan should be formulated to prepare for aggression in advance to ensure all individuals are kept safe and to continue to prevent reinforcement from being attained even if aggression occurs.
Increase the number of extinction trials	Just as additional teaching trials using reinforcement will accelerate skill acquisition, mastery, and maintenance, additional extinction trials will accelerate the extinction process and decrease the target behavior.
Include significant others in extinction	Because significant others are likely to play a role in the consistent delivery of reinforcement for a particular behavior, those same individuals need to be involved in carrying out the extinction protocol.
Guard against unintentional extinction	In the real-time application of extinction procedures, at times, desired behaviors might be placed on extinction along with the target behaviors. It is important, therefore, to clearly identify all forms (topographies) of the target behavior that will be placed on an extinction behavior and ensure that any other appropriate behavior is provided prompt reinforcement.
Maintain extinction-decreased behavior	The most preferred and effective application of escape and attention extinction would be for these procedures to be enforced on a permanent basis. Sensory extinction procedures should also be put into place on a permanent basis but might also be gradually faded and maintained.
Know when not to use extinction (imitation and extreme behaviors)	If there is potential that others will imitate the behaviors being put on extinction (e.g., in a classroom or group home setting), it is necessary to avoid using extinction. Additionally, if the behaviors are extreme (e.g., aggression, property destruction, etc.), it would be necessary to avoid implementing extinction at all to prevent harm from occurring.

Although attention extinction can be highly effective at reducing challenging behaviors, extinction of any kind, when used on its own, does not eliminate the issue of challenging behaviors related to seeking attention. An example may illustrate this point. Let's imagine Jermaine is engaging in high-pitched screaming to obtain attention. The practitioner implements a highly effective attention extinction protocol and the screaming is reduced, but he then begins engaging in tantrums wherein he falls to the ground and hits, kicks, and whines instead, and obtains attention for this new set of behaviors. In this instance, Jermaine was unable to obtain attention through screaming and therefore identified a different behavior to achieve the same outcome. To prevent this substitution of one challenging behavior for another, it is important to not only focus on teaching the individual what *not* to do (using extinction) but also teach them what they *should do* instead of the target behavior. Differential reinforcement is a very useful procedure to address this need.

At this point, you should be clear that positive reinforcement is highly effective when teaching new skills. Specifically, using a procedure of **differential reinforcement** should be used in conjunction with extinction protocols (Cooper, Heron, & Heward, 2007). Differential reinforcement consists of providing reinforcement only when a specific behavior is occurring according to a certain threshold or criterion in terms of its frequency, topography, duration, latency, or magnitude, while placing all other behaviors that do not meet that threshold or criterion on extinction. Essentially, the behavior analyst provides greater amounts of reinforcement according to whether each instance of the behavior reaches or approximates the desired threshold or criterion. There are several different procedures using the principles of differential reinforcement, and each procedure reinforces a different dimension of the behavior being differentially reinforced. These different procedures include **differential reinforcement of alternative behavior (DRA), differential reinforcement of other behavior (DRO), differential reinforcement of incompatible behavior (DRI), and differential reinforcement of low rates of behavior (DRL)**.

DIFFERENTIAL REINFORCEMENT OF ALTERNATIVE BEHAVIOR (DRA)

In order to discuss DRA in more detail, we will return to exploring the most appropriate differential reinforcement procedure for use in the case of Jermaine, whose screaming behavior has been effectively reduced using attention extinction. Because Jermaine's screaming behavior needs to be replaced with a new behavior, we should consider which differential reinforcement procedure to use to teach him to engage in more appropriate requests for attention. Using DRA with Jermaine to teach him to request attention in an appropriate manner would be very helpful because we are going to need to introduce a new behavior to Jermaine's repertoire. In this case, the new behavior will be considered the "alternative behavior" that would be the more socially appropriate, functionally equivalent, behavior to gain attention. Perhaps, as his alternative behavior, Jermaine could be taught to approach his peers or family members at school and/or home and say "come and play with me" or something similar to request attention. If, on each occasion that Jermaine engages in this more appropriate manner of seeking attention, he receives a longer amount of high-quality attention, he will continue engaging in the alternative behavior. Implementers of differential reinforcement will need to match the amount and/or quality of reinforcement to the quality of Jermaine's request.

DIFFERENTIAL REINFORCEMENT OF OTHER BEHAVIOR (DRO)

Whereas DRA focuses on teaching a specific alternative behavior, DRO is a procedure based on providing reinforcement any time the target behavior is not being displayed. So, in the case of Jermaine, reinforcement would be delivered during a specific period of time when he is not engaging in high-pitched screaming (and therefore is engaging in any "other" behavior). Perhaps those working with Jermaine could set an alarm for every three minutes (as this is the average observed length of time Jermaine has spent without screaming) and provide him with high-quality attention when he does not engage in screaming behavior during the previous three-minute period.

DIFFERENTIAL REINFORCEMENT OF INCOMPATIBLE BEHAVIOR (DRI)

Another differential reinforcement procedure can be used to reinforce behaviors that cannot occur at the same time as a target behavior, or are *incompatible* with the target behavior. Imagine you were attempting to decrease the occurrence of a learner's loud clapping behavior. You would consider what other behavior could be reinforced that cannot occur at the same time as the loud clapping behavior. A behavior incompatible with clapping would be placing one's hands in their pant pockets, since, if one's hands are in their pants pockets, they cannot also clap them. Using DRI, a practitioner would differentially reinforce every occasion when the learner's hands were in his or her pockets (and therefore not clapping). Considering the case of Jermaine, if a practitioner opted to use DRI, they would need to identify a behavior incompatible with high-pitched screaming. Perhaps a behavior like humming or chewing would be an appropriate alternative, as it is not possible for Jermaine to hum or chew while also engaging in a high-pitched scream.

DIFFERENTIAL REINFORCEMENT OF LOW RATES OF BEHAVIOR (DRL)

In other cases, it may be that the behavior need not be eliminated completely, and therefore low rates of the behavior would be an acceptable frequency to maintain. An example of this would be a learner who raises his or her hand to respond to each and every question in a class and also to share his or her opinions even when the teacher is engaging in a structured lecture. The behavior of raising one's hand is actually socially appropriate, and it is likely that any teacher would appreciate this behavior maintaining over time. Therefore, it is not necessary that a new behavior be taught, or that the absence of the behavior or an incompatible behavior be reinforced. In this case, it is the *excessive frequency* of hand raising that is the issue to be addressed and lower rates of the behavior would be preferred, hence DRL would be the procedure to use. DRL would occur by measuring the inter-response time (IRT) (duration between occurrences of the behavior) and then only reinforcing occurrences of the behavior *after* that length of time has elapsed. Therefore, if the learner who raises his or her hand does so repeatedly after only an elapsed time of one minute has passed since the previous hand raise, the teacher would only call on the learner after one minute has passed since the last hand raise. In the case of Jermaine, since he is seeking attention every three minutes or so, attention would only be provided after three minutes had passed from the previous behavior's occurrence. (That said, it is unlikely that high-pitched screaming would ever be a behavior sought to be maintained at low rates, since a complete elimination of the behavior would likely be the objective.) Over time, the IRT would be determined to gradually increase until the reinforcement is being delivered less frequently.

NONCONTINGENT POSITIVE REINFORCEMENT

As was discussed in the guidelines for implementing extinction, there are ethical limitations to implementing extinction, even when a procedure of differential reinforcement is combined in the intervention package. For instance, extinction should never be applied to cases where an individual is aggressive and an extinction burst could result in significant harm to others or the environment. The alternative in those cases would be to recommend **non-contingent reinforcement (NCR)**. Non-contingent positive reinforcement consists of providing reinforcement on a fixed schedule regardless of the occurrence of the behavior Cooper, Heron, & Heward (2007). NCR can be used with positive, negative, and automatic reinforcement. In the case of addressing attention-maintained behavior, NCR with positive reinforcement should be considered, wherein the individual would receive attention initially on a fixed schedule. In a classroom or busy home setting, this can be accomplished by 1) having the teacher or parent set a timer, and 2) providing check-ins with the individual to provide brief, high quality interactions that result in a steady provision of attention. When the individual is consistently receiving attention that is reinforcing, he or she will be less likely to seek it using less appropriate alternative behaviors. Over time, as the behavior is reduced, the fixed interval schedule can be changed to a variable schedule of reinforcement and ultimately faded. Additional procedural recommendations are outlined in Table 11.3 and apply to NCR with positive, negative, and automatic reinforcement.

Table 11.3 Procedural Recommendations for Using Non-contingent Reinforcement Effectively (Cooper, Heron, & Heward, 2007)

Recommendations	Explanation
Consider the amount and quality of reinforcing stimuli	Determining the appropriate amount and degree of quality of the reinforcing stimuli when using a NCR procedure is critical to ensure that reinforcement remains effective. Data collection at baseline and throughout the intervention should demonstrate reduction in the target behavior. If this data does not demonstrate reduction, it is possible that the amount and quality of reinforcing stimuli be adjusted so that the learner has contact with an amount and level of quality of reinforcement that will effectively reduce the behavior.
Pair NCR with extinction	Combining extinction with NCR may increase the effectiveness of both procedures.
Continue to conduct preference assessments	That which is reinforcing for a particular learner is likely to change over time. Therefore, it is important to continue to conduct frequent preference assessments to evaluate the effectiveness of the provided reinforcer in the NCR procedure.
Functional behavior assessment	NCR is only effective if the function of the behavior is accurately identified. It is therefore critical to conduct an FBA to determine the function of the behavior prior to implementing NCR.
Emphasizing NCR	Creating an environment, rich or dense, with reinforcement is likely to have a greater effect on the behavior when using NCR.
Time-based NCR schedules	NCR procedures generally start with a fixed-time schedule wherein the reinforcer is delivered on a set schedule (e.g., every thirty seconds). However, a variable-time or variable-interval schedule, wherein reinforcement is delivered on a variable time schedule that averages the original fixed time or fixed number of responses, can be more effective over time after a reduction in the behavior is observed.
Thinning time-based schedules	Once a reduction in the behavior is observed, it is also possible to gradually increase the amount of time between each delivery of reinforcement, therefore thinning the amount of reinforcement delivered across a session. This will gradually return the learner to a more natural state and schedule of reinforcement.
Setting terminal criteria	When thinning a schedule of reinforcement, it is helpful to identify an arbitrary criterion to reach that approximates a schedule of reinforcement that would be encountered in the natural environment. For instance, if it is expected that an individual occupying space with others may receive social attention every five to ten minutes, then the terminal criteria for the NCR schedule would fall within that range. In other words, once the schedule is thinned such that reinforcement is being delivered every seven minutes (and the behavior remains effectively reduced or eliminated), one could determine that the NCR procedure be terminated.

Interventions to address escape-maintained behaviors.

ESCAPE EXTINCTION AND DIFFERENTIAL REINFORCEMENT OF ALTERNATIVE BEHAVIOR

Behaviors maintained by escape or negative reinforcement can also be affected by extinction protocols combined with DRA. Extinction, when it is applied to escape-maintained behaviors, is referred to as **escape extinction**. Essentially, escape extinction consists of withdrawing or removing the reinforcement obtained by escaping an aversive event, such as a task demand, other environmental events, or stimuli. All of the same guidelines provided previously in this chapter by Cooper, Heron, and Heward (2007) would apply to escape extinction, but there are some nuances to applying the intervention in cases where the behavior is maintained by negative reinforcement.

The procedure for escape extinction essentially boils down to changing the contingency of escape from an event or stimulus that the individual finds to be aversive. It is necessary to clearly identify the stimulus and/or event that has been determined to be aversive or non-preferred and operationally define the topography of an acceptable behavioral response to the aversive antecedent. To prevent escape from the aversive stimulus and/or event, the individual is prompted through the process of engaging in the expected behavior. For example, if a learner, Jillian, is presented with the aversive task demand of interrupting her play to use the bathroom, she will be presented with the task demand "Time to go to the potty," will be physically guided to comply, and any behaviors that were previously maintained by escape will be ignored and will not result in bathroom avoidance.

NON-CONTINGENT NEGATIVE REINFORCEMENT

If a behavior is found to be occurring in order for the learner to escape a task demand or aversive stimuli, it is possible that NCR with negative reinforcement may be implemented to effectively reduce the behavior. NCR with negative reinforcement consists of removing the task demand on a regular schedule. Providing frequent opportunities to escape the task demand will increase compliance with the demand over time. Returning to the example of Jillian who is refusing to use the bathroom, providing a fixed schedule of opportunities to escape (getting to take a "break" from completing the task of going to the bathroom) will likely decrease the escape behavior.

FUNCTIONAL COMMUNICATION TRAINING

Functional communication training (FCT) is an intervention that is a bedrock tool in our system of creating behavior change and educating individuals with developmental disabilities in particular. It consists of teaching the individual to make requests for the items and activities they are seeking in an appropriate manner, which supports appropriate social behavior in general. FCT is implemented by first identifying the tangible reinforcers and then systematically teaching the individual to request them using a means that requires the least amount of effort for the individual and is most readily understood by those around them. Examples of methods of communication include teaching the individual to exchange pictures (e.g., using the Picture Exchange Communication System; PECS (Bondy & Frost, 1994)), using American Sign Language (ASL) or adapted ASL, using augmentative and alternative communication devices, or simply vocal communication. Once the appropriate method for communication is determined (following skills and developmental assessments, consultation with speech and language pathologists, and the consideration of input by the family and caregivers of the individual), the requests are taught using DRA along with extinction of behaviors that do not meet the standards of the new form of request (e.g., whining or other challenging behaviors will be ignored, while functional requests will be reinforced promptly).

INTERVENTIONS TO ADDRESS BEHAVIORS MAINTAINED BY AUTOMATIC/SENSORY REINFORCEMENT

Behaviors maintained by automatic/sensory reinforcement can be problematic to address, given that the automaticity of the contingency is difficult to interrupt consistently. In other words, if an individual engages in a self-limited behavior, such as finger-flicking, unless there is a person standing with him or her at all times to prevent finger-flicking, the behavior is likely to occur when the individual is alone or direct attention is not being provided to prevent the behavior from occurring. For these reasons, it is important to consider a few of the interventions already discussed, as well as contextualize some more specific interventions directly to address behaviors resulting in automatic reinforcement.

NONCONTINGENT AUTOMATIC REINFORCEMENT

Depending on the nature of the behavior and the potential for the procedure to be implemented regularly, NCR for automatic reinforcement may serve to be a viable option to decrease the occurrence of a particular behavior maintained by automatic reinforcement. Non-contingent automatic reinforcement consists of providing free access to the stimuli required to engage in the behavior. Often, providing this free access will greatly decrease the occurrence of the behavior because the individual achieves a satiated state, which serves to abolish their motivation to engage in the behavior.

SCHEDULED ACCESS

Although NCR is often effective at reducing the motivation to engage in the behavior, some behaviors cannot be reinforced non-contingently and require certain conditions to be met in order to engage in the behavior or receive reinforcement. Some examples may be individuals receiving automatic reinforcement from watching water running or from toilets being flushed. In these cases where the behavior can only occur in a specific setting—such as a bathroom—access can be provided to the reinforcer on a particular schedule. Additionally, it is inappropriate to engage in other behaviors in public. For the safety of the individual and those around them, an automatically reinforcing behavior such as masturbation (or another behavior that may adversely impact the dignity of the individual if performed publicly), should be restricted to occur in private settings. Allowing access to opportunities to engage in this behavior in private would ensure that the automatic reinforcement is accessed at regular intervals in the day, thus decreasing the probability and motivation for it to occur at other intervals outside of the prescribed schedule.

RESPONSE BLOCKING AND REDIRECTION

Response blocking consists of interrupting the completion of a target behavior by physically blocking its occurrence (Cooper, Heron, & Heward, 2007). For example, in the case of self-injurious skin-picking, response blocking would occur by having a practitioner or caregiver position themselves closely to the individual and physically block the individual from making contact with their own skin as they attempt to pick. By preventing contact through the interruption of the contact with the skin to complete the picking behavior (reinforcement), extinction has occurred.

A frequent concern when applying response blocking is the increased likelihood that the individual may respond aggressively to the behavior being physically blocked. Hagopian and Adelinis (2001) evaluated the effects of the application of response blocking alone to response blocking with redirection to a behavior maintained by automatic reinforcement. The combination of response blocking and redirection, versus response blocking alone, resulted in more effective behavior change.

Summary

This chapter brought closure to the FBA process by exploring how the results of each stage of the FBA can be applied to the practice of selecting and designing intervention. It should be clear now that the interventions selected should serve to both decrease the occurrence of the target behavior and also increase the occurrence of functional replacement behaviors. The examples explored in this chapter highlight the need to base decisions regarding intervention on the identified function of the behavior, instead of the topography or form of the behavior. You are encouraged to complete the review activities to both test your knowledge and further develop your critical thinking and analysis when it comes to addressing realistic case study scenarios.

Definition of Key Terms

- **function-based interventions:** interventions designed to specifically address the identified function of the behavior, versus the topography, or form, of the behavior
- **functional equivalence:** behaviors that differ in topography, but achieve the same function
- **replacement behaviors:** functionally equivalent behaviors that are more desirable than the target behavior
- **attention extinction:** the withdrawal or removal of reinforcement of a behavior previously reinforced by attention with the resulting effect of decreasing the behavior
- **extinction burst:** an increase in the behavior's frequency, duration, and/or magnitude following the implementation of an extinction procedure
- **spontaneous recovery:** an effect of extinction when the behavior abruptly occurs again following a period when the behavior had been significantly reduced or eliminated
- **Differential Reinforcement of Alternative Behaviors (DRA):** a differential reinforcement procedure wherein a different behavior than the target behavior is reinforced
- **Differential Reinforcement of Other Behaviors (DRO):** a differential reinforcement procedure wherein the learner is provided reinforcement when there is an absence of the target behavior
- **Differential Reinforcement of Incompatible Behaviors (DRI):** a differential reinforcement procedure wherein a behavior that cannot occur at the same time as the target behavior is reinforced
- **Differential Reinforcement of Low Rates of Behavior (DRL):** a differential reinforcement procedure wherein low rates of the target behavior are reinforced
- **non-contingent positive reinforcement:** a procedure wherein positive reinforcement is delivered whether the target behavior occurs or not
- **non-contingent negative reinforcement:** a procedure wherein negative reinforcement is delivered whether the target behavior occurs or not
- **non-contingent automatic reinforcement:** a procedure wherein automatic reinforcement is delivered whether the target behavior occurs or not
- **escape extinction:** the withdrawal or removal of reinforcement of a behavior previously reinforced by escape with the resulting effect of decreasing the behavior
- **response blocking:** a procedure wherein another individual physically blocks a behavior from occurring

Test Your Understanding

Level 1: Knowledge

1. True or False: Effective interventions are designed based on the function of the behavior.
2. True or False: Functional equivalence relates to all functions serving an equal, competing purpose for the individual.
3. True or False: Functional replacement behaviors are those that are more socially appropriate while still serving the original function of the behavior.

Level 2: Comprehension

1. Which of the following two behaviors are functionally equivalent? (Choose all that apply.)
   a. Making dinner at home and ordering a meal at a restaurant
   b. Waving to someone across the room and running away from them
   c. Visiting your favorite social media site and calling your best friend to talk about your weekend instead of writing your report for your ABA course
   d. Singing in the car when you're alone and singing to yourself in the shower
2. Which of the following interventions would serve as a functional replacement behavior to a learner who is engaging in hitting to gain attention from others? (Choose all that apply.)
   a. Teaching the individual to greet others to recruit others' attention
   b. Teaching the individual to tap other people on the shoulder to gain others' attention
   c. Teaching the individual to say the names of classmates to gain others' attention
   d. Teaching the individual to say "I want to hit you" so there will be fair warning
3. Which of the following interventions would serve as a functional replacement behavior to a learner who is engaging in high-pitched, long-duration screaming to escape task demands? (Choose all that apply.)
   a. Teaching the individual to request a break from the task after part of it is completed
   b. Teaching the individual to delegate the task to others so they can work on a task for which they have a stronger skill set
   c. Teaching the individual to keep their mouth closed
   d. Teaching the individual new skills so the task will become easier
4. Which of the following interventions would serve as a functional replacement behavior to a learner who is engaging in urinating in their pants to experience automatic/sensory reinforcement?
   a. Teaching the individual to use the bathroom and then request to sit in a pool of warm water or use a cup of water to dampen their pants
   b. Teaching the individual to use the bathroom on more regular intervals
   c. Teaching the individual to change their clothes after they urinate in their pants
   d. All of the above
5. Which of the following interventions would serve as a functional replacement behavior to a learner who is engaging in whining to obtain their favorite snack foods? (Choose all that apply.)
   a. Teaching the individual to select healthier foods
   b. Teaching them to prefer healthy foods
   c. Teaching the individual to request their favorite snack foods without whining
   d. Teaching the individual to wait until designated meal times to eat

Level 3: Application

1. Generate a list of function-based interventions that may be recommended to decrease the occurrence of self-injurious hand-biting that is maintained by escape from task demands at school. Be sure to create two lists: one that outlines interventions to decrease the behavior and one that outlines interventions to increase a specific replacement behavior.
2. Generate a list of function-based interventions that may be recommended to decrease the occurrence of tantrums (hitting, kicking, screaming) maintained by access to favorite activities (watching movies or playing games on iPad) during leisure time at home. Be sure to create two lists: one that

outlines interventions to decrease the behavior and one that outlines interventions to increase a specific replacement behavior.

3. Generate a list of function-based interventions that may be recommended to decrease the occurrence of elopement (running away from caregiver) in public settings that serves the function of attention. Be sure to create two lists: one that outlines interventions to decrease the behavior and one that outlines interventions to increase a specific replacement behavior.

4. Generate a list of function-based interventions that may be recommended to decrease the occurrence of non-functional vocalizations (singing Christmas carols at a loud volume) to serve the function of automatic/sensory reinforcement. Be sure to create two lists: one that outlines interventions to decrease the behavior and one that outlines interventions to increase a specific replacement behavior.

5. Make a video recording of the oral explanation of how to identify functionally equivalent replacement behaviors and interventions to address specific functions of behavior and submit this recording for review. General tips: Students should take care to address the camera as though they are speaking with either a consumer of ABA services or a supervisee (imagine that the camera is the individual with whom you would be speaking). Students may elect to use props to demonstrate the way in which data should be collected or use other materials relating to how the behavior change procedure should be implemented. In the event that these props or data collection sheets are referenced in the video, these items should be made visible on camera.

In-Class Small Group Discussion Questions/Exercises

Create small groups (perhaps four or five students) and discuss the following topics, allowing 10 to 15 minutes to complete the response.

1. Within your group, each team member should share the lists generated as responses in the Application section in the "Review of Concepts" area of this chapter. Work to evaluate your team members' responses and consider the following:
   a. Are the suggested interventions to decrease the behavior evidence based? If so, what literature can you identify to support the intervention's use to address the indicated function of the behavior?
   b. Are the suggested replacement behaviors functionally equivalent to the target behavior? Why or why not? If so, what literature can you identify to support the intervention's use to address the indicated function of the behavior?
   c. Compose and submit a final list of intervention recommendations based upon your discussion as a team.

References

Baer, D.M., Wolf, M. M., & Risley, T.R. (1968). Some current dimensions of applied behavior analysis. *Journal of applied behavior analysis*, 1(1), 91.

Behavior Analyst Certification Board® (2014). *Professional and ethical compliance code for behavior analysts.* Littleton, CO: Author.

Bondy, A.S., & Frost, L.A. (1994). The picture exchange communication system. *Focus on Autism and Other Developmental Disabilities, 9*(3), 1–19.

Carr, E.G. (1988). Functional equivalence as a mechanism of response generalization. *Generalization and maintenance: Life-style changes in applied settings*, 221–241.

Cooper J.O., Heron, T.E, & Heward, W.L. (2007). *Applied behavior analysis* (2nd ed.). Upper Saddle River, NJ: Pearson.

Hagopian, L.P., & Adelinis, J.D. (2001). Response blocking with and without redirection for the treatment of pica. *Journal of Applied Behavior Analysis, 34*(4), 527–530.

Horner, R.H., & Day, H.M. (1991). The effects of response efficiency on functionally equivalent competing behaviors. *Journal of Applied Behavior Analysis, 24*(4), 719–732.

Ingram, K., Lewis-Palmer, T., & Sugai, G. (2005). Function-based intervention planning: Comparing the effectiveness of FBA function-based and non—function-based intervention plans. *Journal of Positive Behavior Interventions, 7*(4), 224–236.

Iwata, B.A., Pace, G.M., Cowdery, G.E., & Miltenberger, R.G. (1994). What makes extinction work: An analysis of procedural form and function. *Journal of Applied Behavior Analysis, 27*(1), 131–144.

Lerman, D.C., Iwata, B.A., & Wallace, M.D. (1999). Side effects of extinction: Prevalence of bursting and aggression during the treatment of self-injurious behavior. *Journal of Applied Behavior Analysis, 32*(1), 1–8.

CHAPTER 12

Progress Monitoring and Maintenance

After the FBA process has been completed and the behavior intervention plan has been implemented, the behavior analyst's work is not over. Behavior analysts have a responsibility to continue to monitor the behavior and to promote maintenance of behavior change over time. Progress monitoring occurs by making a commitment to continue to observe and collect data on the target behaviors long after initial behavior change takes place. Continuing to monitor the behavior and remaining focused on the environmental variables that could continue to influence the behavior will ensure the behavior will most likely continue—if the individuals working with the learner on a daily basis vigilantly focus on target behaviors and communicate adverse changes in the behavior over time. Maintenance of behavior change, or **behavior maintenance**, occurs when the environment is altered, or the schedule is thinned to the naturally occurring reinforcers, to ensure that intermittent schedules of reinforcement are in place and that, to the greatest extent possible, rich amounts of natural reinforcement are present in the environment.

There are numerous texts that cover procedures for visual data analysis and progress monitoring in great detail. The content covered in this chapter merely provides an overview of the general considerations involved in evaluating progress and maintenance of behavior change. In this chapter, you will review various tools for progress monitoring, schedules of reinforcement that promote maintenance of behavior change, and visual analysis to ensure that the maintenance data continues to demonstrate behavior change. You will also be shown examples, be provided activities and data to practice applying the principles of progress monitoring and visual analysis, and will be given a venue to teach others about the importance of these concepts. In so doing, you will be continuing to complete the "See one, do one, teach one" model for this stage of the FBA process.

LEARNING OBJECTIVES

After completing the chapter's activities, learners should be able to do the following:

- Describe and evaluate the importance of progress monitoring
- Define and evaluate the principles of visual analysis of data
- Describe and evaluate the importance of behavioral maintenance
- Define intermittent (variable schedules of) reinforcement
- Identify and evaluate natural reinforcers

Progress Monitoring

Behaviors do not occur in a vacuum and are constantly being influenced by changes in the environment, which means that even after an intervention results in a complete elimination of the behavior, the change is not considered permanent. Environmental changes can be salient or inconspicuous, immediate or gradual. Once the behavior has changed, it is still the responsibility of the behavior analyst to remain vigilant and ensure that the progress made is maintained. However, a broad term like "progress monitoring" can be relatively vague, and it is necessary to properly define what is expected in the process of monitoring behavioral progress. Because there are an unlimited—in fact, infinite—number of situations where target behaviors could be identified and addressed, there are not strict rules regarding how often or with which tools behavior analysts should use when monitoring progress. Instead of taking into account every possible scenario where progress monitoring would be required, it is instead recommended that behavior analysts consider a few major factors and monitor on a systematic and inclusive basis. Two key components are involved in this approach.

First, creating a system by which the behavior is evaluated systematically and consistently, such as a schedule, would be effective in terms of maintaining a consistent record of the behavior's occurrence long after it leaves the crosshairs of a behavior intervention plan. For example, perhaps in order to monitor a learner's behavior of interrupting during conversations after it has been effectively decreased using attention extinction and differential reinforcement of alternative behavior, the behavior analyst will create a schedule of evaluating interrupting behavior three times per week. By creating a rule of when to evaluate the behavior and for how long, the behavior analyst will continue to collect less-intensive, but still valuable, probe data on the behavior's occurrence. Graphing those data over time will allow for a more broad analysis to be conducted and will allow for action to be taken to intervene if the behavior begins to increase according to a trend.

Another consideration in progress monitoring is teaching those around the individual to continue to collect objective, anecdotal A-B-C data on the occurrence of the behavior. This can be accomplished by ensuring that regularly used data sheets (such as A-B-C data recording forms) include an area for the target behavior to be indicated using a check-mark or a blank space to include a narrative description of the behavior. When team members are involved in a behavior change program whereby the behavior is effectively reduced, there is the possibility for bias or failure to recognize slow and steady re-emergence of the target behavior, or for a new topographical variation of the target behavior to emerge unnoticed.

For these reasons, recording and asking those around the individual to record instances of concerning behavior, over time will allow for additional monitoring to take place without a great deal of additional effort.

The primary method of monitoring and analyzing progress in behavior analysis is through visual analysis of the graphed data. There are several criteria for review that have been put forth by single subject design researchers in ABA. Parsonson and Baer (1978; 1992) included several criteria for consideration when visually analyzing behavioral data. Most of these criteria consisted of an analysis of the **stability** or **variability**, **level**, and **trend** of the baseline and intervention **conditions**, as well as all follow-up data collected after intervention has ended. In the sections that follow, each of these criteria will be explored further. First, however, it is important to assess the presentation of the graphed data, as the way that data are formatted can affect the manner in which the data are analyzed and interpreted. Richards, Taylor, and Ramasamy (2014) published four questions research practitioners may ask themselves as they evaluate the appropriateness, accuracy, and utility of graphed data. These questions are provided in Table 12.1 with additional explanation than was provided by Richards et al. (2014).

Table 12.1 Questions about Graphed Data Prior to Conducting Visual Analysis

Question	Explanation
Are the legend, axes, and all phases labeled clearly?	All graphs should be labeled clearly so that any reviewer of the graph would be able to determine the data plotted on the graph. Specifically, axes labels, phases (or conditions), and specific data paths (using a legend) should be labeled with concise yet clear titles.
Have you tracked the data visually to ensure that all data points are connected appropriately and whether the data points include aggregated data across observations, a single observation, a daily observation, etc.?	All data points should be formatted in such a way that each consecutive data point should be connected with a line. This line forms the data path that will be analyzed; therefore, it is important that the data points that are connected with a line are actually intended to be grouped together in the manner in which they will be analyzed. The research practitioner should visually track the data points and paths and ensure that data points that should be connected are, and data points that should be separated to represent separate observations are not connected with a line.
Is the scaling of the y-axis (i.e., dependent variable) appropriate?	Because the dependent variable (most often the target behavior, which is the focus of behavior change) is plotted along the y-axis of a graph, it is necessary that the scale of the y-axis accurately represents changes in performance according to clinical significance. In other words, a small change in behavior (e.g., a reduction of the frequency of kicking from nine times per day to eight times the next day) should be represented visually as a small change on the graph. Similarly, a significant change in the behavior (a reduction of the frequency of kicking from nine times per day to zero occurrences the next day) should be represented visually as a big change, or sharp decline in the occurrence of the behavior. A major concern when evaluating the scale of the y-axis would be if a reviewer of the graphed data observes a sharp decline in the plotted data, but the actual reduction according to the frequency data is minimal and only appears significant due to the range of the y-axis being too small. Or, if the scaling of the y-axis under-represented a significant change in the behavior due to the range of the y-axis being too large.
Do the data depict the performance of an individual or a group treated as a single subject? In the latter case, is the range or variability of the individual performances within the group also included?	Typically, when an individualized BIP has been implemented, the data collected to monitor progress of the behavior intervention plan are data based on the performance of an individual, not a group. Nevertheless, the occasion may arise wherein a group intervention is implemented and requires progress monitoring. Therefore, when examining graphed data on group performance, clarity about the performance of each individual in a group intervention would be necessary to consider.

Now that the critical questions evaluating the appropriateness of the graphed data have been posed, we will explore the additional critical elements to examine when conducting the visual analysis of the data.

Table 12.1: Source: Steve Richards, Ronald L. Taylor, and Rangasamy Ramasamy, *Single Subject Research: Applications In Educational and Clinical Settings*, 2014, Wadsworth/Thomson Learning.

NUMBER OF DATA POINTS IN EACH CONDITION

An accurate visual analysis of data depends on there being a sufficient number of data points in order to interpret a pattern of behavior in the baseline (pre-intervention), intervention, and follow-up (post-intervention) stages. There is not a hard and fast rule regarding the minimum number of data points to qualify as "sufficient," because that number will vary depending on the characteristics of the data as well as the behavior itself. However, generally, the more consistent, or stable, the data in a baseline condition, the more confident one can be using a fewer number of data points (e.g., if three consecutive days of baseline data are collected and the behavior occurred at the exact same amount, then one can be relatively confident that three data points will be sufficient and represent an accurate account of the behavior's occurrence at baseline). Overall, however, a greater number of data points in any condition should increase confidence that an analysis of the data in that condition is accurate (Cooper, Heron, & Heward, 2007).

STABILITY OF THE BASELINE CONDITIONS

The entire goal of a behavior change procedure is to change some dimension(s) (i.e., frequency, duration, magnitude) of the behavior from its baseline occurrence. Therefore, the basic focus of the visual analysis of a graph should be on the comparison of the baseline and intervention conditions of the graph. For this reason, prior to implementing intervention, the practitioner should evaluate the baseline data (as plotted on the graph) to ensure that the data are stable. If the data are not stable and are instead inconsistent or variable, it will be challenging to see a contrast between the baseline and intervention stages if behavior change actually occurred. Therefore, it is critical that the baseline data are stable in order to draw that comparison with greater confidence.

VARIABILITY WITHIN THE INTERVENTION CONDITIONS

Again, because the goal of any behavior change procedure is for it to actually result in a change in the behavior, a focus of visual analysis should be on evaluating whether the behavior changes as a result of the intervention being introduced. In other words, if the baseline data are stable for six consecutive sessions, and on the seventh session (when intervention is introduced) the behavior changes (either increases or decreases), the change could be considered to have occurred as a result of the introduction of the intervention (versus any other reason). Nevertheless, more data points should be collected across subsequent sessions, and the variability of the data collected during the intervention condition should also be assessed. When an intervention is implemented, the immediate effect can introduce initial variability to the behavior. For instance, extinction (as discussed in Chapter 11) presents a predictable, well-documented effect of an initial decrease in the behavior's occurrence followed by a sharp, abrupt increase in the occurrence of the behavior, known as an extinction burst. Therefore, some variability in the intervention condition would be expected when using this procedure; others in the intervention may require longer periods of time to demonstrate effect. For this reason, it is important to continue to implement the intervention until the data becomes stable. However, if, after the intervention has been conducted systematically, consistently, and with fidelity, there is continued variability in the intervention condition, it will be important for the team to reassess whether the intervention is indeed effective and whether it should be modified or terminated.

VARIABILITY BETWEEN CONDITIONS

Any number of circumstances could occur before and/or during the implementation of a behavior change intervention, which could result in both the baseline and intervention conditions being stable, only one condition being stable, or both conditions being variable. Clearly, a stable baseline condition that is immediately followed by an intervention condition reflecting a change in the data path (either in terms of the level or trend of the data) that is also stable will evoke the greatest confidence that behavior change occurred as a result of the intervention. However this ideal circumstance may not occur frequently, and therefore it is necessary to assess the variability across conditions to determine whether the behavior change can be attributed to the intervention alone, and whether the behavior change is likely to continue.

CHANGES IN TREND WITHIN CONDITIONS

Changes in trend, when the direction of the data path within a condition is not ideal, indicates a lack of experimental control, suggesting the intervention is not responsible for the change in the behavior. Therefore, any change in the trend of a data path within the baseline or intervention condition should result in the practitioner continuing to collect additional data and/or consider alternate explanations for the change in the trend. In any event, such a change within a condition should cause additional speculation from the practitioner.

ANALYSIS OF DATA ACROSS SIMILAR CONDITIONS

Quite simply, when a learner is in a similar condition, one would expect similarity in the pattern of responding. Therefore, similar conditions should result in similar data points, levels, and trends. In the context of our discussion of behavioral maintenance and progress monitoring, the analysis of the similarity of the intervention and post-intervention data paths is critical, as practitioners would hope to see that any pattern of behavior observed in the intervention condition would continue to occur post-intervention.

EVALUATION OF THE OVERALL PATTERN OF DATA

Just as is the case with any analysis, it is important for practitioners to consider the overall pattern of data in addition to focusing on individual data points. Essentially, this implies that although one should evaluate and attempt to explain small oddities in a data path, practitioners should not reject an entire data set if these oddities are present. An attempt to explain such anomalies is helpful, however, if the overall pattern of data is able to be interpreted according to the previous principles discussed in this section, you can, and should, interpret those findings while placing less value on the occasional odd data point.

Behavior Maintenance

Maintenance of behavior change does not automatically occur without a sustained change in the environment that previously reinforced the behavior. Usually, a sustained change in an environment does not occur without special consideration in the form of planned modifications. For instance, let's suppose your friend is attempting to lose weight. He would like to eliminate his consumption of foods that contain artificial sugar and fat (consuming only raw produce), and would like to increase his time spent running. After following a strict regimen of following through with both of those behavioral goals for two months, your friend reports he has lost an impressive twenty pounds. Now that he's lost the weight, he laments the fact that he has grown tired of the diet he is eating and craves to eat pizza and cake again. Additionally, the grueling runs he had programmed for himself have taken their toll on his morning routine and evening social life, and he would like to cut back on the number of days he is running from five to one. In short, although your friend accomplished an incredible feat of losing twenty pounds in two months, that level of change (i.e., the weight loss) will not be maintained because it was accomplished without the consideration of behavior maintenance. In other words, your friend has not incorporated sufficient reinforcement to continue to eat low-fat and low-sugar foods or to continue to run on a frequent basis. In his case, the effort involved to maintain this behavior is far exceeding the reinforcement he needs to maintain the behaviors (namely, variety in his diet and the inclusion of a few foods that he previously enjoyed, and a more moderate exercise routine that will have less of an impact on his morning routine or evening social opportunities).

Prior to beginning any behavior change program, and especially after fading the intervention completely, it is critically important to plan for behavior maintenance by considering specific variables that were in place as the intervention was occurring and arranging for reinforcement to occur naturally. Often, behavior change is considered to be easier than behavior maintenance, as the challenges to creating long-standing behavior change are highly individualized. A list of some of those challenges as well as strategies to address them are outlined in Table 12.2.

Table 12.2 Challenges Associated with Behavioral Maintenance and Strategies to Address Them

Challenge	Strategy
A change in the schedule of reinforcement post-intervention	Simply put, behaviors continue to occur as long as they are reinforced. Therefore, behavior maintenance will continue to occur as long as the schedule of reinforcement remains sufficiently thick to provide the learner with contact to reinforcement. Once an intervention ends, often the reinforcement schedule changes as well. It is therefore important to consider ways in which the behavior will continue to be reinforced by recruiting resources in the natural environment.
A lack of natural reinforcers present in the post-intervention environment	Natural reinforcers are those that do not require additional planning or artificial planning in order to be accessed. If, following the end of an intervention, the behavior does not result in reinforcement, the behavior will likely return to pre-intervention levels. However, if natural reinforcers are identified and taught to be accessed in the intervention phase, the behavior is likely to be maintained
The post-intervention environment is significantly different than the intervention environment	When a behavior change occurs as an intervention is being implemented, the stimuli in the environment wherein the intervention occurred have likely controlled the occurrence of the behavior. Therefore, to the greatest extent possible, the more similar the intervention and post-intervention environments are, the more likely the behavior will maintain post-intervention (as those same stimuli will be present and will be likely to continue to evoke the behavior).

Returning to the previous example of our friend who has lost weight and is considering abandoning the behaviors he acquired that resulted in his weight loss (e.g., healthy eating and exercise), perhaps the concepts of **intermittent (or variable schedules of) reinforcement** and **natural reinforcers** should be explored to possibly assist him.

INTERMITTENT/VARIABLE SCHEDULES OF REINFORCEMENT

All behaviors that receive reinforcement are subjected to a reinforcement schedule. Whether pre-ordained or completely incidental, the reinforcement schedule affects the behavior's occurrence. Fixed schedules of reinforcement are in effect when a behavior results in reinforcement either after a fixed number of responses or a fixed amount of time. An example of a fixed ratio reinforcement schedule is the completion of a five-question math homework sheet—once the five math questions are answered, the individual can be finished with their homework to do other activities or receive a different source of reinforcement, perhaps through a consistent grading process. An example of a fixed interval reinforcement schedule would be a typical payroll process, wherein employees are paid after two weeks of work. The schedule of reinforcement (in this case, monetary compensation) is provided according to a fixed duration of time passing (and, presumably, effective job performance). The corresponding alternative to the continuous schedule of reinforcement, where reinforcement is delivered on a fixed schedule, is the intermittent schedule of reinforcement. This reinforcement schedule consists of some, but not all, instances of the behavior resulting in reinforcement. Instead of being fixed schedules, these are variable schedules of reinforcement. There are two types: variable ratio and variable interval. Variable ratio schedules of reinforcement are those schedules that result in reinforcement of an average number of responses. An example of a variable ratio schedule of reinforcement would be when the child has learned to politely use the word "please" to make their requests, her mother would reinforce saying "good job using the word please" an average of every three responses to continue to maintain appropriate manners. And, for example, in the case of a child who has learned to refrain from standing up and screaming at circle time, the teacher would place the child's behavior on a variable interval response and would provide reinforcement on an average of every five minutes. This particular schedule will increase the stability and potential for maintenance of the behavior, due to the behavior no longer being dependent on reinforcement occurring after each occurrence of the behavior.

NATURAL REINFORCERS

Behaviors are likely to maintain when the reinforcement they produce occurs naturally. In other words, when the individual's behavior results in consequences that are desirable, the individual will continue to engage in the behavior. Examples of natural reinforcers can be found across all realms of life. For instance, after thirty minutes of exercise, most people experience a rush of endorphins, which have positive effects on cortisol stress levels and mood. In that case, the endorphin rush (or runner's high) is a natural reinforcing consequence to running. For first-graders with attention-maintained problem behaviors, being taught to play functionally with toys will result in the ability to join play with peers. The peer attention that results from playing with peers functionally is a natural reinforcer. Natural reinforcers are desirable to identify when implementing an intervention and maintenance program, because if the environment can be enriched with reinforcers that occur naturally, there will not be a need for specific or artificial support to deliver reinforcement.

Summary

It is hopefully clear by now that behavior analysts work to change behaviors for the long term. The responsibility to continue to monitor the behavior change and promote the behavior's maintenance still falls on the behavior analyst. Fortunately, many of the daily tasks of a behavior analyst, such as ongoing observation and data collection, lend themselves easily to this work. To minimize some of the burden that behavior analysts face in working to maintain behaviors following behavior change, it is possible to program for maintenance and generalization during the intervention itself. This is accomplished by ensuring that intermittent schedules of reinforcement are in place and that natural reinforcement is available in the environment. It is recommended you continue with the review exercises provided at the end of this chapter to more fully explore these concepts and their application.

Definition of Key Terms

- **visual analysis:** an approach for interpreting the results of behavioral performance data that systematically evaluate the trend, level, and stability/variability
- **stability:** the degree to which frequent measures of the same behavior result in similar or consistent outcomes
- **variability:** the degree to which frequent measures of the same behavior result in different outcomes
- **level:** the value of the y-axis around which a series of data points gather
- **trend:** the direction of a data path (e.g., increasing, decreasing, or flat trend) as well as its degree (e.g., steep, gradual)
- **condition:** the phase of a behavior change procedure that describes the planned circumstances in the environment wherein the behavior takes place (e.g., baseline, intervention, follow-up condition)
- **behavior maintenance:** occurs when a learner continues to emit the behavior over time after the reinforcer has faded
- **natural reinforcers:** reinforcing events that directly relate to the behavior itself; wherein the reinforcement is derived directly from the behavior (e.g., a natural reinforcer of the behavior of learning to turn on a television is the reinforcement of accessing a favorite television show)
- **intermittent schedule of reinforcement:** a schedule of reinforcement wherein reinforcement is delivered following occurrence of some, but not all, instances of the behavior

Test Your Understanding

Level 1: Knowledge

1. True or False: Intermittent schedules of reinforcement consist of reinforcing the behavior occasionally.
2. True or False: Fixed schedules of reinforcement are most effective when attempting to maintain the occurrence of a behavior over time.
3. True or False: Natural reinforcers are those that assist in behavioral maintenance without specific planning and forethought needed to provide reinforcement.
4. True or False: As long as a behavior was effectively reduced and a functional replacement behavior was effectively taught, behavioral maintenance will occur automatically.
5. True or False: Technology can be used to assist in both to monitor progress and to promote behavioral maintenance.

Level 2: Comprehension

1. Which of the following is a natural reinforcer?
   a. A bag of candy following an "A" grade on a spelling test
   b. Requesting "help" when completing a puzzle and receiving assistance from the teacher
   c. Earning the opportunity to watch a movie after using the bathroom successfully
   d. None of the above

2. Which of the following demonstrates an intermittent reinforcement schedule?
   a. After each minute that Caitlyn remains sitting at circle time, her teacher provides her one piece of cookie
   b. Every three days that John makes his bed, he earns another sticker on his chart and after five stickers, he will get to go out to the movies
   c. Charlotte's teacher provides her with verbal praise an average of once every five minutes
   d. None of the above

Level 3: Application

1. Review the example provided in this chapter regarding your friend who recently changed his eating and exercise behavior. Consider the concepts of progress monitoring, behavioral maintenance, intermittent, and natural reinforcers. In this scenario, what would you recommend your friend do to promote maintenance of these behaviors? Specifically, how would an effective intermittent reinforcement schedule look? And, what might be natural reinforcers that could be made more meaningful or salient? (Hint: Perhaps consider your role as a friend who could provide social reinforcement.)
2. Consider a case where a learner's aggressive hitting behavior was put on extinction and a differential reinforcement procedure was taught to have him request attention more appropriately. What would you expect the graphed baseline and intervention data to look like if a behavior change occurred and was maintained? Draw the graph you would expect to see, specifically indicating the baseline, intervention, and follow-up phases and explain what you would expect the level, trend, and stability of the data to be.
3. Make a video recording of the oral explanation of how what you would expect the graphed data to be if a behavior was being maintained and what it would be if it was not being maintained. Be specific with respect to the trend, level, and stability of the data paths and explain why each is an indicator of the confidence practitioners can have in their interpretation of the behavior pattern. General tips: Students should take care to address the camera as though they are speaking with either a consumer of ABA services or a supervisee (imagine that the camera is the individual with whom you would be speaking). Students may elect to use props to demonstrate the way in which data should be collected or use other materials relating to how the behavior change procedure should be implemented. In the event that these props or data collection sheets are referenced in the video, these items should be made visible on camera.

In-Class Small Group Discussion Questions/Exercises

Create small groups (perhaps four or five students) and discuss the following topics, allowing 10 to 15 minutes to complete the response.

1. Please consider a recent behavior that you sought to change (either the behavior of a learner or yourself). Has the behavior maintained? Why do you think it has? Did you make efforts to maintain it? Share this information with your team members, and, as a team, discuss themes and identify whether natural reinforcers are present and/or if an intermittent reinforcement schedule can be identified.

References

Cooper J.O., Heron T.E., and Heward, W.L. (2007). *Applied behavior analysis* (2nd ed.). Upper Saddle River, NJ: Pearson.

Parsonson, B.S., & Baer, D.M. (1978). The analysis and presentation of graphic data. In T.R. Kratchowill (Ed.), *Single-subject research: Strategies for evaluating change* (pp. 101–165). New York, NY: Academic Press.

Parsonson, B.S., & Baer, D.M. (1992). The visual analysis of data and current research into the stimuli controlling it. In T.R. Kratchowill & J.R. Levin (Eds.), *Single-case research design and analysis: New directions for psychology and education* (pp. 15–40). Hillsdale, NJ: Lawrence Erlbaum.

Richards, S.B., Taylor, R.L., & Ramasamy, R. (2014). *Single subject research* (2nd ed.). Belmont, CA: Wadsworth.

CHAPTER 13

Special Considerations

F unctional behavior assessment (FBA) is a procedure that employs several different processes and results in various products of data for analysis. The benefit of mastering ABA is that it is a science and methodology that applies to all organisms that exhibit behavior. Because FBA is a cornerstone to the assessment process in ABA, its applications are wide-ranging. In this chapter, we will discuss the different populations that may benefit from FBA, settings in which it can be conducted, and important safety considerations in carrying it out. In so doing, we will carry out the "See one, do one, teach one" process employed in previous chapters of this text.

LEARNING OBJECTIVES

After completing the chapter's activities, learners should be able to do the following:

- Describe and evaluate both the different populations that may benefit from FBA and the target behaviors that were the focus of assessment

- Identify and analyze settings in which FBA can be conducted

- Describe and apply important safety considerations in carrying out FBA

Populations and Behaviors

Most often, when one considers FBA, the primary population as the focus of the assessment would be individuals with developmental or cognitive impairment. This is because the reason for the specific target behavior can be challenging to identify when the individual who is the focus of the assessment is not able to report on the occurrence of the behavior and more general approaches to behavior change or management are not effective. Although there is a preponderance of reports of functional behavioral assessment being used most often with individuals with developmental disabilities, specifically autism, there are notable studies that have been conducted with individuals with other diagnoses.

Hanley, Iwata, and McCord's (2003) review of the literature of published functional analysis reports reveals that the practice of conducting behavioral assessment has been applied to a wide range of individuals with various developmental, physical, and psychiatric disorders. This review included 277 empirical studies reporting functional analyses conducted with children and adults, including participants with a range of diagnoses, including developmental disability, autism, and no disability. The range of behaviors assessed included self-injury, aggression, disruption, vocalizations, property destruction, stereotypy, noncompliance, tantrums, elopement, pica, and other behaviors. The information provided in this study indicates that there is a wide range of behavior problems that can reliably be assessed using FBA and that a wide variety of populations can benefit from this practice.

There are other examples of FBA being used in groups not related to developmental disorder. For example, Heinssen (2002) examined collaborative behavior interventions to increasing medication compliance in a patient in her mid-thirties with schizophrenia. The intervention began with an FBA, consisting of gathering information from various sources and examining the environmental variables influencing medication compliance. Interestingly, in the process of completing the FBA, the patient herself indicated barriers to her medication compliance as being a lack of belief that the medication was effective. The FBA results in this study also presented evidence that the patient had not developed effective methods to cue her to take her medication daily and her existing memory deficit only contributed to this issue. The intervention therefore consisted of creating automatic visual and auditory cues to evoke medication compliance behavior. Although this brief case study included a focus on cognitive explanations for the lack of medication compliance (versus objective, measurable accounts of behavior, as behavior analysts would), this application highlights a potential area where FBA could be used to address problems with medication compliance not only in psychiatric patients, but patients struggling with medication compliance for any other reason.

Additional applications along the same theme of medication compliance could be extended to individuals with insulin-dependent diabetes. A situation where an FBA would be particularly useful may be with adolescents who are perhaps unlikely to leave social settings to take their medication, but are unlikely to self-report the function of escape as their lack of medication compliance to their parents or medical professionals. Therefore, medical professionals may benefit from adopting the FBA process to evaluate their patients' medication compliance behavior and design interventions to address the identified function.

For yet another application of FBA, we can turn to a different setting entirely, a human services staff office, wherein an FBA was conducted to examine the underlying function of late arrival to staff meetings (Fienup, Luiselli, Joy, Smythe, & Stein, 2013). The results of the FBA were shared with the staff members who then collaborated to develop an intervention plan to specifically address the tardy arrival behavior. The intervention specifically targeted the functions identified by providing reminders, reinforcement for attendance, and meeting termination criteria to assist in transitioning the end of the meeting. This application is an example of a completely different population—human services professionals—who used FBA to identify the function of their behavior and specifically tailored intervention to address it. Hopefully it is clear that FBA is a process that can be applied to a diverse set of circumstances where behavior change is necessary for individuals to improve their functioning.

Settings

Again, because the scientific methodology of ABA is universal, it can be applied to any individual exhibiting behavior. Because individuals engage in behavior across a wide range of settings and locations, it is important to consider the ways in which FBAs should be executed in different settings. FBA is most often conducted in settings such as schools, homes, community locations, vocational settings, group homes, and outpatient clinics. Additionally, as was explored in the additional examples of where FBA could be conducted, there is also the consideration of additional settings like hospitals, offices, geriatric assisted living centers, substance abuse treatment facilities, and correctional facilities. Essentially, FBA can be conducted in any setting where a target behavior has been identified.

Aside from careful consideration and adherence to the ethical guidelines provided by the Behavior Analyst Certification Board®, it is also necessary to consider additional factors specific to the setting itself. For instance, in a school setting, it is important to consider the safety of the individual, members of the team, and any bystanders to the assessment process first. Examples of those considerations will be reviewed in the next section. Next, it is important to recognize that the FBA should be conducted in a manner that creates minimal distractions and does not hinder learning. There is also a need to ensure that the team has reasonable control over the environment to properly manipulate stimuli to carry out the environmental conditions to record reliable data. It will be important for the team to carry out a dry-run or practice session of the direct assessment process and functional analysis conditions, especially to identify variables that will need to be considered and addressed prior to carrying out the evaluation.

Safety Considerations

FBA is frequently used to assess the function of aggressive behaviors in order to apply function-based interventions. Aggressive behaviors are frequently the focus of behavioral assessment because of the risks involved in the behavior continuing to occur—namely, risk of harm to self and/or others. Therefore, it is important to accurately identify the function prior to attempting any form of intervention to address it. Given the precision required to identify the function of this class of behaviors, it is most often necessary to conduct a functional analysis to test the functional hypothesis that has been obtained following indirect and direct assessment. The very nature of functional analysis implies that the problem behavior will be evoked following specifically programmed environmental conditions; therefore, the behavioral analyst needs to think through potential concerns about unnecessarily risking the safety of all persons involved in the functional analysis and of the individual himself or herself (Betz & Fisher, 2011). In light of this consideration, Hausman and colleagues (2015) conducted a retrospective review of ninety-nine inpatient applications of functional analysis, specifically focusing on analyzing the contingencies surrounding cases of individuals exhibiting self-injurious behavior. The focus of the study was on identifying the reports of safety concerns as well as safeguards applied to potentially prevent harm. Approximately two-thirds of the patients whose cases were reviewed were male, and eighty-one of the ninety-nine reports were from individuals with an autism diagnosis; however, many had concomitant diagnoses such as intellectual disability, stereotypic movement disorder with self-injury, attention-deficit hyperactivity disorder, and other mood and genetic disorders. The sample of cases reviewed included individuals who ranged from three years to over twenty years of age. The report indicated that when injuries occurred, they usually were not severe, and that more injuries occurred outside of the functional analysis than during it.

Perhaps the most consequential finding of this study was the common-practice safeguards while conducting functional analysis with individuals with self-injury. The first safeguard included examination of injuries, which occurred before the functional analysis conditions were run, immediately after injuries were incurred (to provide treatment), as well as nightly. Additionally, functional analysis sessions were planned to include a high ratio of staff to patient to provide sufficient support to prevent escalation of the behaviors. Session termination criteria were also developed for each individual patient to ensure that the team had clear guidelines for what would constitute a need to end the session. Finally, clear safety guidelines were provided to ensure patient and staff safety for each condition of the functional analysis.

Summary

Functional behavior assessment (FBA) can be applied to a wide range of different populations, used across different settings, and requires specific considerations depending on the application. In this chapter, the application of FBA to different populations it may benefit, the settings in which it can be conducted, and considerations in carrying it out were all reviewed. You are encouraged to complete the review exercises at the end of this chapter to clarify your understanding and mastery.

Test Your Understanding

Level 1: Knowledge

1. True or False: The use of ABA to assess and treat behavior should be limited to individuals with developmental disabilities.
2. True or False: There have been more published reports of FBAs being conducted with individuals with developmental disabilities than typically developing individuals.
3. True or False: FBAs can only be ethically conducted in schools by Board Certified Behavior Analysts®.
4. True or False: It is safe to conduct standard FBAs with individuals with aggression without additional considerations, since FBA was designed with these behaviors in mind.
5. True or False: Certain stages of the FBA process can be ethically carried out by anyone with proper training, but the functional analysis should always be conducted by a Board Certified Behavior Analyst®.

Level 2: Comprehension

1. Which of the following populations would benefit from an FBA if the behavior they were exhibiting was socially significant?
   a. Individuals with Down Syndrome
   b. Individuals with Cerebral Palsy
   c. Individuals with obesity
   d. All of the above

2. Which of the following behaviors have been target behaviors in an FBA?
   a. Self-injury
   b. Pica
   c. Property destruction
   d. All of the above

Level 3: Application

1. Review the safety considerations for completing a functional analysis on self-injurious behavior. Do any of these considerations surprise you? Are there any considerations you think should be added?
2. Imagine you will need to conduct a functional assessment for an individual who is engaging in fire-setting behavior to gain attention. What safety considerations would you review with your team? What precautions would you put into place in the environment?
3. Consider the various types of individuals who would benefit from FBA and the settings in which the FBA would be conducted that were covered in this chapter. Select one of these examples and describe the considerations that would need to be taken into account from an ethical and practical perspective to carry out the FBA and interpret its results.
4. Make a video recording of the oral explanation of the various special considerations, applications, and circumstances wherein FBA could be conducted. Be specific when describing what challenges would be present and what resources may be at your disposal in the application you describe. General tips: Students should take care to address the camera as though they are speaking with either a consumer of ABA services or a supervisee (imagine that the camera is the individual with whom you would be speaking). Students may elect to use props to demonstrate the way in which data should be collected or use other materials relating to how the behavior change procedure should be implemented. In the event that these props or data collection sheets are referenced in the video, these items should be made visible on camera.

References

Betz, A.M., & Fisher, W.W. (2011). Functional analysis: History and methods. In W.W. Fisher, C.C. Piazza, & H.S. Roane (Eds.), *Handbook of applied behavior analysis* (pp. 206–225). New York, NY: Guilford Press.

Fienup, D.M., Luiselli, J.K., Joy, M., Smythe, D., & Stein, R. (2013). Functional assessment and intervention for organizational behavior change: Improving the timeliness of staff meetings at a human services organization. *Journal of organizational behavior management, 33*(4), 252–264.

Hanley, G.P., Iwata, B.A., & McCord, B.E. (2003). Functional analysis of problem behavior: A review. *Journal of Applied Behavior Analysis, 36*(2), 147–185.

Hausman, N.L., Fisher, L.B., Donaldson, J.M., Cox, J.R., Lugo, M., & Wiskow, K.M. (2015). The safety of functional analyses of self-injurious behavior. *Journal of Applied Behavior Analysis, 48*(1), 107–114.

Heinssen, R.K. (2002). Improving medication compliance of a patient with schizophrenia through collaborative behavioral therapy. *Psychiatric Services, 53*(3), 255–257.